INDUSTRIALISM and
INDUSTRIAL MAN

INDUSTRIALISM and INDUSTRIAL MAN

The Problems of Labor and Management in Economic Growth

Clark Kerr, John T. Dunlop,

Frederick H. Harbison, and Charles A. Myers

1960

HARVARD UNIVERSITY PRESS · Cambridge, Massachusetts

Distributed in Great Britain by
Oxford University Press
London

Library of Congress Catalog Card Number 60–15239

Printed in the United States of America

Contents

Charts

INDUSTRIALISM and
INDUSTRIAL MAN

INTRODUCTION

The world is entering a new age — the age of total industrialization. Each generation lives at only one moment of history; but many members of our generation are trying to stand back and view the total panorama as it extends into the dim past and into the even dimmer future, as well as to assess the present.

An age of change is an age of speculation and of decisions. The African nationalist lawyer in prison in Southern Rhodesia, the young intellectual at the Imperial University in Tokyo, the economist working on the next five-year plan for India, the party intellectual in Belgrade, the aristocrat in Teheran, the military commander in Karachi, and thousands of others are seeking to divine the course of history and to make decisions in the light of some understanding of the time, the place, the forces, and the goals. The authors of this book share these interests and have explored them widely with many persons in this country and abroad.

We wish to speak in this volume to many persons of many persuasions and in a number of countries. In particular, we hope to speak to the intellectuals, the managers, the government officials and labor leaders who today or tomorrow will run their countries, now in the midst of great transformation. Originally we planned to speak on the subject of labor-management-state relations alone. But these relations exist in context; they are not discrete phenomena in society; they are, by and large, determinate results rather than determining forces. To study these relations, accordingly, it is necessary to study their contexts. This has led us to examine the industrialization process, in several of its many forms, and to develop a view of industrialism itself.*

We offer here, consequently, a view of the nature of the met-

* In this volume industrialization refers to the process of transition from the traditional society toward industrialism, which is an abstraction — a limit approached by industrialization.

1

amorphosis which everywhere is bending and shaping the lives of men into new channels; a view particularly related to the roles of the managers and the managed in new societies, but extending also to the inherent nature of these industrializing societies themselves. To grasp what we wanted to understand we found we needed a more general interpretation of the current social processes. This led us to create a framework of our own which draws on the ideas of many others but which is, in its totality, new and different.

We are concerned with industrialization rather than the full range of sectors of an emerging economy. We recognize the critical role of agricultural transformations, as a source of capital, manpower, and as an index of development. ". . . . an agricultural revolution — a marked rise in productivity per worker in agriculture — is a pre-condition of the industrial revolution for any sizable region in the world. . . ."* But agricultural economic developments are largely beyond our projected scope.

Our approach to an explanation of the different arrangements men have devised to combine their efforts in the development of the new industrial processes depends on a concept of the logic of industrialism, of the strategies of the elites who severally guide the process at this stage in history, and of the crucial cultural and environmental conditions which characterize particular societies. We see societies at many stages of development, under several types of leadership, meeting many universal problems, offering ideologies to explain and guide and defend the different ways they meet their problems; but we find within this apparent diversity, patterns of behavior which allow explanation and comparison and understanding of what is universal, what is related to the common strategies of industrialization, and what is unique. There may be no social laws, but there are social consistencies.

We project a future, still long distant, of a world-wide society of pluralistic industrialism; a society where diversity and uniformity still struggle for supremacy and where managers and managed still carry on their endless tug of war; but where the titanic battles which mark our period of transition have already passed into the pages of history.

* Simon Kuznets, *Six Lectures on Economic Growth* (The Free Press of Glencoe, Illinois, 1959), pp. 59–60.

We present our views as an aid toward understanding certain aspects of this current moment in history and possibly, as an assistance to some of those who would guide this moment to its next stage in the continuing transformation of man's life in industrial society. This foreword will explain how we came to write this book, how we abandoned some ideas along the way, and how we developed new ones to take their place.

As American labor economists, the four of us have written this book and given general direction to the project out of which it has developed because of a profound dissatisfaction. All of us, particularly in the period of World War II and the years immediately following, had done the usual things. We had worked for the government in manpower, wage stabilization, and dispute settlement programs. We had made studies of American wage structures, labor-management relations and labor markets. We had taught from the standard textbooks; even written some. We had arbitrated labor disputes in many industries and throughout the nation. But it was all largely related to the here and the now — the contemporary American scene. There was little historical perspective for the broad sweep of industrialization. There was somewhat more comparative perspective, and the experience of Britain, as the "mother country," was well impressed on our minds, particularly because of the classic work of the Webbs. But Britain and the United States have served less and less as the model for industrial society and for its labor movement.

We began wondering whether we really understood the American system of industrial relations and particularly its uniqueness. Why was it so different from others elsewhere — Germany, Israel, the Soviet Union, Argentina? If it was so "good," why did people elsewhere reject it; or at least why did they resist it? The United States government, industry, or organized labor had gone into Japan, Germany, Peru, Australia and tried to take with them the American industrial relations pattern; but it was either not accepted or, if it were, only at the most superficial level. American representatives would initiate a plan and it would develop quite differently than expected.

We had no adequate intellectual framework to understand what happened and why. Why did the Germans insist on works councils instead of bona fide plant level unions? Why did the Japanese have a dual labor market — or virtually no labor market at all, as we understood the term? And why did the Australians insist on compulsory arbitration, which we knew from our own experience could not work? Why managerial paternalism in Peru, which ran against all concepts of the proper separation of workers and management? We thought we knew from experience at Pullman and Hershey that it would not work.

This was not the way General Motors or the Machinists' Union or the Department of Labor operated.

Why?

We had learned from Commons and Perlman and Hoxie about the importance of "job control" unionism; and from Hoxie about the variety of unions in the United States. But "job control," rather than being a universal principle, was almost specific to our own country, and business unionism was hardly known elsewhere. Marx had said that labor would get more radical all the time; but it was becoming more conservative. "Should American unions be more job-centered or more active in politics?" — this was the great issue in debates over the "Theory of the Labor Movement." The debate divided the Perlmanites and the Marxists; but it became a less and less exciting debate. The works of standard economists drew our attention to imperfections in the labor market and the role of wages in depression and in inflation. As labor economists we talked about these problems too; but the problems existed in a much larger and a changing context. What was this context?

These were some of the dissatisfactions that the four of us shared. We discussed the problems with Dr. Thomas H. Carroll, vice-president of the Ford Foundation, who took an interest in our ideas and has continued to do so throughout. We told him we would like to help bring a more international perspective to American labor economics. Through the understanding of other industrial relations systems we might then understand our own better; and, as Americans worked abroad in the labor relations area, there might be, hopefully, some new suggestions for an appreciation of other situations and a consequent greater ability to work within them effectively. We pointed out that effective operation was particularly important to Americans, since

the world is torn between two great approaches to the organization of industrial society.

This was the origin of the project which came to be known
as the "Inter-university Study of Labor Problems in Economic
Development." We were, of course, reacting to a general new
sweep of curiosity among social scientists. After World War II
economic development once again became one of the great
themes of men's interests in many places. More specifically, Americans were discovering that the world was as round politically
and economically as it was geographically. And so we began
doing in our own field what so many other American social scientists were doing in theirs.

Our approach was in some respects, however, unique. We
were four economists conducting a project jointly and developing our ideas together. That it progressed at all is a testimony
both to our intolerance of each other's pet ideas and to our tolerance for each other as individuals. We had almost endless and
often heated discussions in which each developed his views; but
they always ended up as "our views."

This volume is only one of the many results of the project, as
the Appendix demonstrates. Some of several separate studies were
undertaken by one or another of the four of us, but most were
the work of other scholars drawn from several American universities and from among scholars abroad — in Great Britain,
Sweden, Lebanon, India, Egypt, Germany, and Italy. We divided the studies into "country studies" (Japan, West Africa,
Indonesia, India, Egypt, and others) and into "cross-cut studies"
(wage structures, management organization and ideologies, the
American corporation abroad, industrial relations systems, among
others). In addition, there have been a number of conferences
conducted in the United States and abroad — Istanbul, Beirut,
Teheran, Karachi, New Delhi, Jakarta, Tokyo. In some of these
conferences abroad we brought together in the same room for the
first time representatives of labor, management, government, and
the universities for discussion of common problems.

Consequently this book must be viewed as a part of a project.
To begin with, it stands as a summary of the views of the four
of us at this particular stage. It is not documented in detail because the output of the total project largely supplies the docu-

mentation. Beyond that, the ideas are partly ours, but partly they are the summation and restatement of views of other authors in the series and of the many participants in the numerous conferences. They particularly reflect the impact of the late Lloyd Fisher, who was our colleague in planning the study in its initial stages. One of his favorite sayings was that "truth is more likely to emerge out of error than out of confusion." Lloyd Fisher was never confused; and we benefited both from the exploration of his errors and the lucidity of his truths.

We started with these questions:

(1) How is an industrial work force recruited and settled into industrial life?

(2) What is the pattern of worker protest in the course of developing an industrial work force?

(3) Who gets proprietorship over protest and who controls it?

(4) How do the policies and practices of management affect the development and expression of protest? What are the policies and practices of the state and what effect do they have?

(5) How does the culture of a country affect the process of recruiting a labor force and the nature and pattern of labor protest?

We did not end up with these as our central questions. In our exploration of what was to us *terra incognita*, we failed to find some things we expected to find, but we found some other things instead. The book itself is concerned with what we think we did find. It may be of interest to note in advance some of the concepts we discarded along the way; and this list includes some of the ideas we cherished most dearly at the start.

The major point we "unlearned" had been one of our central themes at the outset. Protest was not such a dominant aspect of industrialization, and it did not have such an effect on the course of society as we once thought. Its rise and manipulation were not as central as we thought; it was less decisive to the social process. Marx, of course, had said that protest peaked in the inevitable revolution. But it was not only Marx who emphasized labor protest. Labor historians generally had concentrated on strikes and labor's political activity. To the anti-Marxist "Wisconsin school" of Commons and Perlman, labor protest was also a crucial force. The question was who should control its use — the workers themselves for their own purposes or the intellectuals for theirs? There was some evidence that this was a significant question — the Luddites, the Chartists, the New Unionism, and the rise of a Labor Party had animated a century of British history. Also in the United States, the Molly Maguires, the anarchists, the socialists, and John L. Lewis had helped to write our social annals.

But labor protest, on a closer look, is on the decline as industrialization around the world proceeds at an ever faster pace. In the mid-twentieth century, workers do not destroy machines. The protest of today is more in favor of industrialization than against it. This is partly because industrialization is accepted, even demanded, today as it was not a century ago in Britain or half a century ago in the United States. In Israel, Ghana, and Yugoslavia labor organizations seek to assist the industrialization process. Also, twentieth-century industrialization is often more "humanitarian" than when Manchester and Birmingham were the centers of the Industrial Revolution. Its managers are now more professional and use new methods to develop a labor force. Today men know more about how to control protest, as well as how to suppress it in its more organized forms — the Soviet Union has industrialized and China is industrializing without organized strikes. A controlled labor movement has become more common. Modern industrialization is less related to the traditionally strike-prone industries — textiles, lumbering, mining, water transport. Labor protest in some situations may still be a potent force, however, particularly in times of crisis. The potentialities of protest cannot safely be ignored by the leaders of industrialization, particularly when they confront the challenge of rival contenders for leadership. There is likely to be a "peaking of protest" in any individual case of industrialization, but it may not be a very high peak nor difficult to control. The analysis of the adjustments required of workers in process of industrialization provides a new demonstration of the adaptability of man. The industrializers need not shake in their boots before the raised fists of the new industrial workers.

Instead of concentrating so much on protest, we turned to the really universal phenomenon affecting workers — the inevitable structuring of the managers and the managed in the course of industrialization. Everywhere there develops a complex web of rules binding the worker into the industrial process, to his job, to his community, to patterns of behavior. Who makes the rules? What is the nature of these rules? Not the handling of protest, but the structuring of the labor force is *the* labor problem in economic development.

So we turned from concentration on protest to the problem of providing a structure for the managers and the managed. Who sets the structure? Commons and Perlman said that the demands of labor today were the rules of society tomorrow. But in some places labor did not participate in rule-making at all and yet the labor force was given its form. Elsewhere, labor organizations participated in the rule-making system but within the context largely given by the surrounding society. Who then gave the context to society? This led us to an examination of the various industrializing elites* — who they were, what strategies they followed, how they approached the worker. We turned from labor to management as the "seed of the future." Labor seldom really leads society into its future. It may pull and haul on the leaders, but management broadly defined has the greater role and responsibility in shaping the course of industrialization.

We changed our program in other less crucial, but still important ways. On closer examination, the recruitment and development of a labor force did not seem so difficult as we once thought. Men from the "bush" drove trucks. Up to a certain level, skills came easily — social as well as technical. Men appeared more readily adaptable to the industrial system — the Bedouin from the desert, the Fellah from the countryside, the Bantu from the jungle, the Indian from the village. Rather than being difficult to recruit, the would-be workers more often were found pounding on the gates to be let inside the new factory system.

Nor were preexisting cultures serious "impediments" to economic development. Witnessing some transformations, it would

* In this volume an "industrializing elite" refers to the leaders of the industrialization process. These leaders vary from one society to another, but they include the political leaders, industrial organization builders, top military officers, associated intellectuals, and sometimes leaders of labor organizations. Every industrializing elite will require technicians, administrators, and bureaucrats.

appear that nothing changes so fast as customs. Family and religion, the two immutables, made their adaptations. When cultural factors were significant, their significance was usually greatest at the earlier stages of industrialization. The new culture, even without the Draconian methods of the Communists, sooner or later took the place of the old. Instead, more crucial determining factors for the formation of the labor force and the development of management appeared to be the population situation, the starting point of industrialization, the pace of economic growth and the strategies of the industrializing elite.

It was obvious that there was an East and a West. Which would come to dominate the industrializing world? What were the best tactics for the West in the labor management area? At first this was for us the great policy issue. But the East, it turned out, was several things and not static; the West even more diverse. Instead of two worlds, there were several in the middle of this century of great transformation; and each of these several worlds was in transition. Certainly Britain, the United States, and the Soviet Union were not the only models in the world for the newly emerging economies. We began to develop, in particular, a sense of the importance of nationalism as a very real force at this stage in the history of the world. We also developed a sense of the decline of the importance of competing ideologies. More and more, the questions are technical as well as philosophical. How can this problem best be handled? How can the transition to industrialism best be made, given these conditions? The ideological differences are of great importance; but there is a new realization of the similarity of many problems and of the similarity of some solutions. Rather than two fixed points, there are several changing ones; and technicians are taking their place along with the social theorists.

Like ideologies, the great personality — the one great figure around whom historians so frequently weave their story — began to seem less important. Instead of ideologies and dominant personalities, we became increasingly attentive to the inherent nature of the particular industrializing system and the basic strategy and forces at work within it.

Many of our original convictions turned into nothing but once-held prejudices. "Free trade unions" under some conditions become no more than Communist unions sabotaging efforts at economic development. Should they be that free? Completely free trade unions are sometimes not possible or desirable at certain stages in the industrialization drive. And "free enterprise" in the absence of effective competition can engage in the most outrageous exploitation of workers and consumers. The "free labor market" may result, under some conditions, in extremely heavy turnover of workers, and even anarchy and demoralization. The "free worker," in our sense, cannot exist in some social systems; in others he might exist, but to his detriment. Some "paternalism" is basic to certain systems, to certain industries (mining, ocean transport), and to certain stages (raw workers taken from highly primitive conditions). The "political strike," as it exists under colonialism, may not only be inherent in the situation, but the only effective manner of attaining some transfer of power to the indigenous population. The "heavy hand of the state" over trade unions and enterprises may be the only substitute, at times, for the "invisible hand" of market competition which we have so long preferred. And some generals, in some situations, may be by far the best leaders of an industrializing nation, all doctrine of civilian control of the military to the contrary.

Thus we came to be much more conscious of the significance of time and place in the evaluation of some judgments, and of all slogans. The whole world cannot be like the United States or the Soviet Union, or India, and one should not be morally indignant about it. Works councils may fit Germany; a degree of employer paternalism, the Northern Rhodesian copper mines; dependent workers, the Japanese system; state planning of economic development, the current stage of Pakistani evolution. Wisdom sometimes begins when passion ends.

A new design gradually emerged in our effort to organize what we knew into the universal, the related, and the unique. As we looked around, certain things were happening everywhere. There was always a web of rules, and some rules were repeated again and again. There were some quite obvious uniformities in the several patterns of industrialization. Generally these uniformities seemed to arise out of the uniformity of the basic technology itself.

Other things, although not universal, began to fall into patterns. There were plant-oriented organizations of workers in both Germany and Japan; the worker was treated as an "independent" person in both Great Britain and the United States. Labor organizations were under strong government control in both Egypt and Pakistan. We began to organize this diversity into systems characterized by the nature of the different guiding industrializing elites. We identified five ideal types. Developments in several countries were related to each other because of the similarity of the strategy and approach of their industrializing elites. At the end of Chapters 3 through 9 are charts which seek to summarize each chapter in terms of the consistent approaches of each industrializing elite to certain common problems.

There were also developments which were unique to the individual situation. These seemed to have their explanations too, mostly within the cultural pattern of the particular country or in its historical, economic and demographic setting. We sought to identify the major forces at work.

Thus we identify the universal with the "logic of industrialism"; the related with the strategies of the "industrializing elites"; and the unique with specific cultures and environments. In all this we were trying to go beyond the topographical studies describing the lay of the land in the individual countries; to go beyond saying that in Nigeria it was this way and in Turkey that. Looking at one country at a time, each situation appeared historically unique and the totality of the detail was almost incomprehensible. We sought a system of ideas which would help to make it more nearly comprehensible.

Having set up our system of explanation, we proceeded to examine the nature of management, the process of developing the labor force, the response of the workers to the process, and the patterns of labor-management-state relations that emerge. A few problems came to interest us a good deal more than we expected: How should education adjust to the need for high-level manpower? Once labor was on the job, how could its pace of work be raised and maintained? What could be done with chronically excess supplies of labor? In the United States, we take more or less for granted an adequate educational system, a reasonable pace of work, and a rough balance of supply and demand in the labor market. In a number of industrializing countries, however, these are issues. Also, from the perspective of the nation emerging into industrialization, the recruitment and proper motivation of managers and the development of consensus in society are major problems.

Finally, we turned to considering, very briefly, the origins of the varous lines of development. Marx had seen a unilinear course to history; we see a multilinear one. There are several roads, each of which leads to industrialism. But why is one taken rather than another? And where do they all lead? Do they all converge in the end and, if so, where? In the contest between the uniformity of the logic of industrialism and the diversity of approaches among the industrializing elite, which wins out?

The great transformation of society continues apace and no one can really know how it will all turn out. But we are all curious. *The Communist Manifesto, Brave New World, 1984* — all offer their versions. In our final chapter we will offer some comments, but neither as a manifesto nor as a sure prediction. We are witnessing an immense social process and a great change in man's approach to it — from the early hatred of the new machines, to an intense desire for "modernization" and, perhaps, later, to a sense of mastery over the process itself. Man's view of the process shifts as the process moves along.

We offer here an approach to an understanding of industrial relations which seeks to draw on the experience of several countries rather than of one or a few; and a way of looking at the problem which seeks to place labor-management-state relations in the context of the imperatives of industrialism, the desires of the controlling elites and the demands of the particular environment. We offer this approach as one more attempt to comprehend the swirl of events around us. It is a progress report on our explorations to date, a report that is subject to change, for we have become acutely conscious of our own changing views.

This approach runs against tradition; against Marx, the Webbs, Commons and Perlman, and Mayo, alike. We have redefined the labor problem as the structuring of the managers and the managed under industrialization rather than as the response of unions to capitalism; we have suggested several lines of development rather than a single one — toward communism or socialism or job control or human relations. The followers of each of the standard traditions will of necessity take issue with our approach. We acknowledge this in advance and gladly. They all share, however, our concern to comprehend the world-wide variations in industrial relations systems and the great historical changes affecting them.

We live in a diverse and moving world and the description, alone, of the here and now is not enough.

PART I

UNITY AND DIVERSITY IN INDUSTRIALIZATION

The industrial system everywhere has its managers, its managed, and a pattern of interaction between them. The pattern varies from one nation to another and from one time to another in the same nation. Are these patterns and variations subject to any general explanation or only to description? Part I seeks to offer a framework of general explanation by setting forth what is universal, what is related to common strategies of industrialization, what is unique, and why.

Marx, who set forth the most famous and internationally influential explanation of social relations in the process of industrialization, concentrated on what he considered to be universal; and this included what was for him all the essential elements. There was one road and one destination. His scope of interest was wider than the present study, but he considered many issues which are of central interest to this volume. Chapter 1 ("The Task of Interpretation") compares and contrasts the differing views on some of these common issues.

Industrialization in any country displays many of the same features. Industrializing countries are more nearly like each other, however varied they may be, than they are like commercial or agricultural or hunting and fishing economies. Chapter 2 ("The Logic of Industrialism") sets forth these universal traits. One of the central traits is the inevitable and eternal separation of industrial men into managers and the managed.

At this stage in history, however, there are major differences in the way industrializing societies are organized; and these differences add both variety and conflict to the world scene. Many of these differences can be explained by the character of the industrializing elite who are in charge from one country to another — who they are, what goals they seek, what strategies they follow, and how they approach labor-management-state relations. Chapter 3 ("The Industrializing Elites and Their Strategies") sets forth five "ideal types" of elites and their characteristic approaches.

The anthropologists and the historians consistently view each society or each period as unique to itself, and to an extent they are. Uniqueness may not be the total story, but it is an important part of it. Chapter 4 ("The Conflict of Cultures in Industrialization") and Chapter 5 ("Shaping the Industrialization Process") deal with factors which encourage uniqueness in each industrializing society in general and in labor-management-state relations in particular. Religion and family arrangements, source of capital, and comparative availability of labor, among other forces, can have significant impacts. Chapter 4 treats with the meeting of the old and the new cultures; Chapter 5 with the economic, historical, and demographic factors which variously influence the industrializing process and labor-management-state relations in the course of this process. These cultural and environmental forces have direct impact on industrial relations and indirect impact through their interaction on the separate industrializing elites.

This framework is intended to assist in the understanding of labor-management-state relations within countries and among countries. Why are the United States, Great Britain, the Soviet Union, Germany, and Japan alike in some respects; the United States and Great Britain, or Germany and Japan in others; and in what respects is each unique?

CHAPTER 1

THE TASK OF INTERPRETATION

We live in the midst of enormous transformations to industrial society; the peoples of the world are everywhere on the march toward industrialism. They aspire to higher living standards. They yearn to throw off economic backwardness, illiteracy, and disease. The economically underdeveloped countries are dedicated to reducing rapidly the inequalities that have been growing in the past century between the few rich Western nations and the poor countries which comprise the mass of humanity. They know they face desperate tasks, and they must run twice as hard to narrow the large gap because the advanced countries continue to make spectacular gains. Their leaders preach dedication and hard work. They are committed to an industrial future and they have high expectations. They are launched on a long course that they realize is certain to change their communities into new and as yet not fully known societies.

Great Britain is the first and the classical case of industrialization. It was the first to cross the great divide from an agricultural and commercial society toward an industrial society. "What is certain is that by 1830 Britain had, in one way or another, obtained a body of wage-paid workers, acclimatized to factory conditions and able to move from place to place, and from employment to employment, as occasion required."[1] In the years before World War I, the industrialization process spread widely from its British center through the Western World and to Japan. The international commodity, capital and labor markets, were decisive mechanisms in the propagation of economic development to the United States, Canada, Australia, and parts of South America, not only from Great Britain but also from other emerging industrial countries, notably France and Germany. Industrialization spread out largely by diffusion rather than by independent social invention.

In the interwar years the Soviet Union embarked on a rapid and harsh industrialization program, building upon a base from the old regime, under new leadership and creating new institutions. After World War II, ambitious industrializing programs were adopted by nations and regions in Asia, Africa, and the Middle East. The relatively backward areas of economically advanced countries, such as southern Italy, have also embarked on a course toward industrialism. However, no country is yet fully industrialized; all economies, including the United States and Great Britain, are still to some extent underdeveloped.

In the 1850's the world had essentially one model of successful industrialization: that led by middle-class capitalists. Today the newly industrializing countries have a wide variety of prescriptions, a range of political and economic forms, and a growing body of industrializing experience from which to choose. Experimentation with methods of achieving the industrial society continues to grow, as the recent history of India, Jugoslavia, China, Brazil, and Egypt illustrates. This diversity of experience not only enriches the policy-making within countries and by international agencies, but it also affords a growing body of material well suited to the comparative study of the industrialization process and the interrelations of workers, managers, and governments.

The new industrializing man is more highly educated, enjoys better health, lives longer, and has more leisure than members of traditional societies. His living standards are materially higher, and he is insistently impatient to achieve the ever higher expectations commonly generated in the industrializing society. But industrializing man also sentences himself to hard work. Whether he be worker or manager, he is required to conform to an elaborate web of rules at the work place and in the community. His more highly developed potentialities struggle with leveling conformity.

The industrializing nations have a sense of urgency, even of desperation — some more than others. They have come to recognize, as did the Japanese leaders of the Meiji restoration, that industrial technology overwhelms; they must master it or face oblivion. A military defense now requires a relatively advanced industrial technology. The military bases and operations of the great powers have demonstrated to the farthest corners of the globe, no less than the truck and the tin can, the invincibility of the giant of industrialization. Nonindustrial societies are ultimately destined to be consigned to the rear ranks of nations.

The actual course of the transition to an industrial society may be seen as an interaction between the imperatives of the industrialization process and a preexisting culture. In every case of industrialization there are numerous points of conflict and of accommodation. In the language of Toynbee, there is an encounter between civilizations. There is a struggle for dominance between the new industrial order and the preexisting order. "The adjustment of institutions to changing economic circumstances may be a painful process. It is neither balanced nor complete. . . . The new and the old are mixed illogically and in curious proportions, which differ widely from society to society."[9] The battleground is at a variety of points and levels: religious and ethical values, family system, class alignments, educational system, government structure, and legal system. In this interaction, the old society will be revamped to a greater or lesser extent, or, in extreme cases, it may be largely swept away. The accommodation between the old and the new may also create a distinctive industrializing society, and the process and speed of industrialization in turn may be cause as well as effect in the accommodation of the old and new. An insistent question of the transition concerns which institutions of the traditional society shall be preserved, transformed, and modified, and which shall be sacrificed.

To recognize the invincibility of the industrialization process is not necessarily to approve or to advocate industrialism. It may be argued from some value systems that economic development is undesirable or secured at too high a price of social and political changes in the traditional society. As individuals we may not approve of all the implications of the mature industrial society. But an argument against industrialization in general is now futile, for the world has firmly set its face toward the industrial society, and there is no turning back. The next century is likely to see, despite the obstacles and masses of people involved, an even more dramatic transformation in the countries recently embarked on the road to industrialization than occurred in England in the century after 1750 and in the United States after 1850. Most countries are moving relentlessly through a transition period toward industrialism. They are traveling at different speeds and on different roads, but they all aspire to reach the industrial society. For some the journey will be shorter or easier than for others, but for all the full transition to industrialism will be a long passage.

The Central Questions

Men have sought throughout history to place the immediate events of their times in a longer vista and to relate the developments in their communities to those in other areas. It is by this process that we give meaning to what happens. The task is never finished, for we must continually reassess perspectives and ideas in the light of changing developments.

It is always difficult for one age to see its own place in the stream of history. The interpretation of contemporaneous events tends to suffer from myopia and distortions. The course and potentialities of the Renaissance in Western Europe or the Industrial Revolution in England were not well understood by contemporary observers. Nor is our day likely to perceive with ease the full implications of the great events of our times. Yet it is vital to seek coherent interpretations of these developments and to expose each new analysis to critical review and revision.

The interpretation and meaning ascribed to contemporaneous events is more than a speculative exercise. Courses of action and policies imply one view of events rather than another. It is well that competing frames of reference for current developments be made explicit.

Any general interpretation of the industrialization process and its relation to workers and managers must provide answers to a group of questions:

   (1) What are the main features of systems of interpretation of industrialization, or of capitalism, which was its first form? What contribution do these explications make to an understanding of the diverse patterns of relations now emerging among managers, workers, and governments?

   (2) Does industrialism have an inner logic? What are the

inherent tendencies of the industrialization process, and what impact do they necessarily have upon workers, managers, and governments?

(3) Who are the leaders who plan the strategy and direct the march to industrialism? What are the implications of each strategy for the relations among workers, managers, and governments?

(4) What are the areas of conflict between the traditional culture and industrialization? How are these conflicts resolved? How do the conflicts between the old and the new societies affect the pattern of relations among workers, managers, and governments?

(5) What are the principal decisions made in the course of the transition? What are the major questions which confront a country seeking to industrialize, and how do the ways in which these problems are handled influence the relations among workers, managers, and governments?

(6) What is the role of enterprise management in the industrializing society? What are the consequences of alternative policies and philosophies of managements upon economic development and the pattern of industrial relations? How are enterprise managers generated and developed?

(7) How is an industrial labor force recruited, developed, and motivated in the course of industrialization?

(8) What are the responses of workers in the industrialization process? Who organizes them? Into what types of institutions are they organized and around what ideas?

(9) What are the major patterns of interrelations that are established among workers, managers, and governments in the industrialization process?

(10) Do industrializing societies, regardless of their origins and leadership, tend to become more similar to each other, or do they retain the variations of their pre-industrial background or develop new diversities?

These ten groups of questions are considered in turn in the ten chapters of this volume. The discussion of these questions taken as a whole is designed to provide a coherent and general theory of industrialization and its impact on managers and workers. The first comprehensive interpretation of the industrialization process was provided by Karl Marx at the outset of the classic British case. While Marx had something to say concerning the questions listed above, he was interested in a considerably wider range of issues, and his system raised different questions and used quite different concepts. The central interests of this volume are narrower in scope and more specialized to the inter-relations among workers, managers and governments. The present analysis, however, is able to draw upon an additional century of experience with industrialization in many countries and under diverse leaders. It also has the benefit of the reflections of several generations of scholars seeking the inner logic and the inherent tendencies of the industrialization process.

The Marxian Interpretation

Marx was largely influenced by British conditions existing in the first half of the nineteenth century.[3] Marx regarded the case as a general model since "The country that is more developed industrially only shows, to the less developed, the image of its own future."[4]

After the passage of a century, Marxian views on the industrial process are still widely accepted. One third of the globe is ruled by leaders who are committed to the dogma. The Marxian ideology has had great appeal to large groups of workers and intellectuals of Western Europe over whom, however, its doctrinaire hold is now waning. It commands many converts and wide allegiance among the intellectuals and sectors of the labor movements in many newly industrializing countries. The Marxian view of the industrialization process — and its implications for the relations of workers, managers and governments — will be briefly stated, together with an occasional reference to other writers in order to compare and to contrast it with the ideas advanced in this volume.[5]

An Analytical Model of Social Development. Marx applied deductive methods to long-run economic and social processes. The preface to *Capital* states that it is the ". . . ultimate aim of this work, to lay bare the economic law of motion of modern society." He was concerned to develop the logical implications inherent in the "capitalist mode of production." Marx's thought was thus concerned with long-run developments. ". . . it tries to uncover the mechanism that, by its mere working and without the aid of external factors, turns any given state of society into another."[6] A recognition of the long-term tendencies inherent in early industrialization under capitalist or bourgeoisie leadership, regardless of whether the particular deductions have always proved to be historically valid in retrospect, was a considerable intellectual achievement apart from its role as propaganda. For Marx ". . . the fundamental view of the capitalist process (is) one which, in principle, involves ceaseless accumulation accompanied by changes in methods of production. . . . The way is paved for regarding the 'end product' as a revolutionary reconstitution of society. . . ."[7]

The application of deductive methods to long-run processes was not, of course, distinctive to Marx; he adopted the methods of Ricardo and the classical economists and was the first to develop an explicit model of the capitalist process. The more recent writings of Veblen and Schumpeter illustrate more or less comprehensive models of capitalist development. Indeed, ". . . . we cannot approach historical reality except through a search of regularities and deviations from regularities, that is to say, by conceiving it in terms of constructs of our mind, of patterns, or models."[8] One of the principal deficiencies, even in the classic studies of relations between workers and managers, such as those of the Webbs and Commons, is that they have lacked the perspective of a long-run deductive model of the industrialization process.

Central Role of Technology. Changes in the methods of production necessarily change the structure of society. The technology of the capitalists is superior to earlier forms. Moreover, "The bourgeoisie cannot exist without constantly revolutionising the instruments of production, and thereby the relations of production, and with them the whole relations of society."[9] Among the transformations in society created by the bourgeoisie and explicitly noted by Marx and Engels are the following: "the physician, the lawyer, the priest, the poet, the man of science" are converted into "paid wage-labourers"; the family relation has been reduced to a mere money relation; the bourgeoisie has subjected the country to the rule of the towns"; "It compels all nations on pain of extinction, to adopt the bourgeois mode of production"; "a cosmopolitan character to production and consumption in every country"; "The bourgeoisie, wherever it has got the upper hand, has put an end to all feudal, patriarchal, idyllic relations." But the bourgeoisie also produce the proletariat: "its own gravediggers. Its fall and the victory of the proletariat are equally inevitable."

For Veblen, changes in technology are the key generators of institutional changes. ". . . the machine discipline acts to disintegrate the institutional heritage, of all degrees of antiquity and authenticity — whether it be the institutions that embody the principles of natural liberty or those that comprise the residue of more archaic principles of conduct still current in civilized life."[10] Tannenbaum makes the application to workers more directly: "The machine, however, seems to know no limits. It is invading a constantly increasing portion of the community's activities. It constantly compels new adjustments for more and more people. . . . Where men used to have land or commerce in common they now have the machine, and as the feudal organization represented the expression of the dominance of land, as capitalism represented and represents the dominance of commerce — so the labor movement is the blind and unplanned readjustment of men to a new economic center of gravity. . . . The labor movement is the result, and the machine is the major cause."[11]

Degradation of the Industrial Worker. The logic of the capitalist mode of production yields certain necessary results on the workers and in the relations of workers and capitalists:

[The workman] becomes an appendage of the machine, and it is only the most simple, most monotonous, and most easily acquired knack, that is required of him. (*Manifesto*, p. 65). . . . Hence, in the place of the hierarchy of specialized workmen that characterizes manufacture, there steps, in the automatic factory, a tendency to equalise and reduce to one and the same level every kind of work that has to be done by the minders of the machines . . . (*Capital*, p. 420). The more modern industry becomes developed, the more is the labour of men superseded by that of women (*Manifesto*, p. 66). . . . The various interests and conditions of life within the ranks of the proletariat are more and more equalised, in proportion as machinery obliterates all distinctions of labour, and nearly everywhere reduces wages to the same low level (*Manifesto*, p. 69). . . . The essential division is, into workmen who are actually employed on the machines (among whom are included a few who look after the engine), and into mere attendants (almost exclusively children) of these workmen. . . . In addition to these two principal classes, there is a numerically unimportant class of persons, whose occupation is to look after the whole of the machinery and repair it from time to time such as engineers, mechanics, joiners, etc. (*Capital*, p. 420). . . . machinery is the surest means of lengthening the working day. . . . lengthening of the working day went hand in hand with increasing the intensity of factory labour (*Capital*, pp. 408–9). . . . Factory legislation, that first conscious and methodical reaction of society against the spontaneously developed form of the process of production, is, as we have seen, just as much the necessary product of modern industry as cotton yarn, self-actors, and the electric telegraph (p. 480).[12]

These quotations from the *Manifesto* and *Capital* envisage as the consequence of capitalist production longer hours, greater intensity of work, the destruction of the hierarchy of specialized workmen in pre-industrial society and the leveling of skill, a minor number of skilled labor, engineers, and managers, and the use of women and children for a growing number of unskilled tending and feeding jobs. The impact of the factory system upon workers is a persistent theme of serious students of the capitalist process, legislative investigations, and pamphleteers.

Inevitable Protest and Revolution. There is necessarily a tendency toward increasing misery for the working class. The capitalist process of accumulation inherently reduces the lot of the laborer. Mechanization destroys his skill. Business crises are increasingly severe. The industrial reserve army, recruited primarily from those displaced by machinery, exert a continuous downward pressure on wage rates and preclude wage increases. "Within the capitalist system all methods for raising social productiveness of labor are brought about at the cost of the individual laborer. . . . Accumulation of wealth at one pole is, therefore, at the same time accumulation of misery, agony of toil, slavery, ignorance, brutality, mental degradation, at the opposite pole, i.e., on the side of the class that produces its own product in the form of capital."[13]

Marx sees the discontent of the proletariat growing through a series of stages until it eventually erupts into open revolution, and "the violent overthrow of the bourgeoisie lays the foundation for the sway of the proletariat."[14] At first the "contest" is carried on by individual laborers, then by the work people of a factory, then by one trade in a locality, then workers organize into trade unions, and finally into a political party. The proletariat are joined by ideological bourgeois who comprehend "the historical movement as a whole." Open revolution breaks out as the culmination of the capitalist contradictions. The increasing misery of the working class, the falling rate of profit, the increasingly severe crises, the increasing class and political organization of workers, under the vanguard of the communists, creates increasing discontent and protest among workers through the capitalist period.[15]

The State: Past and Future. The state under capitalism in the Marxian view, is an apparatus of the oppression of one class by another. "Political power, properly so called, is merely the organized power of one class for oppressing another."[16] The highest purpose of the state is the protection of private property;[17] it is an instrument of class domination. "Property confers upon its owners freedom from labor and the disposal over the labor of others, and this is the essence of all social dominance whatever form it may assume. It follows that the protection of property is fundamentally the assurance of social domination to owners over non-owners."[18] Thus, in the Marxian view, the capitalist state must be overthrown by revolution.

In the good society which Marx believed to be the final and inevitable result of the dialectical process, there would no longer be a division of society into economic classes. Since he held the state to be an instrument of class coercion, and all classes based fundamentally on economic power, the state would no longer be necessary and would "wither away." "The society that is to reorganize production on the basis of free and equal association of the producers, will transfer the machinery of state where it will then belong into the Museum of Antiquities by the side of the spinning wheel and the bronze age."[19]

World-Wide Imperialism. Changes in technique introduced under the bourgeoisie necessarily tend to create world-wide markets and a world-wide community. There could never be a closed capitalist system. "The bourgeoisie has through its exploitation of the world market given a cosmopolitan character to production and consumption in every country. . . . In place of the local and national seclusion and self-sufficiency, we have intercourse in every direction, universal interdependence of nations. And as in material, so also in intellectual production."[20]

Among advanced capitalist countries, in which accumulation is at high rates, capital is exported to backward regions where wages are low and profits high. An active colonial policy is created. But these exports lead to an uneven and one-sided production pattern in colonial areas; natural resources and trade are exploited, and some public works are created. An indigenous bourgeoisie arises which seeks to encourage native industries. But handicraft industry is destroyed by imports and the native population is driven out of the land. "The interests of both native bourgeoisie and native masses are sacrificed to the needs of capital in the advanced countries."[21] The rivalry and contradictions of advanced capitalist colonial powers characterize imperialism and world conflict.

There are at least three aspects of the work of Marx which are vital to subsequent analysis of the industrialization process. (1) In applying deductive methods to long-run economic and social processes, he illustrated the potentialities of a powerful tool of analysis. The method compels attention to the inner logic and necessities of the industrialization process. The time horizon is not a short period but rather the long run, the end consequences of the working out of the industrialization process which is industrialism.

(2) Changes in technology introduced in the course of industrialization do have fundamental consequences for many features of a traditional society: its family system, educational processes, and scheme of values. This insight is fruitful for tracing the wider consequences of changes in methods of production. The economic interpretation of history, however, need not be so mechanically applied as to render it an absolute principle. Moreover, it must be recognized that changes in technology are not entirely autonomous; they are frequently related to other changes in the larger society.

(3) The emphasis upon the process of capital accumulation, as distinct from Marx's preoccupation with "The General Law of

Capitalist Accumulation," is a contribution to the understanding of industrialization under any political form. The source and the rate of "surplus value" is pivotal to each case of industrialization. It is fruitful to analyze each country which is industrializing in terms of the sources of capital that have been marshalled for industrial growth at varying stages in its development. The relative reliance varies widely in different countries among capital from abroad, reduced worker consumption, profits, a specialized extractive resource such as oil, and agriculture.

The Necessity for a New View

A century or more has passed since the early stages of the first instance of industrialization under middle-class leadership which so influenced Marx's formulations. Also, a century of advance in theoretical economics has replaced the Ricardian system which Marx adopted as a starting point. The intervening years have seen industrialization take an increasing variety of economic and political forms. There are infinitely more data on which to formulate a general view of the industrialization process and its impacts upon workers, managers, and governments. The advantage of first-hand observation and detailed discussions in a number of industrializing countries now provides a more solid basis for valid generalization.

The following points compare and contrast the major features of the Marxian interpretation of the capitalist process with the analytical framework to be developed in this volume. No attempt is made in this chapter, however, to answer the ten questions listed earlier or to sketch a rounded view of the analysis.

Industrialization Rather Than Capitalism. This volume is concerned with the industrialization process rather than with the "Process of Capitalist Production" which was the subtitle to Marx's *Capital.* It is not the process of capitalist production but rather industrialization in many guises which is of contemporary interest. In our times it is no longer the specter of Communism which is haunting Europe, but rather emerging industrialization in many forms that is confronting the whole world. The giant of industrialization[22] is stalking the earth, transforming almost all the features of older and traditional societies.

Rising Levels of Skill and Responsibility. The technology of modern industry tends to raise substantially and progressively the average levels of skills and responsibilities of a work force. It also tends to raise the proportion of highly skilled and responsible employees. While some older handicraft skills may be destroyed and the transitions may be painful, new skills and new responsibilities are created. Modern technology is displacing highly repetitive tasks with new machinery and processes and is creating new skills at high levels to design, install, maintain and service such automatic processes. The distinction between machine operatives and attendants tends to disappear. New industries and occupations are continually being created by modern industry, and white-collar and service occupations, outside a factory milieu, come to bulk very large.

Growing Proportion of Technical and Managerial Personnel. Modern industry requires a rapidly increasing number and a high proportion of technical, professional, and managerial personnel. This is equally true whether ownership is private or public. This staff is concerned with the functions of planning, organization, direction, training, and research that have become indispensable to modern factory production and to urban communities. Neither this group, nor the skilled manual workers, can be referred to as "a numerically unimportant class of persons." On the contrary, they are a group continuously increasing in size and significance. They require an ever higher degree of formal education and training, and substantial resources in the community tend to be devoted to their development.

New Wealth and Leisure. Industrialization is technically so superior to earlier forms of production that it tends under any political and economic system to raise materially the level of wages, to reduce the hours of work, and to raise living standards as measured by such conventional means as life expectancy, health, and education. While policies of rapid industrialization may divert for a period all "surplus" to further industrial expansion in heavy industry, eventually improvements in living standards cannot be longer delayed. The prospects are for increased well-being rather than for increased misery. Indeed, much of the early resistance to industrialization has disappeared, even in economically backward countries, as economic development has become a policy of these regions and as individuals seek and expect the benefits associated with industrialization.

The Decline of Overt Protest. The discontent of workers, reflected in disruptive forms of protest, tends to be greatest in the early stages of industrialization and tends to decline as workers become more accustomed to industrialization. The partially committed industrial worker, with strong ties to the extended family and village, unaccustomed to urban life and to the discipline and mores of the factory, is more likely to reflect open revolt against industrial life than the seasoned worker more familiar with the ways of the factory, more understanding of the reasons for the web of factory rules, more reconciled to factory life, more motivated by urban and monetary considerations and less attached to the traditional and rural society. The worker in process of the early stages of industrialization is more prone to absenteeism, prolonged and sporadic withdrawal from industrial work, wildcat stoppages, naked violence, and destruction of machines and property. In later periods, industrial workers tend to be more disciplined in their withdrawal of effort and in the use of the strike. The extent of protest does not tend to rise with increasing industrialization, reaching the crescendo of revolution with a mature work force fully committed to factory and urban life. Rather, turning Marx on his head, protest tends to peak early. The initial generations of industrial workers tend to be critical from the perspective of concern with the revolutionary consequences of the transition to the industrial society.

Greater Role of Enterprise Managers. Industrial managers, private or public, and their technical and professional associates, rather than industrial workers, have the more significant and decisive role in industrialization. Again, turning Marx on his head, they are the "vanguard" of the future. It is they who largely create and apply the new technology, who determine the transformations in skills and responsibilities, who influence the impact of such changes upon the work force and who exercise leadership in a technological society. This is not to imply that workers and their organizations exercise no influence on the course of industrialization. They perform the vital role of protest, of calling attention to both the direct and unforeseen consequences of managerial decisions upon workers and the larger community. But, except for crisis periods, this is essentially a more restricted and passive role. The initiative for the technological revolution and its consequences for the work force are concentrated more largely in the hands of managers. This view places an even heavier responsibility upon industrial managers, upon their selection, training, and norms of conduct, be they private or public.

The Omnipresent State. Industrialization involves a large role for government not only to treat with the technological complexities of modern industry, or with developmental programs, but also as a consequence of the goods and services demanded in the industrializing society, such as education and health services, and directly in the regulation of the relations between managers and workers. Modern industrialization does not see the withering away of the state and its bureaucracy; rather the role of governmental agencies is expanded and enhanced. Industrial relations seldom concern the relations of workers (and their organizations) and managers solely. Typically, there is a three-way relation, including state agencies.

The Eternal Classes. No classless society arises under industrialism, even if a revolution is executed to eliminate a class.[23] Workers are never freed from restraints; they never lose their "chains" in the work place. Industrialization requires and develops a distinctive web of rules to constrain and to direct the industrial work force, and workers have or may have more or less influence in shaping these rules. The industrializing society whatever its political form, demands high-skilled technologists and lower-skilled manual workers, and requires managers and the managed.

Many Roads to Industrialism. The course of industrialization does not follow a single mold or prescribed pattern. Underdeveloped countries need not grow in all important respects in "the image" of any particular advanced country. There is a variety of leaders of industrialization movements, with different objectives, starting with societies at varying degrees of backwardness, confronting different obstacles, proceeding at quite different rates of speed, and using a variety of political and social forms. Nor does the industrialization process end in a single stereotype revolution.

Pluralistic Industrialism. The industrializing society does not in the end create political uniformity and standardized interests. Workers do not develop a monolithic solidarity, although the advanced industrializing society eliminates many of the regional, linguistic, and nationalist internal differences of an earlier stage of development. New differentiations appear as diverse occupational, cultural, and associational interests arise in a society of higher incomes, more leisure, and higher standards of education. The society nearing industrialism is pluralistic in its interests, with a wide range for individual freedom outside the work place.

An interpretation of the industrialization process developed during the early stages of the first instance of industrialization is not likely to be appropriate or applicable after a century of experience.[24] No rigid model or dogma is satisfying to the dynamic industrialization process in new settings, in new and varied forms and with new leaders. There is need to rethink the logic of the industrialization process and its consequences for workers, managers, and their interrelations with governments. The views set forth in this and later chapters are designed to assist in a new analysis of the industrialization process and its consequences for industrial man.

CHAPTER 2

THE LOGIC OF INDUSTRIALISM

Industrialization refers to the actual course of transition from the traditional society toward industrialism. Industrialism is an abstraction, a limit approached through historical industrialization. Industrialism is the concept of the fully industrialized society, that which the industrialization process inherently tends to create. Even the most economically advanced countries today are to some degree and in some respects underdeveloped. They contain features derived from earlier stages of development which obscure the pure logic of the industrialization process.

The central purpose of this chapter is to state the imperatives intrinsic in the industrialization process; the logic of the process taken as a whole constitutes industrialism. The present purpose is not to predict the actual course of the future, or to approximate the most probable industrial society of 1984, 2060, or 2460. Neither is the task to extrapolate the course of development of any contemporary society, now highly or slightly industrialized, through the long transition period to the fully industrialized society.

The present objective is rather analytical and deductive. Given the character of science and technology and the requirements inherent in modern methods of production and distribution, what may be deduced as to the necessary or the likely characteristics of workers and managers and their interrelations, in societies that continue to industrialize? What are the inherent tendencies and implications of industrialization for the work place — factory, office, laboratory, site, transport, or mine — and the larger community? Assuming the transition stage of industrialization to have passed, what would be the principal features of the new society?

In the actual course of history the inherent tendencies of the industrial process are not likely, at least for a very long

time, to be fully realized. Industrialization ordinarily develops
in an existing and established society; even in an "empty country" immigrants bring along many traits of an old society. The
existing societies shape and constrain the full implications and
inherent features of the industrialization process. The leaders of
economic development influence the directions and the rate of
industrial growth, and the existing resources and the contemporaneous developments in other countries are also likely to affect
actual events in an industrialization. These influences do not
vitiate the significance of the underlying tendencies within industrialization generally. Indeed, an understanding of the logic
of the industrialization process (industrialism) is requisite to an
appreciation of the full measure of the influence of historical, cultural, and economic factors on the actual course of industrialization.

The Industrial Work Force

The industrialization process utilizes a level of technology far
in advance of that of earlier societies. Moreover, the associated
scientific revolution generates continual and rapid changes in production methods, products, and in technology. The continuing
changes in science and the technology and production methods
inherent in industrialization have a number of decisive consequences for workers, managers, the state, and their interrelation.

The science and technology of industrialization is based upon
research organizations: universities, research institutes, laborato-
ries, and specialized departments of enterprises. The methods
and procedures of scientific research are likewise applied to a
variety of economic and social problems. It is an axiom of scientific inquiry that the frontiers of knowledge are virtually
limitless, and research experience shows that accretions to knowledge yield further unsuspected relations and conclusions in un-
ending vistas. While individual research projects or fields of
inquiry may be played out, the totality of research appears to
defy any diminishing returns. A dynamic science creates changes
in technology which defy prediction and appear to stretch
without limit into the future.

The industrial system requires a wide range of skills and professional competency broadly distributed throughout the work force. These specialized human resources are indispensable to the science, technology, and production methods of industrialism. Indeed, the creation of such a highly skilled and professional labor force is one of the major problems of a society in transition to industrialism. The absence of a specialized and highly qualified labor force is no less serious an impediment to industrial growth than a shortage of capital goods. The professional, technical, and managerial component of the labor force, private and public, is particularly strategic since it largely carries the responsibility of developing and ordering the manual and clerical labor force.

Mobility and the Open Society. The science and technology of the industrial society is never static; it generates continual, rapid, widespread changes in production methods and products, which in turn create frequent changes in the skills, responsibilities and occupations of the work force. Some are made redundant and new ones are created. Both insecurites of obsolescence and gains from new and expanding fields reflect the highly dynamic qualities of jobs and occupations. The work force is confronted with repeated object lessons of the general futility of fighting these changes, and in the industrial society the work force comes to be reconciled, by and large, to adaptations required by the repeated changes in ways of earning a living generated by technology and science. But there may be continuing conflict over the timing of change and the division of the gains. The industrial society requires continual training and retraining of the work force; the content of an occupation or job classification is seldom set for life, as in the traditional society. Its occupational mobility is associated with a high degree of geographical movement in a work force and with social mobility in the larger community both upwards and downwards.

The industrial society tends to be an open society, inconsistent with the assignment of managers or workers to occupations or to jobs by traditional caste, racial groups, by sex or by family status. There is no place for the extended family in the industrial society; it is on balance an impediment to requisite mobility. The primary family constitutes a larger and more mobile labor force. The function of the family under industrialism is constricted: it engages in very little production; it provides little, if any, formal education and occupational training; the family business is substantially displaced by professional management. ". . . economic growth and a transference of women's work from the household to the market go closely hand in hand."[1] In the industrial society the primary family is largely a source of labor supply, a unit of decision-making for household expenditures, and a unit of cultural activity.

This society is always in flux and in motion as a result of its science and technology. It is continuously rearranging what people do for a living, where they work and where they live, and on what they spend their incomes. Their children come to expect to live different lives from their parents, so rapid and extensive are the changes. But mobility in the industrial society is not random; it comes to be organized and governed by a complex of rules of the work community.

Education — The Handmaiden of Industrialism. Industrialization requires an educational system functionally related to the skills and professions imperative to its technology. Such an educational system is not primarily concerned with conserving traditional values or perpetuating the classics; it does not adopt a static view of society, and it does not place great emphasis on training in the traditional law. The higher educational system of the industrial society stresses the natural sciences, engineering, medicine, managerial training, whether private or public, and administrative law. It must steadily adapt to new disciplines and fields of specialization. There is a relatively smaller place for the humanities and arts, and the social sciences are strongly related to the training of managerial groups and technicians for the enterprise and the government. The increased leisure time of industrialism, however, can afford a broader public appreciation of the humanities and the arts.

In the industrial order, as in all societies, there is debate over the curriculum in higher education and over what the youth is to be taught, at least on the narrow grounds of selecting the programs that provide most effectively for the range of careers. The largest part of the higher educational system tends to be specialized and designed to produce the very large volume of the professionals, technicians, and managers required in the industrial society. There is a case for some degree of generality in the educational system because of the rapidity of change and growth of knowledge during the course of a career. A technically trained work force needs to be able to follow and adapt to changes in its specialities and to learn to shift to new fields. Generality is also requisite for those coordinating and leading the specialists.

The industrial society tends to create an increasing level of general education for all citizens, not only because it facilitates training and flexibility in the work force, but also because as incomes rise natural curiosity increases the demand for formal education, and education becomes one of the principal means of vertical social mobility in a technical world. "This demand for a certain minimum of culture is created by the conditions of the capitalist mode of production itself, with its high technique, complexity, flexibility, mobility, rapidity of development of world competition, and so forth."[2] It will be observed that the industrial society tends to transform drastically the educational system of the pre-industrial society. Further, the high level of technical and general education requisite to the industrial society cannot but have significant consequences for political life. The means of mass communication play a significant role both in raising standards of general education and in conditioning political activity and shaping political control.

Research organizations develop scientific, professional, technical, and managerial specialists indispensable to the operation and administration of the industrial society. The industrial society requires increasing numbers of this high-level manpower, and the areas of specialization continue to multiply. The relations of workers, managers, and governments even develop into a field of significant specialization, and a discipline of industrial relations emerges. Technicians in industrial relations are formally trained for a place in all organizations participating in the labor market.

The Structure of the Labor Force. The labor force of the industrial society is highly differentiated by occupations and job classifications, by rates of compensation, and by a variety of relative rights and duties in the work place community. The labor force is not a homogeneous mass of workers and managers freely substitutable for each other. It is impossible to consider the individual worker or manager in isolation from his place in the complex of responsibilities, relative compensation, and differentiated rights in the work community.[3] The labor force in industrialism has form and structure vastly different from the traditional society.

The variety of skills, responsibilities, and working conditions at the work place of enterprises requires an ordering or a hierarchy. There are successive levels of authority of managers and the managed, as well as considerable specialization of function at each level of the hierarchy of the work place. There is a related differentiation according to compensation; enterprises establish a wage and salary schedule which differentiates groups of workers and managers. Job evaluation and salary plans symbolize the ordering of the industrial work force by function and compensation.[4]

The work force in the industrial society is also structured in the sense that movement within the work community is subjected to a set of rules; hiring, temporary layoffs, permanent redundance, promotions, shift changes, transfers, and retirement are applied to individual workers and managers according to their position, station, seniority, technical competency, or some other measure of status in a group rather than in random fashion. Not all jobs are open at all times to all bidders except in the structureless market. The ports of entry from outside into an enterprise are limited, and priorities in selection are established. Movement tends to be relatively easier within certain groupings of jobs than among these job families in an enterprise. Job families may be defined differently according as movement is promotion, layoff, or transfer. The relative rights of workers and their protection in particular jobs constitute a complex structuring of job relationships at their work places.

The industrial system changes the hours of work that prevail in agriculture. The technology and the demands of the industrial community require around-the-clock manning at some operations. The silent night of pre-industrial society yields to the insistent requirements of continuous operations. The work force is geared to shift operations and the community to a changed attitude toward working at night. Even the holidays and religious days of the traditional society do not escape transformation.

Scale of Society

The technology and specialization of the industrial society are necessarily and distinctively associated with large-scale organizations. Although large cities antedate industrialism, the metropolitan area characteristically arises in the course of industrialization. The largest organization of industrialism in a country is the national government machinery. Economic activity is carried on by large-scale enterprises which require extensive coordination of managers and the managed. A wide variety of rules and norms are essential to secure coordination and compliance within enterprises and to achieve their objectives in the larger community.

Urban Dominance. The industrial society is an urban society. While substantial cities have been created as commercial and religious centers,[5] urban ways come to permeate the whole of industrial society. The industrial society is concentrated in metropolitan areas with their suburbs and satellite communities. Rapid means of transportation and mass communication tend to reduce the variance of subcultures in the society, particularly those based on geography and the contrast between farm and city.

In the industrial society agriculture is simply another industry; it is not a "way of life" to be preserved for its own value or because it constituted a traditional and antecedent form of society. Agriculture serves the sole purpose of providing a variety of agricultural outputs for the economy; it is not even certain that it fulfills the function of supplying industrial manpower which it does in the transitional stages. Agricultural units of production (farms) tend to be specialized according to products, and the general farm, substantially self-sufficient, has little place in the industrial society. Indeed, the proportion of the work force engaged in agriculture is a rough index of the degree of industrialization of a society.[6] Allowance should be made for economies concentrating in particular agricultural products as a consequence of international specialization. "To the economic eye a community which needs to have the majority of its people working on the land is merely demonstrating its inefficiency."[7]

The industrial society tends to adopt the values, folkways, and heroes of the city and comes to shed those of agriculture and the farm. Even the art and music of the pure industrial society can be expected to be substantially different from the pre-industrial society. The industrial society frees itself from its agricultural antecedents.

Large Role for Government. The industrial society is necessarily characterized by a substantial range and scale of activities by the government. In a society of advanced technology there are, by virtue of this technology, a larger number of activities for government; for instance, the need for roads and highways, the provision for airports, the regulation of traffic, radio and television, a result of modern means of communication. Urban development has the same consequences. Technology also creates a more complex problem for a military establishment, extending in many directions the activities of government. The more integrated character of the world increases the activities significant to international relations and hence typically the scope of governmental activities. The scale of some scientific applications and the capital needs of new technologies tend to increase the scope of public agencies. As income rises, the demand of consumers may be for services largely provided by governments, such as education, parks, roads and health services.

The industrial society and individual freedom, however, are not necessarily to be regarded as antagonists. A high degree of discipline in the work place imposed by a web of rules and a large range of governmental activities is fully consistent with a larger freedom for the individual in greater leisure, a greater range of choice in occupations and place of residence, a greater range of alternatives in goods and services on which to use income, and a very wide range of subgroups or associations in which to choose participation. It is a mistake to regard the industrial society as antithetical to individual freedom by citing ways in which the scope of public and private governments has increased without also noting ways in which the industrial society expands individual freedom.

The role of government in countries entering upon industrialization, regardless of political form, may therefore be expected to be greater than before. There is wisdom in the observation: ". . . it is extremely unlikely that the highly modernized systems of the world today could have developed indigenously on the basis of any system other than ones that relied very heavily indeed on private individual operations, and it is extremely unlikely that latecomers can carry out such development without relying very heavily on public operations."[8]

The Web of Rules. The production of goods and services in the industrial society is largely in the hands of large-scale organizations. They consist of hierarchies of those with authority to direct, including staff advisers, and those with the function of following such directions. There are relatively few managers, and there are a great many to be managed. The managers and the managed are connected by an elaborate web of rules that is made the more intricate and complex by technology, specialization, and the large-scale operations.

A network of relationships between managers and the managed and a complex of substantive rules is required to make the industrial system operative at the work place, quite apart from the issues concerned with who formulates or promulgates these rules. At any one time, the rights and duties of workers and of managers, indeed of all those in the hierarchy, must be established and understood by all those involved in the hierarchy. Answers must be provided to the many questions that arise in the course of operating a complex organization with managers and workers, and procedures are required to provide promptly such answers. The web of rules of the work place concerns compensation, discipline, layoffs, transfers and promotions, grievances, and a vast array of matters, some common to all work places and others specialized for the type of activity — factory, airline, railroad, mine, or office — and to the specific establishment. The rules also establish norms of output, pace, and performance. Moreover, the web of rules is never static, and procedures arise for the orderly change of these rules. The industrial system creates an elaborate "government" at the work place and work community. It is often said that primitive societies have extensive rules, customs, and taboos, but a study of the industrial society reflects an even greater complex and a different set of detailed rules.

The web of rules established at a work place may be viewed partially as the consequence of the technological features and market or budgetary constraints of the work place, which are in a large measure common to all types of industrializing countries, and also partially the consequence of the particular resources, political and economic forms of the country, and its path to industrialism. The relative strength of these factors, and their mode of interaction, is significant to an understanding of any particular industrial society. The industrial system tends to develop a common set of rules under common technological and economic conditions. Cultural and national differences are less significant to the web of rules, the further a country is along the road toward industrialism.

Governments tend to have a significant role in determining the substantive rules of the work community or in establishing the procedures and responsibilities of those with this power. In the fully industrialized society, regardless of the relative balance and roles of enterprise managers, workers, and the government in the transition, all three tend to have a significant part in the establishment, adaptation, and administration of the rules of the work place and work community. The industrial relations system of the industrial society is genuinely tripartite (See Chapters 9, 10).

Consensus in Society

The industrial society, as any established society, develops a distinctive consensus which relates individuals and groups to each other and provides a common body of ideas, beliefs, and value judgments integrated into a whole. There must be a consensus to permit the industrial society to function. Various forms of the industrial society may create some distinctive features of an ideology, but all industrialized societies have some common values. In the pure industrial society science and technical knowledge have high values, and those engaged in advancing science and in applying it to industrial processes have high prestige and receive high rewards in the society. The pure industrial society eliminates taboos against technical change, and it places high values on being "modern," "up-to-date," and in "progress" for their own sake.

Education also has a high value in the industrial society because of the fundamental importance of science and the utility
of education as a means of social mobility. The industrial society
is an open community encouraging occupational and geographic
mobility and social mobility. In this sense industrialism must be
flexible and competitive; it is against tradition and status based
upon family, class, religion, race, or caste. The industrial society
is pluralistic, with a great variety of associations and groups and
of large-scale operations; the individual is attached to a variety of
such groups and organizations.

The pure industrial society places a high value on output of
goods and services, and the "demonstration effect" is very strong
on the part of individuals and groups seeking to imitate the
standards of those with higher income levels.

In the industrial society the work force at the work place is
dedicated to hard work, to maintain a high pace of work and a
keen sense of individual responsibility for performance of assigned
norms and tasks. The ethic of hard work and a rapid work pace
at the work place is required by the logic of industrialization.
Industrial countries may differ with respect to the ideals and
drives which underlie the devotion to duty and responsibility for
performance, but industrialism requires an ideology and ethic
which motivate and command individual members of the work
force at the work place. Strict supervision and exacting management imposed on a lethargic work force will not suffice; the personal responsibility for performance and the achievement of
norms of quantity and quality of output must be implanted within workers, front-line supervisors, and top managers to be truly
effective.[9]

It is not by accident that the leaders of industrializing countries today exhort their peoples to hard work. "This generation
is sentenced to hard labor" (Nehru). "We shall march forward
as one people who have vowed to work and to proceed on a holy
march of industrializing . . ." (Nasser). "The chief preoccupation
of every Communist regime between the Elbe and the China Sea
is how to make people work; how to induce them to sow, harvest,
mine, build, manufacture and so forth. It is the most vital problem
which confronts them day in, day out, and it shapes their domestic
policies and to a considerable extent their attitude toward the

outside world."[10] There are many substitutes and counterparts for the Protestant ethic.

The Western tradition has been to harness the drive of individualism; the Communist method combines in varying proportions at varying times money incentives, devotion to a revolutionary creed, and the compulsion of terror. Regardless of the means that are used in the industrializing process, the industrial society achieves at the work place a pace of work and a personal responsibility exercised by individual workers and managers seldom known in economic activity in traditional societies.

The function of making explicit a consensus and of combining discrete beliefs and convictions into a reasonably consistent body of ideas is the task of intellectuals in every society. Industrial society does not uniquely create intellectuals; they exist in all societies in some degree. There are probably more intellectuals, at least potentially, in the industrial society on account of the higher levels of general education, higher income levels, and greater leisure. There are also new patrons to the intellectuals as compared to pre-industrial society. A diversity of markets for intellectuals — the university, enterprise, labor organization, voluntary association, government, and self-employment — tends to displace the old aristocratic patrons. The function of formulating and restating the major values, premises, and consensus of a society from time to time, of sweeping away the old and adopting the new or reconciling the industrial processes with the old order, plays a significant role in industrialization. The intellectuals accordingly are an influential group in the process of the creation and molding of the new industrial society.

Population

The fully developed industrial society confronts no serious population problem. Just as primitive societies have birth rates and death rates relatively equivalent at high levels (35 to 40 per thousand), so in the mature industrial society birth rates and death rates are likely to be relatively comparable (10 per thousand), and result in only a moderate rate of growth in population. Population problems are of particular significance to the society moving from pre-industrial to the industrial status. It may well be that a rise in population is necessarily associated with the beginnings of the industrialization process. But constraint on the rate of population growth, except in an "empty country," is essential to cross the threshhold to the industrial society. Thus, industrialization creates a population problem at the outset which must in turn be solved or else the community cannot enter the promised land. The severity of the problem varies greatly, depending on whether an "empty" territory is being industrialized with immigration (the United States and Australia) or whether a "crowded" region is seeking to industrialize (India and Java).

World-Wide Industrialism

The industrial society is world-wide. The science and the technology on which it is based know no national boundaries; they speak in a universal language. "[Science] is nonnational, nonlocal and, although one would not say noncultural, singularly independent of the form of government, the immediate tradition, or the affective life of a people."[11] There can be few technological secrets, at least for very long, as the atomic field has well demonstrated. The industrial society is an integrated world, to use Myrdal's phrase.[12] The differences in language and dress, which themselves are much reduced, are in contrast to the common characteristics produced by the automobile, airplane, tin can, electric lights and power, and other features of industrialization. The factories and metropolitan centers are focal points for the diffusion of industrial society. It is a common experience that the metropolitan centers of the world appear so familiar and so similar. The same might be said more often of the work places of modern industry, save that they are much less frequented by tourists and travelers.

The industrial society spreads out from centers of advanced technology in a variety of ways. The normal channels of trade in the markets for commodities, services, and capital may not be relatively as significant today as they were in the propagation of industrialization from England, Germany, and France before World War I, but they are still important. Governmental development programs constitute a channel of growing importance. The training of students, the temporary resort to foreign experts, and the demonstration effect produced by exchanges of persons are further means of spreading the industrial society. The character of military defense in a world of advanced technology and the worldwide scope of military conflict have been a significant means of diffusing modern technology and the industrial society. The training of a work force to build bases and to maintain motor vehicles and aircraft involves the establishment of important beachheads for industrialization.

The extreme discrepancies in methods of production which now exist between more advanced and less industrialized countries will tend to be eliminated in the pure industrial society, although significant differences in income levels and in the specialization of activity are likely to remain.

Industrialization transforms an old society or an empty country and creates the new industrial society; the inherent features of industrialization tend to create the pure industrial society whose major characteristics have been outlined in this chapter. This pattern of abstractions constitutes the logic of industrialism.

The actual course of events, however, is never likely to create the precise society constructed by deduction. No two cases of industrialization can be expected to be identical. Industrialization may be under the control of different leaders with different methods and policies and proceed at different rates of development. The old societies have different characteristics and resources, and they start from varying levels of economic development or varying degrees of backwardness, and they may strengthen or weaken or give direction to these inherent tendencies of industrialization in different ways. The place the society starts from and the route it follows are likely to affect its industrial features for many years, but all industrializing societies respond to the inherent logic of industrialism itself.

The empire of industrialism will embrace the whole world; and such similarities as it decrees will penetrate the outermost points of its sphere of influence, and its sphere comes to be universal. Not one, however, but several roads lead into this new and ultimate empire.

CHAPTER 3

THE INDUSTRIALIZING ELITES
AND THEIR STRATEGIES

Industrialism has as its greatest imperative the conquest of the old by the new; and it is compelling mankind to march through history at an ever faster rate. But it sets only the general direction of this march. It does not, at least at this stage in its history, set the specific route of the march or the exact pace to be followed. What these routes are and what their implications are in the area of labor-management-state relations need to be seen from some broad perspective; the general nature of the route defines many of the specifics which otherwise appear miscellaneous and even accidental. A separable issue is why one route or another is chosen by or accepted by or forced upon men (see Chapter 10). We shall be concerned here only with the general character and the broad consequences of the route, however determined, rather than with the ultimate sources of that determination.

Industrialism is introduced by either native or alien elites; by groups of men who seek to conquer the society through the superiority of the new means of production. A war between the old society and the new, the old elites and the new, takes place whether the conquest is an internal or an external one. The new, in the long run and under one auspice or another, is always bound to win. The great dramatic issue is not whether industrialism will emerge supreme but rather which elite will seize and maintain control of the process and what its strategical approach to the organization of industrialization will be.

The ideological conflict which is so characteristic of our age is a natural accompaniment of the diverse routes taken toward industrial society under the leadership of diverse elites. Contending ideologies are fashioned as men seek to guide this historical process by conscious effort, to explain it to themselves, and to justify it to others. The construction of these ideologies is largely the task of the intellectuals who try to divine and make explicit and rationalize the essence of the alternative routes. But the ideologies are not used only to guide, to understand and to justify, but also as weapons of war among the proponents of the several routes; and thus the inherent conflict is sharpened and the lines are hardened. These ideologies become weapons of defense and attack for the general staffs guiding or trying to guide the routes to be taken. The routes become crusades as well as diverging pathways. Men debate and protest and fight with each other almost every step of the way. This has been a large share of the history of the past century and will be a good share of the history of the next.

The Dynamic Elites and Social Conquest

Industrialization is always at first of necessity undertaken by a minority group — the colonial company, the indigenous entrepreneur, the government agency, the military unit. It cannot come into full bloom overnight except, perhaps, in small societies with unusual natural resources which attract external capital, like Kuwait; but even there an initiating human agent is requisite. Usually industrialization starts in a restricted geographical area or sector of a society as a small subculture initiated by a subordinated group which then spreads into new areas and new sectors until it is the dominating system of production affecting almost all the relations of men within the society.[1]

The subordinated group which initiates the industrialization process is, of course, a product of the particular culture found in the pre-industrial society or is a foreign elite. The range of issues which confronts the leaders of industrialization are shaped, in part, by and are seen through cultural and economic constraints, the subjects of Chapters 4 and 5. Members of the various elites do make choices, but they are shaped by their strategies and their values and by the fact that the culture, the economic environment and history have made these persons leaders (See Chapter 10). The conjuncture of these cultural and economic variables is, in fact, implicit in the concept of an elite, and the typology of elites which is used throughout this volume reflects this interrelatedness.

There are at the start of the march toward industrialism some important minorities, of course, who do not wish to move in this direction at all, but their influence can only be local and relatively temporary. They are usually found among the leaders of the older society, the land owners, the "medicine men," the higher artisans, the aristocrats. They are the static minorities. They can delay and by their delay affect the location within society of the new initiative, but they cannot prevent the transformation in the long run; and their delaying efforts are only likely to make the inevitable transition more traumatic.

The technology of industrialization requires dynamic elites for its introduction and extension into a society. The human agents who successfully introduce and extend the new technology have great influence in the society. They can guide and direct it within reasonable limits to suit their wishes. Consequently it is of considerable significance who introduces the new system and what their wishes may be.

Thus a crucial factor in any industrializing society is which elites become the initiators of industrialization, and how they view their role and the nature of the "good society." The universal questions are these:

(1) Who leads the march to industrialism?
(2) What is the purpose of the march?
(3) How is the march organized?

The answers to these three basic questions depend in part on cultural and economic preconditions; they also depend in some measure on the aspirations of the newly emerging group of industrial employees, ever more numerous and more powerful. They wish progress, and they also wish participation. Some elites promise more of one or the other or of both than do others. And promise and delivery do not always coincide. Consequently the routes the industrial workers prefer to take are subject to change — now one and now another; here one and here another. Much of the turmoil of the last century was caused, and much of the turmoil of the next century will be caused, as this group debates its preferences, changes or is led to change its preferences, and attempts to assert them. The industrial workers, however, are a conditioning, not a determining influence. But they can have a clear impact on the election, the performance, and the survival of the dynamic elites. The peasants, also, are, except at certain times of crisis, an even more passive force in the industrialization process but, unlike the workers, they are a declining element.

At this juncture in history there are five ideal types of elites who customarily and variously take the leadership of the industrialization process. These are the initiators, the manipulators, the prime movers:

(1) Dynastic elite
(2) The middle class
(3) The revolutionary intellectuals
(4) The colonial administrators
(5) The nationalist leaders

The fourth group, at least in its pure form, is particularly transitory in its span of leadership; and the longer range competitors are probably found among the other four. They have the greater survival value but they also may turn out to be, as history unfolds, transient instruments of the transformation; for industrialization is relatively new to man and what form it will finally take cannot yet be clearly seen.

It should be understood that each of these elite groups may have associated with it or indeed may be composed of several elements — political leaders, industrial managers, military officers, religious figures, top civil servants, leaders of labor organizations, associated intellectuals, among others; and thus when we speak of a certain type of elite we refer more to the character of its central orientation than to the specific individuals who constitute it at any moment of time.

Each of these elite groups has a strategy by which it seeks to order the surrounding society in a consistent and compatible fashion. This strategical perspective, if the society is to end up with a cultural consistency, must pervade the entire culture. It needs to penetrate and order the cultural totality; to become the dominant theme in the culture. Otherwise there is internal tension, conflict, and restlessness. It is partly because the colonial managers do not have in their positions and in their outlooks the possibilities for developing a cultural consistency that they are perishable elements; their base of operation is too foreign and too narrow.

An internal conflict between the new culture, with its dominant theme set by the industrializing elite, and the old culture is inevitably fought on many fronts — the economic, political, religious, intellectual; and an external conflict between alternative ideologies of industrialism tends to be fought on all fronts at once. Consistency at home and compatibility abroad, since industrialism will inevitably in the end be a world-wide system, are two insistent imperatives felt in greater or lesser degrees by each dominant group; imperatives which press on the instinct to survive. Each industrializing system becomes a "way of life," no matter what its specific form, and a "way of life" demands internal acceptance and external protection if it is to function successfully in the long run. The only ultimate external protection is a world organized along reasonably compatible lines. These are the internal and external aspects of the historical battle over the character of the industrial society — the effort to secure internal consistency and to assure external compatibility.

Management types, protest forms, labor organization typologies, rule-making relationships, all relate to the central themes of industrialization and cannot be fully understood outside the context of these themes; else the individual phenomena appear largely unrelated to each other and are explained singly only by history. But there is a consistency which binds them all more or less firmly together and the elucidation of this consistency is the first, but not the last, step in the analysis of the separate types, forms, typologies, and relationships. All things are not possible in all situations.

These five types of industrialization, it should be noted, are "ideal" situations, and, as such, no individual historical case corresponds fully to any one of them. But most individual cases may be understood better in relation to one of these types. They abstract from reality, but by reducing complexity and by making comparisons they can also illuminate reality. They give order to our task of comprehending the forms of industrialization and their varying impacts in the labor-management-state area.

It should be borne in mind that these five ideal types of industrialization ignore much important detail in individual cases; they do not correspond exactly to any single actual case; many cases are, to a degree, mixtures; and several societies have changed, and will continue to change, their essential type over time. Moreover, some elites have developed at an earler point in history than others; consequently comparisons at the same point of time are hazardous.

The Dynastic Elite and The Paternal Community

The members of the dynastic elite are originally drawn from the landed or commercial aristocracy, since agriculture and commerce are usually the preexisting forms of production, or less frequently, from the allied military caste (as the Samurai in Japan) or religious hierarchy, government bureaucracy, or tribal chieftains. This elite group is held together by a common allegiance to the established order. New recruits may be added from time to time from other strata of society and embraced into the aristocracy, but the emphasis is on a closed system based on family and on class. There is a race of rulers — a race apart.

Its orientation is predominantly toward tradition and the preservation of tradition; and this tradition embodies the past, the present, and the future. The dynastic elite is bound to earth and to history. The "realists," within this elite, acknowledge the rise of the industrial system and its eventual dominance. They seek to identify the essentials of the past and to preserve them in the face of the new form of production; but they will make whatever compromises are necessary to permit industrialization to proceed under their guidance. The "traditionalists" among this existing elite group may denounce and seek to defend against the new industrial system. Thus the "realists" and the "traditionalists" in the early stages of industrialization may find themselves locked in combat. Only if the "realists" triumph (and they will start out as a minority within the elite) can this elite avoid liquidation at worst or oblivion at best; and even then their conquering of the new industrialization depends on their own vigor and on the vigor of contending groups.

In addition to "traditionalists" and "realists," a dynastic elite may be composed of "decadents" who are oriented toward personal indulgence, which may be expressed in high living, corruption, attachment to a foreign culture or personal security through foreign investment, rather than toward national tradition or national progress. Only if the "realists" are dominant, and are also strong, competent, and patriotic, is a dynastic elite likely to master the industrialization process, as in Japan and Germany.

If the "realists" get control of the industrialization process, their approach to it is quite distinctive. The emphasis is on personal rule which involves perpetuation of the family that is "born to rule" and of the class within which alliances are made and from which most managerial recruits are obtained. The system rests on tradition but ultimately on the use of power. Such a system under sufficient pressure can become fascist in an effort to maintain internal control, since fascism is oriented toward the elite and toward the use of force, as well as toward action. But the normal emphasis is on the approach of the patriarch toward his family or the benevolent monarch toward his subjects.

The "good society" cherishes the virtues and the symbols of the past and its institutions — the family, the church, private property, the national state. Resting on tradition, the "good society" is a determinate one changing from past forms only to the extent necessary for survival; and, consequently, it is inherently anti-intellectual except for the "Lords Spiritual" who interpret and reinterpret the essence of the past and assess the present in the light of this essence; these "Lords Spiritual" may hold a high place in the society.

Law and order and firm administration are part of the essence of the system, and this leads often to cartels and to a mixture of "private" and "public" affairs in the conduct of economic life. The political system is paternalistic — the paternalistic state — and so also the economic system — the paternalistic enterprise manager. The worker is to be cared for and in return he is expected to be loyal. He is dependent on the manager for his welfare and his leadership. The idea of tension between the enterprise manager and the worker is abhorred; "harmony" is devoutly sought. Rule-making is held, so far as possible, solely in the hands of management; prerogatives of management are sacred. The social and economic systems alike have a clearly stratified hierarchy of superiors and subordinates and a reciprocal series of duties and obligations.

Industrial progress will be no faster than necessary to meet the pressures placed upon the elite; and the strong preference

is for a smooth passage from the pre-industrial to the industrial
society. Industrialization is not fostered for its own sake but for
the survival of the society it is replacing. Fitful and violent
change is anathema; change too must be ordered. Such a system,
however, if under enough external pressure, can make rapid
economic progress. It can select goals and it has the mechanism
to achieve them. It will be subject to substantial internal change,
although the motto must always be "no faster and no farther than
necessary." The two elements which will change least readily
are the two most central to the system — the dynastic elite and
the paternal community.

The dynastic elite will behave differently depending particularly on the amount and nature of the pressure placed upon it.
This pressure may be external or internal. If external, it will largely
come from foreign economic or political and military competition, and in any event, the greater the pressure the greater the
urge for economic progress. If internal, it is less likely to arise
from economic competition (since the system is usually structured against it) than from political pressure from a class-conscious working class or a strong group of independent and
alienated intellectuals, or both. Checked and balanced this way,
the dynastic elite may be unable to maintain its control over the
total culture or wield enough power to be able to set and attain
economic goals. Consequently, internal pressure is likely to be
against economic progress — the greater the pressure the less the
likelihood of economic progress. External pressure aids economic
progress and internal pressure supports political instability.

A central question is whether a dynastic industrializing society
has permanent survival value; although given proper conditions it certainly can continue for substantial periods. Without
internal control it is always unstable and particularly subject to
attack from the extreme left, as in France and in Russia prior
to World War I. Even with considerable internal control under
normal conditions, it may face real crises, as in Germany, in
depression periods, or after military defeats; and then it may
be confronted by the reality or the imminent possibility of being
transformed into our third type, one managed by the revolutionary intellectuals. But, even given continuing control, industrializing society is marked by such fluidity and diversity that a

dynastic elite may gradually lose both its rigidity and its conformity. External competitive pressure can aid this process, as in Germany and Japan, particularly by opening up new avenues for upward social mobility through education and a new job mobility for the worker; and under such pressure, this type of industrializing society may gradually merge into our next.

The Middle Class and The Open Market

The human agents here are members of a new class rising, as in England, in opposition to the old elite, but able to live in coexistence with it. They are most likely to be drawn, at least at first, from commercial or artisan groups already in being, often composed of religious or national minorities — groups which were not entirely integrated into the old elite and groups which are sensitive to the gains to be had from the new means of production. They do not advance on the wings of a rigid ideology; rather they tend to be pragmatic. They favor a structure of economic and political rules which best permits them to pursue their gains. This brings them into conflict with the old order, but they seek to impose their will piecemeal, and their assault is carried out through concentration on specific issues rather than as an explicit social revolution. In their conflict with the old, the new group may find allies among the intellectuals wanting more freedom and the workers wanting more opportunity, particularly for political participation.

The middle-class ideology is economically individualistic and politically egalitarian. Each individual is held to be morally accountable to and for himself, within the limits of the law, which is supposed to apply equally to all members of the community. Each man's responsibility begins and ends with the injunction to make the best use of his opportunities. In practice the rigor of this doctrine is softened by the social and religious beliefs embodied in the culture, but the emphasis is on progress and on the individual. Each man is his own "Lord Spiritual" with the new reliance on personal self-interest instead of community welfare. Instead of the old and the community, there is the new and the self.

Upward mobility within society is fairly directly related to knowledge of opportunities and capacity to make use of them. Family background and wealth are important, not for themselves, but only inasmuch as they tend to affect the range of opportunities open to men. No one is born to rule, but some are destined to manage; and their enterprise management relies more on policies and rules than on personal preference. The system is based heavily upon consent and the appeal in politics and in economics is to self-advantage. Every manager is, in part, a politician adjusting, within the rules of the game, but with some rapidity, to the pressures of individuals, groups, and institutions; mobility and self-interest are at the center of the social process, in practice and in theory.

The "good society" is an indistinct and shifting shadow. It is more a series of means than an end; and the means are reason, self-interest, and a relatively broad toleration of dissent. Relative emphasis is placed on many centers of decision-making power and on a system of checks and balances. The checks and balances in political life involve the separation of church and state and of the legislative, administrative, and judicial authorities; and in economic life the separation of economic units into discrete and competitive entities.

In industrial relations, the worker is relatively independent and is expected to be self-sufficient economically and politically. ". . . he knows that he is the political equal of his employer and he has no intention of subordinating himself by incurring a debt of gratitude. He is in the workshop by virtue of a business transaction and he does not consider the personnel as a family group of which the entrepreneur should be the patriarchal head."[2] The worker is even permitted to be in organized opposition to the enterprise manager — some degree of conflict is built into and accepted by the system; and a whole series of economic and political institutions are in fact devised to channel and settle such conflicts. Rule-making, in society as a whole, may be more or less equally shared — by management, by organizations of workers, and by the state in a pluralistic arrangement.

Progress is taken for granted in the belief that it flows naturally out of the day-to-day decisions of many people. It should not be retarded nor should it be forced unduly by state action. The incentive of self-interest in a competitive and materialistic society is relied upon as a sufficient spur to progress. Thus economic advance is not centrally planned. Such a system will be intermediate in its record of economic growth. It will not be held back by the built-in resistances of some dynastic elite systems but it also is not geared to the forced-draft industrialization of which the third type is capable.

Such a system depends for its more specific aspects on its origin. It may find its origin in an established society (England, Sweden, India). Here there will be more initial conflict between the old elite and the new entrepreneurs,[3] and also more of an attitude of class warfare between capital and labor because of the heritage of ruling-class attitudes. The old generally will have a greater hold and the new will have to struggle harder to gain acceptance. All this conduces to more participation by the state as the arbiter of these conflicts and as the carrier of the aspirations of the working class. Management will be more elitist, labor more class-conscious, and the state more interventionist. Similar patterns of behavior tend to arise when a relatively new but still distinct elite class arises early in the process of industrialization, as in France and certain Latin American countries. These societies have characteristics of both the dynastic elite and middle-class approaches; they are intermediate between our ideal types.

Such a system may originate in a new and relatively classless society (United States, Canada, and New Zealand). From the beginning there is more social mobility, less class-consciousness, and a freer hand for progress. The middle class reigns supreme and eventually nearly everyone is or believes himself to be middle-class; and the market is as open as markets are ever likely to be. This is the more or less pure model of the "middle class and the open market"; and economic progress is likely to be reasonably rapid — the new business and industrial class is given its head. Internal cultural consistency is comparatively readily attained; although where the origin is in a class society, as many as three subcultures may develop beside each other — the subcultures of the aristocracy, the business class, and the working class.

The evolution of the new industrial managers may not be the gradual process experienced in England and the United States, among other countries; it may instead be abrupt, as in Pakistan;

and this is an increasingly important phenomenon. In a rapidly industrializing nation, if the state is not to be the universal entrepreneur, private entrepreneurs must be deliberately developed. They are most likely to be drawn from among the larger merchants who have some capital and some managerial experience. Almost overnight, instead of operating a shop, they are running a modern factory. But they have not had time to accumulate experience and this leads to inefficient use of the new facilities. Nor have they had an opportunity to change their orientation from concentration on a quick profit to the development of a continuing organization concentrating on production, and this leads to an attitude of short-term exploitation of the new situation. Nor has a competitive market grown up around them to restrict greed and compel efficiency, and so the state must step in to control the situation. Also the state may have an additional claim to control through its partial provision of the necessary capital.

In these cases, the new industrial managers must be as much oriented toward the state as toward the market — toward the bureaucrat as toward the consumer; and stifling bureaucratic controls and the possibility of corruption may be among the most insistent problems. Middle-class leadership so created is subject to special strains — the task of learning its new assignments and new attitudes quickly, the likelihood of worker and consumer protest against "exploitation," and the complications associated with dealing with the state as well as the market. The success of the new class will depend, in part, on how fast the industrialization proceeds and thus how soon the discipline of the market can replace that of the state in controlling prices and forcing efficiency. Only when the market has largely taken over as the regulating mechanism can this new class be certain of its future. The larger the segment of the economy made available to the private entrepreneurs, the greater also the chance they may become the primary organizational element in the new society.

Middle-class leadership, extending as it does from the merchant just reaching into production in a newly industrializing economy to the formally trained manager of the long established enterprise in the highly organized society, covers a wide span of managerial types and attitudes. Both the men and their environments are widely different; but there is the same search for profits, the same acceptance of a role for private initiative, the same emphasis on piecemeal adaptation and change. Managerial performance, worker attitudes, and labor-management relations, however, will vary quite considerably.

The Revolutionary Intellectuals and The Centralized State

A new class of intellectuals and associated activists may take over the industrializing process and society in its entirety and sweep away, as fast as they can, the old elite and the old culture. From the beginning they intend to eliminate the former leadership groups and the preexisting cultural arrangements and replace them with a new ruling class and a brand new culture. The new wine shall be in totally new bottles. The principal new bottle is the centralized state.

These intellectuals are self-identified for the task of leadership by their acceptance and espousal of a theory of history. This theory of history specifies for them the place to act, the time to act, and the means to act. Acceptance of this theory of history sets them off from other persons. They are, they contend, the bearers of the virtually inevitable historical process; the possessors of an ideology which they think will make it possible for them to create the future.

The ideology is the cement which holds this class together. It states that the new society is inevitable — a society fully committed to the new technology and the economic and social relations which are thought to be most compatible with its fullest development. Since an ideology is at the center of this class, there must be "high priests" to interpret and apply this ideology to current developments — the "line." The faithfulness with which one follows these interpretations is a main determinant of who belongs to the ruling class and who does not. New recruits to the class are drawn on the basis of ability combined with political reliability.

Once the new class has attained full power to control society in a centralized fashion, the original revolutionary intellectuals give way increasingly to high-level political administrators and bureaucrats as the leaders of the system. A new class still controls the new society but the old revolutionaries and the new bureaucrats may run it rather differently over time. In fact, the revolutionary intellectuals and the bureaucrats to whom they give over power may be almost the antithesis of each other; emphasis on constant change gives way to greater conservatism; debate over basic policy yields place to reinterpretation of received doctrine. This transition is of great importance in the evaluation of this system. But, with both the old intellectuals and the new bureaucrats, instead of the self, there is the ideology, the party, and the state. Once the influence of the original revolutionary intellectuals is gone, the centralized state remains.

If the community under the hereditary leader is the essence of our first type and a balanced institutional mechanism powered by self-interest the essence of our second, then an ideology stressing the demands of the new technology and the supremacy of the dominant interpreters of this ideology is the essence of our third type. If the first type may be said to spring from the land and the second from commerce, then the third finds its source in the manifesto. The party and the leaders of the party are at the center of this society. Internal conflicts, at least ostensibly, are not settled on the basis of personality, or on the basis of ability, but on ideological correctness. The "vision" is the animating force along this road to industrialization. The system rests on the cohesive force of a common ideology among the leaders; the manipulation of economic class interests among the masses; and the use of force when necessary at both levels. Collective thinking and collective force are central to the system.

The "good society" as seen by the proponents of this system is quite determinant, although more as an historical process than as a clear goal. Above all, the new technology must be served. The world conflict is seen in large part as a test of which system can make the best use of the new technology. This means forced-draft industrialization and the construction of a culture which is consistent with the new technology and its fullest utilization — thus education, labor organization, art and literature must all be geared to the system of production in a single-minded fashion. The centralized state is the only mechanism which can fully conquer the old and create the new culture and undertake the forced-draft industrialization; the centralized state under a disciplined bureaucracy supported by the political police.

The society, of necessity, is monolithic — there can be no real separation of economic, political, and religious institutions. Rule-making, generally, and in industrial relations, specifically, is inherently in the hands of the dominant class — the managers of this historical process who have their plans. The worker is again dependent on the enterprise manager, and the enterprise manager in turn on the state, both economically and politically. The worker's highest attribute is a sense of duty. "The Productivity of Labor, in the final analysis, is the most important, the main tool for the victory of the new order."[4] The worker is a "citizen" with many duties and few rights. Tension between the enterprise managers and the workers is suppressed. This society is considered "good" by its proponents because they believe it follows the logic of industrialization to the full and thus has the greatest survival value.

Great stress is placed upon economic progress; history is viewed as a conscious process, subject within limits to central control. History, in making its demands, makes them in fits and jerks. Not only are there strategic constellations of class interest to be manipulated, but also strategic moments of time; and it is part of the task of the Ideology to identify these constellations and these moments. Time is structured into climactic periods. As a consequence, a chiliastic view of history is forced on the followers who must respond to these crucial moments: expectation of the millenium is used as a force in society. There is an historical strategy to which the mass is expected to respond. Time is a series of strategic points and society a chain of more or less strategic interest groups. This type of society is particularly capable of force-draft industrialization, and this may turn out to be both its preeminent survival characteristic and its greatest historical impact.

The system, however, is subject to a gap between the assertions of the ideology and the aspirations of the masses in their historical and geographical environments. Individual variations within this general approach may be identified depending on the attention paid to each of these factors. In the more orthodox version (Soviet Union and China), the ideology and thus the centralized state are preeminent. This calls for a heavy-handed bureaucracy and a strong police arm to get rapid industrialization and to control unrest. The original intellectuals are likely to be most committed to this approach.

The orthodox version may have its costs in internal opposition and sabotage and in external criticism; and so a revision of approach may take place where the masses are served to the extent permitted without endangering minimum adherence to the ideology (Poland and Yugoslavia). There is some decentralization of the bureaucracy, some relaxation of police control, some increase in goods and services available to consumers, some more permissive attitudes toward older cultural and nationalistic traits, and perhaps some resultant slowing of the pace of industrialization. But the central commitment remains to the ideology, the party, and the state. This version is likely to be adopted by the more politically and practically oriented members of the new class, but it is viewed by the more orthodox as a miscellany of expedient concessions which will lead over time to a forsaking of the true faith, for there can be only one road and not several. But as orthodoxy declines, heterogeneity grows.

The Colonial Administrator and The "Home Country"

The colonial elite has been a major instrument for the introduction of industrialization in many areas of the world, supplying capital, techniques, and leadership. The colonial administrator, however, is an alien "alien" — he not only represents a new system of production but also an external society. Consequently, he must carry the weight of two justifications — the justification of the new system and also of his personal intrusion into the indigenous culture. Consequently his role as prime mover can be an unusually difficult one.

The other aspect of the externality of the colonial approach is the essential service to the home country rather than to the indigenous population. The home country may be served by a supply of raw materials, a market for finished products, a source of profits, an outlet for "younger sons" or surplus population, an extension of an ideology and of political and military suzerainty. An alien elite and an alien purpose are the twin features of all colonialism.

We are concerned here with colonial industrialization, not with simple political control (Cyprus);[5] with colonial industrialization in a geographical area with a substantial native population and established culture and not the populating and industrializing of largely empty lands (Canada, Australia). Nor are we concerned with foreign investment, foreign management, and foreign technical assistance under the rules and within the system of the indigenous population; for this is a separate phenomenon. Rather our concern is with foreign control and administration of a society in the course of industrialization.

The colonial approach to industrialization has been and is a diverse one, and so it may be better to identify it as a series of approaches related by the theme of external conquest or attempted conquest of an indigenous culture. The foreignness of the leadership and of the purpose is the essence of this approach to industrialization; and because of this foreignness, the use of force is latent or actual in the direction of the society.

Any colonial power must make several basic decisions. First, is its rule a transitional or a permanent one? Its views on this may change from one period to another. Second, should it develop only a segment of the society (the plantations or copper mines) or should it try to absorb and remake the total society? Should it make the natives "Portuguese" or Communists? Third, should its nationals reside temporarily in the area, as "expatriates," or should they become permanent "settlers," maintaining their own separate cultural patterns and dominant economic and political power? Immigrants who adopt the indigenous culture are neither expatriates nor settlers. The answers to these questions have, of course, their interrelationships and out of these relationships come differing forms of colonialism.

(1) The lightest form of colonialism occurs when the external power plans to stay — or does in fact stay — only temporarily, and while in control develops only a small segment of the society with the use of expatriates. Examples are cocoa exports from Ghana and sugar cane production in the Philippines and the complementary sale of manufactured goods in return. This form of colonialism may serve to introduce for the first time contact with the irreversible process of industrialization but without any severe political repercussions ("segmental colonialism").

Of greater impact is a segmental form of colonialism which

aspires to be permanent. The colonial power makes the investment in transportation, communications, a civil service, and the
like, which is requisite to permanent participation in the economy
but attempts to develop only segments of the productive system
(jute in India, sugar cane in the Fiji Islands and Jamaica, tropical
fruits in the Ivory Coast). The segments of the economy developed are more likely to be the extractive and commercial rather
than the manufacturing. Segmental colonialism has varied quite
considerably in the depths of its penetration; and the depth of
penetration is usually related to the prospective profit to the home
country.

(2) Where "settlers" from the home country become an important element in a colonial system, a new and particularly difficult dimension is added to colonialism ("settler colonialism"),
for it takes on an aspect of true permanence; and, to the service
to the home country, is added service to the "settlers" who may
have quite contrary interests to those of the home country because their views of necessity are more rigidly tied to the *status
quo*. Settler colonialism may seek to encompass only part of an
economy (plantations in Indonesia, farms in Kenya) or it may
seek to absorb the total society as part of the home country
(Algeria). A dual economy and a dual society are created, while
industrialism requires unity and consensus for its fullest development. Rather than concentrating on profit, settler colonialism
comes to concentrate on preservation of the settlers' "way of life."

(3) The heaviest form of colonialism occurs when the home
country seeks to transform the subject area into its own image,
using indigenous leaders and a few expatriates as its human
agents ("total colonialism"). The purpose is the complete and
permanent attachment of the indigenous area to the home country. This may happen with fairly general consent (Hawaii)
or grudging acceptance (Mozambique) or general resistance
(Hungary). If successful, the subject country has been totally
conquered. Industrialization and its guiding elite have become
indigenous and, after a time, the system ceases to be "colonial."
The purpose is full assimilation of the economy and the society,
and its attachment to the home country.

Each of these forms of colonialism has its own logical history.
The first ("segmental colonialism") is by its very nature tran-

sient. It has not penetrated deeply enough to make possible its continuing hold on the economy and the society. It carries the seeds of industrialization, and the seeds of its own destruction. It is alike the creator and the victim of progress. It may continue, however, in a new and changed form: a segment for foreign ownership and management in the economy within a compatible political system operated by the indigenous people. The colonial enterprises may retain their profits by giving up their control of the society. The second ("settler colonialism") has more tenacity and also creates a greater need for tenacity. Whether it can survive anywhere is still in doubt. Past history would indicate the settlers only survive by ceasing to be "settlers," giving up their separate and dominant "way of life," as in the case of the colonies of ancient Greece. The third ("total colonialism"), if successful — and success depends very much on the power and determination of the home country — can be reasonably enduring, as the history of ancient Rome illustrates. The colonialism with the greatest survival possibilities is total colonialism because it ceases, once it is effective, to be colonialism. It becomes the system of the country itself under its own indigenous leaders.

All colonialism, in the end, is either overthrown by the "natives" or ceases to be colonialism by becoming the "native" system or a component part of it.

The characteristic colonialism of the dynastic elite or the middle class is quite different from that of the revolutionary intellectuals. It has been more apt to be directed toward profit on investment or access to raw materials or outlets for finished products for the sake of the "home" market, or to economic advancement for the individual settlers. The revolutionary intellectuals have been more politically oriented, and through the use of indigenous associates more intent on the conquering of the cultural totality of the dependent area. The dynastic elite and the middle class have been more oriented toward the "home market" and the revolutionary intellectuals toward the "home ideology."

The colonial administrators, however, whatever variation in the form of colonialism there may be, have in common with each other service to the home country or ideology, above all. Also in a colonial situation, the power of the government and of the management of enterprises is likely to be rather great in order to handle an indigenous labor force; the worker is likely to be viewed as being in a dependent or at least semidependent status, since the management represents a superior culture; conflict between labor and management, subject to exacerbation by nationalist sentiments, is likely to be severely controlled or suppressed. Labor organizations, when they exist, are likely to be oriented toward nationalist goals.

The indigenous worker, on the other hand, is likely to be treated quite differently as a member of the labor force from one form of colonialism to another. Settler colonialism allows him to rise until he competes with the settlers; the segmental, until he reaches the level of the expatriates; the total, once he is politically reliable, to the very top. Total colonialism is most interested in full and rapid development of the economy, including manufacturing; and the segmental generally the least. Total colonialism also attacks the old culture most aggressively; while settler colonialism may even insist on the maintenance of the old culture (South Africa), and segmental colonialism may more or less ignore the existing culture.

Among all our strategies, the colonial is inherently the most diverse and thus the least subject to the presentation of a unified "ideal type."

The Nationalist Leader and the Guidance of The State

The nationalist leader may also be the agent of industrialization; but the mantle of nationalism may be worn by many different types of persons. All the elites are to a degree and in a way nationalists; the nationalism of the colonial administrator, of course, reflects the home country. There is no single social base for nationalism and no single outlook on the nature of industrialization. Historically important as a mechanism of transition, the nationalist leader may point his society in any one of several directions. Nationalism is more a sentiment than a system of thought. Some other element must enter here before the choice can be made and this usually is the social orientation of the nationalist leaders. Beyond the fact of nationalism is the great question of who rides to power on the magic carpet of nationalism.

Yet nationalism does predispose a society in certain directions, inadequate as it may be as a total philosophy of societal development. First, a nationalist revolt against the old order or a campaign against colonialism usually raises a leader or a small group of leaders to the forefront; men who are the symbols of the new independence and who carry with them the aspirations of the populace; men who are, at least at first, national heroes. They are often charismatic personalities. Their personal influence is great. Given the unstructured situation at the start of a period of great national development, they can guide or form a society within broad limits in accordance with their will; and thus what they will (if they have a will) is a crucial factor in the unfolding of the new society.

Second, instead of classes of people there tends to be a chiliastic mass — a mass with great expectations for sudden improvement but little appreciation of how that improvement will come about; a mass subject to ecstasy and to despair. The goals are extravagant and the means ignored. And the earlier the stage of economic development and the lower the level of education and material standards of the population, the more chiliastic the nature of the mass. The attitude of this mass is open to sudden and erratic change and thus the total situation is an unstable one.

This chiliastic attitude pervades nationalism. The view of history is a climactic one — that men can "take the fortresses of history by storm."[6] There is not only the Man but also the Moment. The act of independence is such a climactic event, and the tendency is to rely on other climactic undertakings (the Aswan Dam approach); history is to be structured as a series of climactic efforts. This tends to lead the industrialization of the society into difficulties arising from an overextension of total efforts and some grave imbalance among individual efforts as the startling advances (a new steel mill or an elaborate new university) are placed ahead of the more prosaic; and industrialization, instead of being a flow, becomes a series of episodes. Instead of duty or self-interest, political and economic activity is organized around patriotic zeal.

Third, while nationalism in and of itself has no social philosophy, and is usually more pragmatic than ideological, it does predispose toward state-directed effort. Nationalism initially is negative — against the old order and the external enemy. This is enough of a platform to gain power but not to rule an economy. Once power is attained there must be a mechanism through which to work and this mechanism is likely to be the state. In fact, it is usually the only available mechanism for a great national effort. There may be no theory in advance as to how to proceed, but there must be a practice, a practice which will involve the state. This tends to lead to the planned economy, to state or state-sponsored investment, to state-controlled labor organizations, to workers dependent on the state for economic benefits and political direction, to state guidance of the new industrialists, to state appeals for hard work and saving, and to a call for unity. The nationalist state requires a civil service in a crucial location within society, and the quality and the source of this civil service is a strategic factor.

The nationalist mantle everywhere appears much the same, but the philosophical orientation and the social base of the leaders who wear it vary greatly. Consequently, the struggle over who wears the mantle is one of great importance, for whoever wins it has power to point the direction of society quite beyond the ordinary. The Communists, in particular, have been conscious of the significance of this struggle and have realized the instability of the masses at this stage in a nation's history. What happens just before and just after the advent to authority of the new nationalist state writes a great deal of subsequent history.

The nationalist leaders may be found among the indigenous hereditary elite, as in Iran; among the liberal–democratic or quasi–socialistic intellectuals, as in India; or among the military commanders, as in Egypt. The first two sets of leaders may be more inclined toward reliance on private capital and initiative and the last toward state capital and initiative; liberal–democratic and quasi–socialistic intellectuals toward freedom for the individual and persuasion, and the hereditary elite and military commanders toward force and discipline and duty and personal rule. Perhaps, also, where labor organizations have been important in the independence struggle, as in Indonesia, and particularly if they are under left-wing influence, the emphasis will be additionally upon state activity. But, in any event, the nationalist economy is likely to be a mixed economy lying somewhere between the private initiative preferred by the middle class and the state control preferred by the revolutionary intellectuals. This may be particularly true where the leaders have risen through nationalist political or military channels, and prior to their advent to power, have had little contact with the theory or practice of managing a society; they thus tend to seek out what works best at the time with few preconceived ideas.

With the state assuming the responsibility for the guidance of the new industrial managers, the new labor force, and the new labor organizations, rule-making is largely in the hands of the state, the worker is viewed as a "patriot" serving a national purpose, and industrial conflict controlled or suppressed.

The "nationalist society" is particularly a plaything of history. Its recent past is of special significance. If the nationalist leaders arise out of a violent rejection of a hereditary dynastic elite, or of settler colonialism, the emphasis is particularly likely to be a negative one stressing hates and fears. If the transition is a more peaceful one, as, for example, a transition out of segmental colonialism, elements of the old system are more likely to be retained and attention turned to positive developments. In any event, however, there is likely to be a negative period when independence from the old, and a lack of social discipline (slack work and heavy consumption) will be the dominant themes. The more violent the act of independence, the longer this period is likely to last with its uncertainty and lack of national concensus about anything except distaste for the old, as in Indonesia and Iraq. More fortunate is the society which can move quickly and firmly into a positive program of national economic development and away from excessive concern over internal and external political developments. But even there, as in Turkey, there are likely to come periods of rapid forward progress and periods of relative stagnation — so important is the influence of the leaders and the national mood to the magnitude of the current effort. If the nationalist approach is to be successful, it must attain a sense of national unity and substantial forward momentum. The tests are how soon the national purpose can be moved from the negative to the positive phase, and then how much effort can be pulled out of the nation, and how sustained that effort will be.

Common to the nationalist road are the nationalist leaders, the chiliastic mass and the state as an instrument of economic development. Common also is the need for clear direction. Yet this clear direction is particularly difficult to attain. The leaders come out of a political background rather than a solidly anchored class or group and are "personalities"; and as the leadership shifts so does the "personality." The mass may alternately expect too much and then too little. And there is no single ready-made ideology for the nationalist conduct of an economy. Consequently, the nationalist approach tends to be a wavering one following an unsteady course. This is particularly true if regional, tribal, or religious differences are added to the uncertainty over social direction.

Any society at any moment of time probably needs some reasonably well-settled theme for its development if it is to move ahead, as is so well illustrated by the case of Indonesia, or of Poland when immobilized between Stalinism and revisionism. Economic progress waits on a firm decision as to the specific approach to be followed; in the case of the nationalist economy, in particular, how much state guidance there will be. There must be a decision. The society which wishes to travel fast must travel one road at a time. There is no good substitute for a strategical concept.

Chart 1 summarizes the major elements of the strategies of the five ideal types of elites.

The Floating Forces — The Intellectuals and The Generals

Two forces — one representing ideas and the other power — are inherently socially unattached on any permanent basis in the struggle for supremacy in organizing industrializing societies. Both the politically minded intellectuals and the generals often can and do align themselves with one and now with another elite and its strategy; and their alignments can be a crucial factor. They wear coats of many colors.

The intellectuals (including the university students) are a particularly volatile element, since they are capable of quite rapid shifts of opinion, quickly sensitive as they are to the social climate. They are almost always divided among themselves. They are capable of extreme reactions to objective situations — more extreme than any other group in society. They are by

CHART 1.

The industrializing elites and their strategies.

Strategic Concepts	Dynastic	Middle-Class	Revolutionary-Intellectuals	Colonial Administrators	Nationalist Leaders
Central strategy of the elite	Preservation of traditional society.	Individual self-advancement.	Forced-draft industralization.	Servicing the "home country."	National independence and progress.
Central characteristic of the society	Paternal community.	Open market.	Centralized state.	Alien system under alien control.	State "guided" development.
Sources of variations in the approach	Nature of external and internal pressures.	Origin in class or classless society; or in rapid industrialization.	Comparative responsiveness to deology, or to desires of masses.	Segmental or total approach; and absence or presence of "settlers."	Negative or positive stage of development.
Basic rule-making authority in labor-management relations	Employer and state.	Employer, union, state.	State.	Colonial administrator and employer.	Largely state.
Elite's view of worker	Dependent.	Independent.	Dutiful producer.	Dependent.	Patriot.
Elite's attitude toward conflict	Suppress.	Accept within rules of game.	Prohibit.	Suppress.	Control.

nature irresponsible, in the sense that they have no continuing commitment to any single institution or philosophical outlook and they are not fully answerable for consequences. They are, as a result, never fully trusted by anybody, including themselves. Yet they have power which can move society.

The intellectuals generate ideas and serve as constant critics of society. They help determine how men think about each other, about history, about the nature of the good society. They spin theories and ideologies, which may or may not bear a close relation to reality and to ethics; they can turn conflicts into crusades. In the modern world with its perfected communications, they are particularly influential since ideas travel fast. The new invaders are not the hordes breaking across a traditional boundary but ideas riding the air waves and the printed page around the world. The new border warfare is between ideas instead of people. Consequently, it is important who best attracts or captures the intellectuals and who uses them most effectively, for they may be a tool as well as a source of danger. What is the quality of the intellectuals on each side and how well are they used? This is an important question for social groups within a nation as well as for the contending systems among nations; and particularly in periods when a society is in crisis or when the contending systems are competing. The intellectuals speak the loudest and are heard the most at the crossroads of social history.

Each of the ideal type elites, even the colonial in Kipling and others, has drawn its intellectual supporters — the romanticists and historicists supporting the dynastic elite and the old culture and the idea of community; the humanitarians and rationalists favoring the liberal-democratic theme and the open society; the revolutionaries aiding Communism and destruction of the old order; and the chauvinists elevating the national state and national character. There have also been those who have withdrawn to the side in disillusionment and bewilderment into nihilism, existentialism, or some other school of thought standing largely aside from the battle over the transformation of society into its industrial mold. But intellectuals are not always free to float as they please, for they may be controlled, and the more authoritarian the society the more effective the control; and the communist as the most authoritarian has the most control. It is part of the essence of communism (and fascism) that the intellectuals must serve the ruling order if they are to serve at all. In these instances they are neither free-floating nor much of a force.

The generals influence society not through ideas, but through the ultimate power of the armed forces. In some societies, aside from the power at their command, they are and are recognized to be the best trained and most patriotic elements in the society and may also be closest to the aspirations of the mass of the people, particularly when the army is one of the few channels for upward social mobility. They often have a reputation for being less corrupt than other elements, for being more dynamic in getting things done, for being able to make decisions, for having trained staff available. They also, like the intellectuals, can transfer their allegiance and support from one group to another, or from one system to another, but are more likely to be attached to the ruling element, whatever it may be. In fact, in some societies the definition of the ruling element is the element with the support of the armed forces. The military tend to be more important in societies which rely heavily on force for their sanction — the dynastic, the communist, the colonial, and the nationalist — than in the liberal-democratic which relies more on consent. In the liberal-democratic system, the military almost of necessity must be under civilian control and is not a significant partisan political factor.

The generals normally stand for law and order, and serve as a reserve force to either back the ruling group or to take over from it if it breaks down. But they may also be a force for reform, often of a populist character, for they have a mass base in the soldiery; and so there may be a Cromwell as well as a Franco. Military reform when it comes tends to be nationalist, disciplinary, and responsive to a great mass wish — like independence or land reform — and not to have a full ideology or an intellectual base or even much knowledge of the complexities of civilian life. Whether supporting the ruling group or supplanting it, the military may insist on industrial modernization, as in Japan and Germany, for the sake of the strength of its armies and thus become an influential factor in economic progress.

The generals, like the intellectuals, are a more crucial factor in a critical period. A crisis, whatever else it may do to other groups — heightens the influence of these two elements. Crisis elevates both; and peace humbles both. Even if the military remains silent in a crisis, it is taking sides and affecting the outcome; while the intellectual attempting to influence events cannot be silent. Since force is most likely to be called upon internally in a period of social transition, the armed forces play a special role under such circumstances. The orientation of their leaders becomes a factor in the front rank, and whoever captures the military leaders may well capture the system. This is particularly true in recent times when the armed power of the soldier so far surpasses the unarmed power of the citizen.

The general is more important at some times — the crises — and in some systems — those based on force — than at other times and in other places. Thus, in a dynastic system under severe internal pressure, the communist society in an internal power struggle, the colonial economy subject to unrest, and the nationalist regime looking for national unity, the role of the generals may be the single conclusive factor. This is not to suggest that they will always all see alike: some of the drama may lie in their internal rivalries. Their role, of course, is also enhanced by external as well as internal warfare. Only the liberal-democratic system in peace can afford to ignore the generals.

These floating forces — the intellectuals and the generals — guide the march to industrialization mostly when the march is faltering or changing course. On other occasions the guidance of the march is left to the other more persistent elements described earlier.

The Decisive Questions

We started with three questions (Who leads the march? What is the purpose of the march? How is the march organized?); we identified four systems which apparently have or may have some survival value (the dynastic elite, the middle class, the revolutionary intellectuals, and the nationalist leaders). Another system (that of the colonial administrators), it was suggested, does not have such survival value and will be effective only in the short run. Colonialism is either overthrown or it ceases to be colonialism. Two other elements (the intellectuals and the generals) were presented as factors of importance in crisis periods, but not as groups which in themselves provide a stable base for industrial advance.

If it takes a reasonably consistent strategic approach to be able to run an industrializing society effectively, then the four major contenders at this moment in history are the dynastic elite, the middle class, the revolutionary intellectuals, and the nationalist leaders. Their respective answers to the three questions might be summarized as follows:

Who leads the march? The dynastic elite answers, those born to lead and they are identified by family and by class. Their rule should be a personal one based on tradition and backed, if necessary, by force. The middle class answers, those who through competitive education and competitive experience most merit leadership responsibility; and their leadership should be based on consent and take place within certain generalized rules of the game. The revolutionary intellectuals reply that it should be those persons who have the superior theory of history and superior strategy for organizing a society in keeping with the demands of industrial technology; and they rest their leadership on force. The nationalist leaders say that it should be the men who through their vision and courage represent the future of the nation; and their power is based on the sense of patriotism they can arouse in the citizens of the nation.

What is the purpose of the march? And how is the march organized? The dynastic elite sees the goal as the preservation of the old order, with its emphasis on the paternal community, to the extent possible, while still keeping control of the new method of production. The method of the paternal community calls for a reasonably strong state intent on preserving internal order and stability, very substantial rule-making authority in the hands of the enterprise managers, and dependent workers owing loyalty to the managers. The middle class understands the goal to be a method which it is expected will, over time, bring the greatest welfare to individuals — the method of the open market in political and economic affairs. The open market entails a heavy emphasis on private as against public effort, a pluralistic distribution of rule-making authority in the industrial relations area among management, labor organizations, and the state, and independent workers motivated by self-interest and capable of undertaking conflict with the employers in the name of this self-interest. The revolutionary intellectuals envision the goal as a totally new society fully compatible with the new technology. This calls for a powerful centralized state which holds in its hands all rule-making authority and which expects the worker to perform his duty and to accept without conflict the decisions of the state, which is held to be acting in his interest. The nationalist leaders see the goal to be the independence and progress of the nation to be achieved under the guidance of the state.

The dynastic elite offers continuity; the middle class, individual choice; the revolutionary intellectuals, high velocity industrialization; and the nationalist leaders, the integrity and advancement of the nation. None of them, however different their essential emphasis, can escape the imperatives of consensus and assimilation. In each case, starting as a minority, they must get the acceptance of the society and become broadly based within a culture which is compatible with their strategic approach. Once this has been done the society becomes internally largely ideologically barren, for there no longer is a basic conflict over the strategic approach to industrial society. The decline of ideology in a society marks the rise in acceptance of the dominant strategy. The decline of ideology in the world will come when there is only one accepted approach to industrialism; and that eventuality, if it ever comes, is still a long distance away.

This chapter has been largely concerned with "ideal types," but each actual situation has grown within a preexisting culture and been affected by it; each has encountered a series of historical and economic facts and been molded by them. The almost infinite variety of realistic experience can only be understood by reference to the variety of cultural, historical, and economic settings. Industrialism in the end may become one, but it certainly will have found its initial beginnings in the many.

CHAPTER 4

THE CONFLICT OF CULTURES
IN INDUSTRIALIZATION

The sweep of industrialization throughout the world transforms the culture of the traditional societies. Each industrializing elite, except the colonialist, emerges from a pre-industrial culture and evolves a strategy toward the changes to be made in the old society. Some elements of the existing culture are more resistant than others to the penetration of industrialization; some elites are more tolerant or place a higher priority upon preserving the traditional values. The nature of the conflict between the old and the new cultures, and the degree of penetration of the traditional by the industrial, depend both on the attraction of the new and the resistance of the old. The different possible outcomes of this conflict have significance for workers and managers in the industrialization process.

Some Critical Elements in the Culture

As the anthropologists define it, "culture" is broader than those features we shall discuss here. In their definition, "Culture. . . . is that complex whole which includes knowledge, belief, art, law, morals, custom, and any other capabilities and habits acquired by man as a member of a society."[1] The present discussion somewhat arbitrarily and more narrowly considers only some aspects of "culture" which are often characterized as primarily noneconomic.

Chapter 2 noted that the logic of industrialism involves certain inherent cultural characteristics. Industrialism develops an ideology oriented toward work and accumulation, emphasizing responsibility to the job and to norms or standards of performance. Individual and work-group effort and accomplishment are rewarded, whereas the pre-industrial societies often demand quite contrary standards because of an other-worldly religious ethic and strong family obligations. Family, caste, or class affiliations determine occupation and social position in the traditional society, whereas individual and group performance are the gauge of success in the advanced industrializing society. These illustrations indicate the many contrasts and conflicts between the industrial and the traditional cultures, but they do not suggest the variety in pre-industrial cultures. Nor do they help to understand how this variety affects the primacy of particular industrializing elites or the probable success of their efforts. There is need to examine in more detail the interrelations between the following five cultural elements and the industrialization process as they affect managers and the managed.

(1) *The family system* — the nuclear as opposed to the composite, joint, or extended family, and its comparative impact on incentives to work and invest, on enterprise organization and activity.

(2) *Class and race* — the effect of class structure and its relative flexibility or rigidity on the industrialization process, and on worker and manager responses.

(3) *Religious and ethical valuations* — toward work, thrift, and the satisfaction of material desires; and toward innovation, change, and the utilization of modern technology.

(4) *Legal concepts* — the relative roles of statute, common and administrative law and codes, in relation to workers and managers.

(5) *Concept of the nation-state* — the extent to which divisive groups in the preexisting culture remain dominant, or are subordinated to national ends in economic development.

The totality of the preexisting or traditional culture is more important than is any one of the above cultural elements in explaining the adaptation to industrialization. The culture as a whole is decisive for resisting or for accelerating the new order. Thus, the long-established cultures found in Asian countries are more resistant to industrialization than was North America where the indigenous people were physically swept aside by European immigrants whose culture was conducive to the economic development of the continent. Where some elements of the preexisting culture were favorable to a change, as in England and later in Japan, the industrial culture moved in more rapidly than it did in either China or

India before 1947. The industrializing elites in both of these latter nations face the problems of inducing major modifications of strong traditional cultures.

Despite strong traditional cultures in many industrializing countries today, the elites also confront widespread aspirations for industrialization. Man in the mid-twentieth century is everywhere demanding the fruits of industrial progress, and nationalist man in the newly emerging independent countries sees industrialization as the road to national recognition, prestige, and power. Ideological resistance to industrialization, which characterized both traditionalist and reform groups during the Industrial Revolution in England and (to a lesser extent) in the United States during the nineteenth century is not a significant force in most countries today. The example of the advanced industrial nations has demonstrated the superiority or invincibility of industrial culture over traditional cultures in the eyes of the economically underdeveloped peoples.

The discussion which follows examines the five cultural elements in relation to the strategies of each ideal type of the industrializing elites.

The Family System

In a few societies, the nuclear family forms a separate and independent unit; but in the great majority of traditional cultures several nuclear families act as an aggregate in their social and economic pursuits. This composite, joint, or extended family is, more often than not, unfavorable to economic growth. It provides shelter and food for all of its members, regardless of their individual contributions, so that the indigent and the indolent alike are cared for in a sort of "social security" system. Working members are expected to pool their earnings for the benefit of everyone in the extended family; individual saving is discouraged. The behavior and careers (including marriage) of its members are the close concern of the elders in the extended family. Family loyalty and obligations take precedence over other loyalties and obligations. Thus, the joint or extended family tends to dilute individual incentives to work, save, and invest.

There are some circumstances, of course, in which the extended family may facilitate the transition to an industrialized society. It may be the main source of initial capital for investment when only close relatives may be trusted or persuaded to lend money. It may offer security and means of adjustment in the industrializing urban areas to new recruits from the villages, as in India or the Belgian Congo. But these advantages are at best temporary; the entrepreneur must eventually tap a wider and less personal capital market; the industrial worker eventually becomes a member of an urban nuclear family. ". . . . economic change is always destructive to a joint family system."[2] The industrializing elites are confronted with the prospect of adapting the industrializing process to the existing family system or of altering the family system in the cause of industrialization.

Traditional Japan was family-oriented, and its industrial change under the guidance of a dynastic elite was geared to the preservation of existing family structure and values. As a result, it is said that when a Japanese goes to work for a firm, he normally expects to remain a part of this industrial or commercial "family" for the rest of his life, and he looks to the employer as the head of this family. There are indications more recently, however, that postwar economic, political, and social changes in Japan have weakened family ties as compared to the prewar period.

In less economically developed countries, the dynastic elite has also geared the structure and management of enterprises to the extended family. Family-dominated enterprises are characteristic of many of the less developed countries. Among the many causes of the relative backwardness of much of French industry is the "backward family enterprise." The role of the extended family in dominating Indian industries is well known. In each case, the extended family's control of an enterprise or group of firms enables less competent members of the family to hold managerial positions for which their training and ability would not otherwise qualify them. The consequence is that outsiders, however competent, seldom progress to high managerial positions in the enterprise; although in some cases the extended family may concentrate on training and developing its more able members for these top managerial posts.

In contrast, the advanced industrial countries with a strong middle-class elite place less emphasis on family connections in developing the structure of an enterprise, or its administrative organization, although family influence is certainly not unknown in enterprises in England, Sweden, and the United States. The point to be stressed is that the culture of industrialism requires selection and advancement on the basis of competence, and this is clearly more evident in the advanced industrial countries. In the pre-industrial society, loyalty and obligations to the composite family are considered "good" and family-oriented behavior is commendable. But in advanced industrializing countries, preference for family members — whether in managerial positions or in industrial employment — is called "nepotism" and considered undesirable.

When the prime movers in industrialization are the revolutionary intellectuals, as in the Soviet Union and more recently in China, they set out deliberately to weaken family loyalties and obligations and to demand primary loyalty to the state as the principal instrument of industrialization. This is clearly evident in recent reports from China, where establishment of "communes" in the villages has sought to break up the ancestral homes in which members of an extended family lived together and to which absent members returned periodically. This destruction of the family was evidently designed to require labor of all its members, as well as to replace loyalty to the family with full allegiance to the totalitarian regime.[3]

The nationalist leaders also seek to modify the joint family, but less drastically and more indirectly. Their efforts to industrialize a newly independent country tend to break down the wider family affiliations as the nuclear family develops in the urban centers. The colonial administrators, on the other hand, have no uniform policy toward the preexisting family structure. Their policies reflect particularly the problems of recruiting a labor force. In India during the British rule the joint family persisted as it had for centuries, until industrialization under nationalist auspices after independence began to weaken it. On the other hand, colonial administrators seeking to exploit natural resources may recruit labor in ways which break family ties, as in parts of Africa.

The logic of the industrialization process requires that selection and promotion be made on the basis of ability and competence. Thus, industrialization inexorably clashes with the joint family; it demands performance and loyalty to the enterprise and to the work group (with its labor organization) and to a nationalist aspiration rather than to the extended family as such. The separation of these functions from the family, the individualization of contract, the movement of production from the home to the factory were steps in the industrialization of the West. Later industrializations may not repeat the identical steps, but weakening or destruction of the extended family and the substitution of new loyalties and affiliations is clearly one of their consequences.

Class and Race

Most societies have distinct social groups composed of individuals with such common characteristics as income, education, occupation or cultural heritage. In addition, every society has a class structure which arranges its social groups in a hierarchical order, or which may cut into the groups themselves and impart stratification within them. There are many bases for stratification, and among these are economic function and status affiliation. Economic activity involves a division of labor, which results in stratification based on occupation, property, income, and so on. Thus, there is an "economic order" which may be distinguished from a "status order" stemming from family lineage, traditional styles of living, and other factors. In the extreme, as in pre-industrial India, the class systems resulting from these two orders may merge in a "caste system" which combines the economic and status ordering — both cemented together by religious sanction.

The culture of industrialization challenges the old hierarchy and replaces it with a new ordering of the classes; professionals, managers, administrators, and industrial workers replace the pre-industrial economic ordering of landowners, merchants and traders, master craftsmen and guild journeymen, apprentices, and peasants.

If traditional class and caste lines are relatively rigid, as in pre-industrial India, or nineteenth-century France and Italy, the more functional class structure of an advanced industrializing society may be slower in developing. This is particularly likely when the dynastic elite is the prime mover toward industrialism. In Japan's industrialization, for example, the paternalism and authoritarianism of the old class structure seem to have been preserved in the factory system.

In contrast, societies such as those of the United States, Canada, and New Zealand which are much newer have relatively open class structures compared to the earlier industrial societies of Western Europe and the later ones of Japan, the Soviet Union, India, China and others, which had pre-industrial class structures of varying degrees of rigidity. Industrial workers in the United States, for example, have moved up the occupational hierarchy in greater numbers than is possible in traditional societies. Even though a majority remain as industrial workers, the possibility of upward and horizontal mobility remains in greater degree, particularly between generations, and the belief in "equal opportunity" persists. A bitterness of class conflict has not plagued labor-management relations to the same degree in the newer societies, as it has in the older ones. When the middle class is in the industrialization driver's seat, as in Britain or Sweden, it tends to be successful in retaining control, in part because it modifies the harshness of class distinctions — often under pressure from labor movements and labor parties which challenge the authority of the ruling class. Where the latter has tried to hang on to its power at all costs, an intense class conflict has resulted in labor-management relations and in politics, as in France and Italy.

The revolutionary intellectuals approach to industrialization involves violent overthrow of the preexisting dominant class, as in the Soviet Union and China. The ruling groups may be physically liquidated, or forced to purge themselves and accept a different status by surrendering their power and wealth as the price of physical survival. But in these societies, a new class is substituted at the top of the social structure, just as other new classes rise to the top in societies which choose a less drastic and more gradual road to industrialism. The "managers of the economy" are a new class, and at the apex is the Communist Party which is dedicated to the perpetuation of its own power. Thus, the society which was to become "classless" develops into one in which the ruling class has a power more absolute than most in history.

When industrialization is under colonial auspices, the class and racial structure from one society is superimposed on or tries to subordinate the class and racial structure of the occupied society. This describes the impact of the British in India or Rhodesia and the Dutch in Indonesia, for example. Racial tensions become intermixed with nationalist conflicts, and spill over into labor-management disputes, especially when management is white and Western, and labor is nonwhite and nationalist in sentiment. The early history of the Indian labor movement is partly explained in these terms. The explosive possibilities of *apartheid* in South Africa represent the extreme case in a spectrum which includes racial and national discrimination in varying degrees in most industrializing societies, whether it be in the southern sections of the United States, in pre-independent India, or in some of the South American nations with large indigenous Indian populations.

The nationalist leaders, of course, seek to exploit these evidences of class and racial discrimination to their political advantage both in the struggle for national independence and in the drive for industrialization. The difficult but successful effort of the Egyptian industrialists to show that they could build a textile industry despite the active discouragement of the British is parallel with the drive of newer nations today to build steel mills to prove their claim to national industrial vigor. The fierce pride of non-Western peoples in their industrial achievements and in their future goals, fanned by nationalist aspirations, is the reaction to centuries of Western domination and treatment of these peoples as backward and indolent. The current Chinese industrialization effort, no less than the present Soviet effort to overtake American productivity levels, is explained partially in these terms. The following quotation from the Peking *People's Daily* (quoted in *The Times,* June 13, 1958, p. 9) is illustrative:

The clarion call for a technological revolution has sounded, and an earth-shaking battle has begun. We shall stir up the minerals which have slumbered underground for hundreds of millions of years . . .

We shall scale the highest peaks of world scientific technique, wipe out poverty, eliminate backwardness and bring to our people a life of the greatest happiness.

While the nationalist leader is mobilizing sentiment against the domination of the foreigner, he may also be seeking the subordination of divisive classes and groups within the new society and the dominance of the new state. Tribal rivalries complicate the national unity of Ghana, and long-standing regional differences pose problems to the leadership of the Yugoslav drive for industrialization. Independent India could not tolerate the continuance of the princely states within the new Indian nation, and it could not countenance the later agitation in 1955–1957 for many separate linguistic states. Similarly, rigid caste distinctions are intolerable in a developing industrial society, and have been denounced by leaders like Gandhi and Nehru. More important than exhortations, however, are the eroding pressures of industrialization itself on caste lines, especially in the cities.

Just as the relationships between management and workers are shaped by industrialization, and influenced by the strategy of the industrializing elite, so also is the role of the intellectuals. In some cases, particularly in the early development of industrialization, intellectuals may be alienated from the emerging industrial society. Historically, they have frequently been in the forefront of protest movements against the excesses of the new industrialization. In middle-class industrializing countries, they have joined with the emerging labor movements in opposing or protesting particular consequences of the industrial society, as did the Fabian Socialists in Britain, or the other Socialist parties in Europe. The communist intellectuals in every country have also spearheaded the protest against industrialization when it proceeds under noncommunist auspices. But once the revolutionary intellectuals gain control, as they have in the Soviet Union and in China, the role of the intellectuals is subordinated to the goals of the party and the state. If this latter point needs documentation, the denunciation by the highest Soviet authorities of the Russian novelists Vlidmir Dudinstev and, later, Boris Pasternak, for departing from glorification of the regime, and the rapid demise of Mao's invitation, "let a hundred flowers bloom," are illustrative. As noted in Chapter 3, the intellectuals under this elite are servants of the industrializing society, not its critics.

When nationalist leaders are the industrializing elite, the intellectuals support industrialization. The industrial society is the promised land, not the anathema it was to a bygone Dickens or Upton Sinclair.

Finally, we have seen how the governmental leaders in these same systems have become a new class superior to all previous groups in class structure. To a lesser extent, this is true in other industrializing societies, where the economic planning and administrative function of government is relatively greater than in the present advanced industrial societies; and this administrative class undertakes to shape labor-management relationships.

Religious and Ethical Valuations

In traditional or pre-industrial societies, organized religion often obliges people to seek other-worldly goals, and the organized priesthood in many Eastern as well as Western religions was the instrument in setting the pattern for the faithful to follow. The traditional religions, reinforced by the related social systems, also emphasized that each person had his "place" and that he had a "duty" to fulfill that was not usually related to economic gain or advancement.

Religious and ethical valuations toward work, particularly with respect to manual labor, were generally not favorable to individual effort aimed toward material progress. Furthermore, in the pre-industrial societies characteristic of much of Asia, there has been a "cyclical theory of time." "If the nature of things is such that everything runs in a cycle, coming back at some later date to precisely where it is now, what is the point in trying to change the present state of affairs?"[4] Deliberately planned change is abhorred; the *status quo* is preserved in economic activity while the individual is directed to subordinate himself to a God or Gods through the established church and in accord with accepted doctrine.

These unfavorable attitudes toward change are related to hostile or lukewarm views on the applicability of science and technology to economic growth. Traditional religions and traditional societies teach that man must accept and adapt to the dictates of supernatural powers. They are unfriendly to the notion that man may utilize his knowledge to manipulate or to adapt to his environment.

Finally, religious and ethical valuations influence the relationship between superior and subordinate, master and servant, manager and worker. In the pre-industrial society, the master expects obedience from the servant and has some obligations of a protective nature toward him. But the subordinate owes unquestioning allegiance to his superior; he must carry out his orders and his wishes.

In varying fashion, the incoming industrial culture builds on, bends, breaks, or destroys these traditional cultural elements. If the dynastic elite is the prime mover toward industrialism, as in Japan during the Meiji restoration, many of the traditional values will be preserved while others change. The authority of superiors, stemming from the restoration of the emperor, was maintained into modern Japan, and the consequent employer-employee relationship in the Japanese factory is vastly different from that found in democratic Western industrial countries. Yet the Japanese did not hesitate to adopt modern technology, and they borrowed heavily from the scientific and industrial knowledge of the West. Traditional religious beliefs did not handicap industrial development, and in modern industrial Japan many of the old customs persist side by side with advanced technology. In Japan, as in France and Italy, the traditional culture favored the dynastic elite as the prime movers toward industrialization, and this elite in turn preserved as much of that culture as possible. In such countries as Spain, and in parts of Latin America and the Islamic world, the power of organized religion has without question helped to preserve the hierarchical relations in the society and has been a factor in the larger strategy of a slow pace of industrialization.

The reverse of this conclusion is, of course, the importance of the "Protestant ethic" for economic growth.[5] The revolution in religious ideas wrought by the Protestant revolution produced the personality of an inner-worldly ascetic, strikingly different from the personality of the other-worldly monk or the inner-worldly, luxury-devoted aristocrat. This inner-worldly ascetic is the prototype of the modern middle class or bourgeois capitalist — pushed on by Calvinist predestination doctrine to accumulate more and more of the materialistic signs of grace. The middle-class capitalist prime movers of industrialization in Britain, Scandinavia, and the United States found these spiritual doctrines congenial to doing what they devoutly believed was God's work on earth — practicing the virtues of thrift, austerity, and capital accumulation. Because the spiritual and intellectual authority of the earlier established church was overthrown or rejected in these countries, the leaders of industrialization could therefore build on the new religious and ethical valuations toward work and accumulation. They helped spread the new gospel to the subordinate groups in the society — especially to the new industrial workers, who were urged to become "independent" and self-reliant, rather than "dependent." Methodism in England, for example, helped industrial workers accept the harshness of the industrial system. Furthermore, the intellectual renaissance, combined with Protestant reformation and the religious dissent, was wholly congenial to the advancement of scientific inquiry and the development of advanced technology. Thus, the cultural stage was set for the world's first industrializing society.

Historically, the revolutionary intellectuals came later in countries like the Soviet Union and more recently China, where pre-existing religious and ethical valuations of the traditional variety seemed to block the prospect of rapid industrialization. So the new elite set out to break and to destroy them by deliberate design, partly because they were so rigid. The revolutionary elite, of course, rejects private thrift and accumulation, substituting state investment; but they are no less "Calvinist" than Western European Protestants in their efforts to encourage hard work. They have clearly accepted for industrialization the valuations implicit in modern science and technology.

In Turkey, with a mixture of the revolutionary and nationalist approaches, "Ataturk's genius as a social planner was to see 'economic development' within a comprehensive behavioral matrix."[6] He destroyed the political and temporal power of the organized religion; he established secular schools; he simplified the alphabet; and he degraded the traditional form of dress by ordering the wearing of Western attire; he introduced radios into people's houses. Through such institutional changes he undermined rural isolation and encouraged modernization.

India has chosen a different route, under the direction of nationalist leaders who stress a "socialist pattern of society" which leans heavily on the middle class rather than on a dynastic elite or on revolutionary intellectuals. Gandhi and Nehru have sought to modify the Hindu ethic in the industrializing society, but not to destroy it. Superficially, Hinduism with its other-worldly emphasis might seem to stultify economic growth, but Indian industrialists who are also devout Hindus do not seem to have been greatly inhibited in seeking economic gains. Similarly, the Moslem religion has not interfered with the development of banking, trading, or commercial and industrial institutions in Egypt. Traditionalist religious values do not seem to have been as serious an obstacle to economic development in the long run as some anthropologists have thought [7]

Legal Concepts

In the traditional society, custom and social norms are more important than written law in governing relationships between individuals and groups. But the advanced society has developed institutions, such as parliaments and legislatures to promulgate statute laws, and courts to interpret and apply them. Written constitutions, as interpreted by the courts, are also part of law; there is administrative law by public agencies, and finally, a system of private law which may be developed by parties such as managers and labor organizations.

The early industrializing societies, under the middle-class elite in Great Britain and the United States, were characterized by laws which respected private property rights and enforced obligations concerning them. Legal concepts extended to the market and applied to functions rather than to persons as individuals. There was legal protection of contract rights growing out of economic activity, and the process favored private capital accumulation and investment. Subsequently, in these industrializing societies, the statute and common law was expanded and modified to limit private property rights when they infringed upon the rights of workers (as well as other groups). Thus, the growth of labor and social legislation progressively restricted the rights of private property.

When the dynastic elites lead the march to industrialism, the legal system is likely to support the existing elite and the national state above individual rights before the law. Indeed, as with other cultural elements, the preexisting legal system may help to explain the rise of a particular state. The Napoleonic legal code, a comprehensive set of rules affecting all types of conduct, has influenced the legal systems of industrial relations in such countries as France and Italy, where state regulation of the terms and conditions of employment and the rights and obligations of employers and unions is much more detailed than in the countries with Anglo-Saxon legal traditions. The German legal system, as applied to industrial relations, emphasized social justice more than individual rights, and this concept is found also in the administration of the detailed "Labor Codes" which have developed in Chile and Brazil.

A nationalist leader in a revolution designed to destroy the preexisting culture in order to further industrialization and national growth may adopt a Western legal system in the modernization process. As one of his many revolutionary reforms, Ataturk abolished Islamic law in Turkey and substituted the Swiss civil code. Turkish judges have a degree of independence guaranteed by the constitution.[8] The Turkish labor code, promulgated in 1936 with 148 articles, was drawn largely from the French labor code, and influenced by conventions approved by the International Labor Organization. Thus a different legal system, particularly as it applied to labor organizations and labor-management relations, was substituted within less than a generation for a traditional Islamic legal system which was found inadequate for a modern industrializing state.

The revolutionary intellectuals in Russia and in China rejected Western legal systems as "bourgeois" appendages of a rejected capitalist economic system. Soviet and Marxist legal theorists have held that "law is no more than a social technique with some advantages and disadvantages in comparison with other possible ways of regulating human behavior, but it is certainly not superior to what it should regulate."[9] Thus the Soviet State may promulgate whatever decrees, laws, and rules are needed to suit the purpose of rapid industrialization and the growth of a powerful national state. There are no superior individual rights guaranteed by law against arbitrary action by the state or its agents. Labor organizations may be severely limited in certain respects, for instance, in regard to strikes, and their duties may be enlarged in other respects as, for example, their pressure for some control at the shop level on the actions of factory managers. Individual workers may be tied to their jobs and prevented from moving to more attractive places at one time; they may be permitted some movement at others.

Colonial administrators impose the legal systems of the home country on the colony, as was common throughout Africa. The substitution of the laws of an industrializing state on the pre-industrial is designed to encourage foreign investment and the orderly handling of business affairs. In labor-management relations, the system of the colonial power may be introduced to settle disputes and possibly (as the Indians charge) to impose labor standards on new industry, thereby reducing competition with the home country. Colonial administrators may seek to regulate the labor market providing for differences in wages and mobility according to racial characteristics as they did in many parts of Africa. When ex-colonial countries win independence, they may take over the legal system of the colonial administrators, as the Indians have done. While compulsory adjudication of labor disputes in India has some distinctively Indian features, it is modeled on the preexisting British court structure and legal system. Much of Indian labor legislation draws upon British experience. The contrast with China, which had no Western-type legal system, is clear. Here "people's courts" dispense a kind of justice quite unrelated to any concept of established legal rights.

With the exception of the communist states, the industrializing societies of the modern world have substituted legal systems, which encourage economic growth through some protection to private property and individual rights, for the pre-industrial system of arbitrary actions (often in the name of the law) of superior over subordinates. Specifically, in the industrial relations systems of modern states, rights and obligations of labor, management, and the state are developed through statutes, codes, court decision, and administrative agencies acting under statutory power. The arbitrary power of the state or its agents is limited by these means, just as their specific powers have been progressively enlarged in many countries. Private law, developed by management and labor organizations as part of a system of industrial relations, is a further limitation on the role of the all-powerful state.

The Concept of the Nation-State

Pre-industrial societies are often divisive; tribal groups, language groups, and geographical regions assert their cohesiveness and independence from central authority. So long as these societies are primarily agricultural or commercial, divisiveness is not such a serious handicap, but the industrializing society requires the permanent central nation–state. If the earlier society has been a colonial one, furthermore, the central state is the instrument of triumphant nationalism.

The emergence of a strong governmental administrative or bureaucratic class goes hand in hand with a more decisive role of the state in industrial development in the twentieth century. The late comers to industrialization, like the Soviet Union, Turkey, India, China, and Egypt, are in a hurry, and state investment in basic industries of an industrializing society seems necessary to them — along with economic planning. The power of the state may also be regarded as necessary to destroy an impeding pre-industrial social structure (as in Russia or China), or to speed up a peaceful transition to an industrial society (as in Turkey under Ataturk and in Egypt since 1947). "Statism" in this sense is a powerful political and ideological concept which appeals to industrially underdeveloped countries everywhere today.

When this concept prevails, the state intervenes actively in the labor-management relationship; first to protect industrial labor with all kinds of social insurance in a sort of state paternalism and then, as industrial labor gets too powerful or independent, to control it, clip its wings, and contain the overt forms of protest by compulsory arbitration of labor disputes and other devices. We need not develop these points in detail here (see

Chapter 9); but the impact of an ideological view of the role of the state on labor-management relations is worth noting.

In the newly-industrializing societies, particularly those which were formerly under colonial rule, nationalism is a potent force in industrial development and has an important bearing on labor-management relations. Nationalism may be an integrating force in underdeveloped economies characterized by wide class and cultural differences between the elite and the masses. The Congress Party of India under Prime Minister Nehru is known as the "Party of Independence" and has therefore been able to take the leadership in welding together India's many separate groups into a unified national effort to achieve more rapid industrial development. The experience of Israel serves as another example of nationalism harnessed for economic development, although in this case the same kind of prior colonial domination was not involved. Similarly, nationalism — fed by anti-Western sentiments — was clearly a powerful force in the industrialization of Japan. Turkey is an example of a Middle Eastern country where national pride was harnessed by Ataturk to attempt economic development on the pattern of the West.

But nationalism may also be a hindrance to economic development if it requires for national pride alone such appurtenances of industrialization as steel mills or automobile assembly plants without sound economic justification. Extreme nationalism may also irrationally reject all forms of external aid, and drive out the technical and managerial resources identified with the former colonial power as the Indonesians did with the Dutch, or the Iranians with Anglo-Iranian Oil Company. The labor policies of a foreign-owned or managed enterprise in a strongly nationalistic newly independent country are targets for special legislation and labor organizations.

Finally, nationalism combined with revolutionary totalitarianism, as in the Soviet Union and China, merely reinforces those pressures for control of labor-management relations which are implicit in the ideology of totalitarianism. The managerial class and leaders of labor organizations are subordinate to the will and the interests of the state — the Soviet or Chinese state, controlled by the Communist Party in each.

The nationalist leader in most industrializing societies is confronted with divergent group pressures in the cultures, such as tribal, regional, minority, and linguistic groups, as well as pressure groups like organized management or labor. The logic of industrialization compels a subordination of these groups to national survival and growth, and one of the dilemmas of modern industrializing societies is the conflict between freedom for these groups in the culture and the centralized controls which rapid industrialization requires.

This chapter has considered what is universal about the cultural changes brought by industrialization and what is related to the impacts upon traditional cultures by the programs of the different ideal types of industrializing elites. The central themes may be summarized in the following points:

(1) The preexisting or traditional culture is limiting but not exclusively determinative of the process of industrialization. It helps to explain the character of the elite which leads the march, and this elite then, in turn, confronts the distinctive problems of industrialization posed by the particular culture. The preexisting culture must adapt or be broken as industrialization proceeds. Cultural impediments are not insuperable barriers to industrialization, but they are frequently significant in explaining the kind of industrialization which develops. The cultural patterns of industrialization may move in rapidly, advance slowly, or be sealed off in a particular society. They may penetrate deeply or shallowly, depending upon the nature and strength of the preexisting culture. In retarded or slowly developing industrial societies, the two conflicting cultures may persist for long periods side by side within the same society, or in different parts of it.

(2) Industrialization imposes its own cultural patterns on the preexisting culture. This transition will be more rapid if the preexisting culture has the following characteristics: (a) a nuclear family system which tends to accentuate individual incentives to work, save, and invest; (b) a relatively open social structure which encourages equality of treatment and advancement on the basis of ability; (c) religious and ethical values which are favorable to economic gain and growth, innovations and scientific change; (d) a legal system which encourages

economic growth through protection of property rights from arbitrary or capricious rule; and (e) a strong central governmental organization and the sense of being a nation which can play a decisive role in economic development. Put in another way, the culture of industrialization is characterized by these factors, and has less difficulty in replacing an older culture if some of the necessary cultural factors are already present or if social revolt has already helped to uproot the older culture.

Conversely, certain cultural factors impede the advance of the industrial culture: (a) an extended family system which weakens industrial incentives to work, save, and invest, and which reserves key managerial positions for family members regardless of relative competence of insiders and outsiders; (b) a class structure based on traditional social status rather than on economic performance; (c) traditional religious and ethical values which emphasize "place" and "duty" unrelated to economic gain or advancement, and oppose change and innovation, particularly in science and technology; (d) traditional customs and social norms which deny individual and property rights and fail to guarantee observance of contracts; (e) divisive groups in the society which hinder or prevent the emergence of a strong nation–state.

(3) The strategies of the different industrializing elites are affected, in part, by the strength and rigidity of the pre-industrial culture. The consequences for cultural change and the resulting impact on labor-management-state relations are great. Thus, the character of the labor organizations and the structure and philosophy of enterprise managements are both significantly influenced by the particular industrializing elite, which, in turn, is partially a consequence of the impediments presented by the pre-industrial culture. These interrelationships are summarized in the accompanying chart (see Chart 2).

(4) The pattern of cultural change has a significant impact upon the character of the labor problems which arise under industrialization. Thus, the following generalizations are suggestive of the impact of cultural factors during the course of industrialization on labor-management-state relations (see Chapters 6–9).

The greater the class distinctions in the old culture, the more intense the industrial conflict.

CHART 2.

Industrializing elites and cultural factors.

Pre-existing cultural traits	Dynastic	Middle-Class	Revolutionary-Intellectuals	Colonial Administrators	Nationalist Leaders
The family system	Preserves joint family.	Weakens wider family; encourages nuclear family.	Destroys traditional family loyalty and responsibility.	Little change, unless breakup through labor recruiting.	Modifies toward nuclear family.
Class and race	Preserves existing class structure.	Modifies, develops fluid classes.	Destroys, and substitutes new elite class.	Substitutes new superior class.	Modifies existing structure – national state gives people sense of common citizenship.
Religious and Ethical valuations	Tends to preserve.	Modifies or builds on.	Breaks or destroys-- new valuations substituted.	Two cultures-- slowly adapt.	Modifies or breaks.
Legal concepts	National law developed to support existing elite and national state.	Developed to protect individual rights-- and the law of the market.	Administrative law-- people's courts.	Two systems: national vs. colonial.	Administrative-- one system.
Concept of nation-state	Great emphasis.	Moderate emphasis.	Great emphasis.	Little emphasis.	Great emphasis.
The total culture	Accepts for most part.	No policy toward the total culture.	Drastically modifies, or destroys.	Encourages dual culture, home and native.	Modifies in part, accepts in part.

The less the emphasis upon work in the old culture, the greater the
need for discipline at the work place.

The greater the emphasis upon the extended family, the slower the
rise of professional management.

The greater the strength of the extended family, the slower the commitment of workers to industrial life.

The more diverse the groups in the old culture, the harsher the role
of the nation-state.

(5) In the past, culture and social structure were changed by
movements of peoples between countries. Today, ideas and institutions which affect culture are moving throughout the world
with the speed of modern means of communication and transportation. Few pre-industrial cultures can be insulated for long
from the spreading cultural patterns of industrialization.

(6) The faster the pace of industrialization, the more likely is
the preexisting culture to be modified or destroyed with the on-
rush of the industrial society. Conversely, the speed of industrialization can be greater if the pre-industrial culture is favorable or
less resistant.

Out of the myriad cultures of the past emerge new and fewer
distinctive cultural patterns. The logic of industrialization decrees a trend toward the nuclear family, a high evaluation on
work, and a heightened sense of the nation as the prime social
unit. The strategies of the several elites may slow or hasten the
transition, may soften or intensify the conflict of the old and the
new; and they also affect the characteristics of the new culture,
particularly the role of class and race distinctions. But regardless
of the resistance or acquiescence of the old culture and the
tolerance or intolerance of the industrializing elites, the pre-industrial cultures sooner or later are largely modified or swept away
and new cultures take their place; new cultures more compatible
with the new technology; and much of the anguish of men and institutions that marks our current period of history derives from
this transition from the old to the new.

The emerging industrialism and the elites that guide it are confronted by and must react to the economic realities of the present
as well as to the cultural heritage of the past, and the next chapter
discusses the nature of these realities and the several typical responses to them.

CHAPTER 5

SHAPING THE INDUSTRIALIZATION PROCESS

Industrializing elites confront a number of related constraints and difficult decisions no matter which strategy they elect enroute to the industrial society. There are no smooth superhighways to the industrial society. But speed on some routes is greater than on others, some roads have been traveled more frequently, and the danger signs are more clearly marked. Some industrializing elites are more generously provided with resources for the journey; some have greater luck or skill in following their course and in logistics, and some are better travelers or have greater zest for the one-way expedition to industrialism. Some elites have elaborate and detailed plans and road maps, while others tend to improvise and feel their way along. Some elites will not reach their destination, falling by the wayside to more acceptable, competent, dedicated, or ruthless leaders. On the record to date, the destination is not necessarily achieved first by the earliest starters nor even by the most opulent travelers.

As on any prolonged journey, those who travel the routes to industrialism are themselves changed in the process, in varying ways and degrees. The present chapter concentrates upon the metamorphosis of economic systems in the course of industrialization, the decisions — not necessarily conscious choices — which most directly shape an economy and the interrelations among workers, managers and governments. The form of the labor market, the level of wages, the rules on discipline, the functions of organizations of workers, and the industrial relations arrangements, for instance, are directly affected by the general strategy of an elite and its related economic policies.

There is so much interdependent change in industrializing economies that attention may be directed toward almost any feature to observe the disappearance of the pre-industrial and the emergence of the new: the introduction of advanced technology; increases in per capita gross national product; a decline in the proportion of the agricultural sector in total output and employment; the emergence of large-scale enterprise and financial organizations; the development of industrial workers and managers; capital accumulation, and so on. While recognizing the essential interdependence of the features of the new economy, the basic indicator is the achievement of a self-generating amount of capital formation. An economy enters the industrial age when the rate of gross capital formation attains a sustained chain reaction in which a significantly larger amount of capital is available each period to increase output than is necessary merely to sustain the old level and composition of production. (This formulation abstracts from population increases and short run fluctuations.) "The central problem in the theory of economic growth is to understand the process by which a community is converted from being a 5 per cent to a 12 per cent saver — with all the changes in attitudes, in institutions and in techniques which accompany this conversion."[1]

Economic constraints are not the only nor necessarily the most serious impediments restricting economic growth; they are, however, the only ones considered in this chapter. At any one period, the economic constraints constitute parameters or conditions given to the industrializing elite that is leading the march. They shape the range of choice in economic policy that is available to the leaders seeking to push capital formation above the critical level of sustaining growth or beyond to ever more rapid expansion. They place in sober proportions the high flying aspirations to achieve industrialism. Among different countries, even at comparable stages of industrialization, there are very marked differences in these constraints upon the major decisions that shape the economy and the strategies of the elites. These constraints are outlined in the next two sections. The first considers economic limitations to development in the short period, and the second section indicates the constraints which arise from the historical timing and circumstances of the beginning of industrialization.

Economic Limitations in the Short Period

In every country, regardless of its stage of economic development, the industrializing elite confronts the following limitations in the short period: (1) the level of technology in the most advanced countries and the level of technology in the particular country; (2) the known natural resources of the country; (3) the educational development as it affects the skill, training, and experience of workers and the skill, organizing ability, and competence of the managerial and professional groups and government personnel; (4) the level of population, its age distribution and the rate at which the population is increasing. Since the above listing treats each country largely as a closed economy, a further factor accordingly needs to be added in an interdependent world; (5) the capacity to borrow funds or to secure grants or gifts from abroad and to export natural resources. In the short period in which these dimensions are given, they constrict the possibilities of economic development, although they by no means uniquely determine the performance of an economy. In the short period, there is not very much which an industrializing elite can do about these dimensions except for grants from abroad. While some variations in style and size are possible, the economic suit must be cut to fit the given cloth.

These factors at a given period tend to influence directly the rate of economic growth of a country. The higher the level of technology, the richer and more highly utilized the natural resources, the higher the levels of education and applied skill in all sectors of the work force, the greater the availability of foreign capital and the greater the proportion of the population in education and in the active work force — in general, the greater the potential for economic growth. The influence of the level of population and its rate of increase on economic growth depends largely upon the ratio of population to other resources; in relatively "empty" countries a rapid rate of population increase may be essential to achieving a rate of capital formation compatible with any economic growth.

Any comparison among countries reveals how large are the differences in the limitations which confront the industrializing elites, even if comparison be somehow restricted to countries in approximately the same stage of economic development. Some countries utilize the most modern technology, while technology in others is backwards in many sectors. Some countries are known to be richly endowed with a wide range of natural resources while others appear to be much less fortunate. The uneven world-distribution of coal, oil, and water power is illustrative. Some countries have a skilled labor force with effective professional managers and public administrators, while other countries lack such resources. In some countries population is small relative to resources with an age distribution that results in a high proportion of the population in the working ages, while in other countries population is dense relative to resources, is increasing at a rapid rate, and the age distribution is relatively highly concentrated among children. Finally, some countries have ready access to scarce factors from abroad and secure generous capital grants or gifts, while other countries must rely almost exclusively on domestic resources. This range of limitations confronting industrializing elites may be expected to result in different rates of economic growth and in different economic policies among countries.

A brief illustration of the significance of these constraints is provided by a comparison of contemporary Iraq and Egypt. In agricultural land, Iraq is potentially rich and Egypt is desperately poor. Egypt must support today four times as many people as Iraq with less agricultural land than Iraq, whereas with even less new investment in dams and irrigation works and more intensive land use than is contemplated in Egypt, Iraq could have an increase in agricultural production of three to four times that which would be technically possible in Egypt. Egypt's comparative position is even less favorable with regard to the availability of capital for investment in economic development. Iraq, in contrast, appears to have an assured flow of funds for investment in needed development projects. Moreover, Egyptian population is increasing at a rate in excess of 2.5 per cent a year. These hard facts have convinced many Egyptians that it is practically and politically impossible to find an internal solution for the country's economic dilemma.

If the two countries are compared in terms of their human resources, the contrast is almost as sharp. But here the advantage lies with Egypt. Egypt has a large and comparatively well-trained body of civil servants, whereas Iraq is handicapped by an acute shortage. In the fields of social welfare, public health, rural community development, and agricultural extension services, Egypt is also far ahead of Iraq. Egypt eclipses Iraq in the field of education. Apart from the foreign-managed oil companies, Iraq has very few skilled workers, technicians, or engineers. By contrast, Egypt has the high-level manpower for substantial industrialization. Human resources constitute the more serious restraint to economic development in Iraq[2] while natural resources are the more restrictive in Egypt. These strictures materially shape the direction of economic policies of any industrializing elite in the two countries.

It must be emphasized that such economic constraints do not necessarily predestine the course or timing of industrialization. The rapid and very high level of development in Japan after 1870 was made against the severe economic limitations of a high density of population, relatively poor natural resources, and a relatively low level of technology. Neither is the delayed economic development of Czarist Russia[3] readily to be understood solely in terms of the short-period economic limitations noted above. As in other spheres of human experience, some handicaps may serve as an added incentive and may be compensated for by the development of skills in other directions. The economic development of Denmark, Switzerland, and England provide many illustrations of the stimulating character of some economic limitations and the compensating shaping of specialized skills and services.

While the five limitations noted above are relatively given and serve to limit and shape the potentialities of economic growth in the short period, they are not fixed over a longer period, and they frequently become the focus of policies designed by an industrializing elite to stimulate growth. Advanced technologies can be borrowed; systematic surveys and explorations may discover hitherto unknown natural resources; education, training, and health programs raise the levels of skill and human performance; capital imports may be increased; and even the rate of increase of population may become the subject of public policies in some countries, although the independent effects of public policies are not well established. Indeed, the prospects for economic growth depend on the capacity of the industrializing elite to overcome these economic limitations and to provide fewer and less stringent constrictions to development. The short-period limitations are the principal locus of longer term economic development policies.

The Onset of Industrialization

The Historical Timing. The chronological date at which a country enters significantly the industrializing process makes a difference to the course of growth.[4] There are different consequences of an early as compared to a late start. Each has some advantages and some unfavorable consequences for industrial growth. It has frequently been noted that a late start has the advantage of permitting industrialization with more advanced technology. It is likely to be more productive, to open up virgin territory with airplanes and modern equipment rather than with covered wagons and the technology of a century and a half ago. To an increasing degree, improvements in technology are capable of being rapidly distributed throughout the world; the present age is better organized for spreading knowledge and technology to those beginning industrialization. Technical assistance, relatively cheaper travel, technical journals, and the exchange of students are illustrative. The opportunity to plan the growth of cities for industrial society may result in many lower social costs relative to those involved in seeking to modernize older urban areas. The advanced industrial countries are dependent upon the advance in the frontiers of technology which is likely to be less rapid than the application of existing technology to a more backward country.

But a late start also involves many disadvantages and limitations to economic growth. In the past century the gap between the most advanced industrializing countries and those now just starting has widened appreciably. A late start has meant a relatively larger handicap and a greater distance to travel. The latecomer is particularly given to borrowing technology and machinery which may be poorly adapted to the relative distribution of resources of the country and which is likely to require a relatively larger importation than would have been necessary with more gradual and indigenous growth of technology. The late comer is faced with the fact that modern technology frequently requires large-scale organizations, comprised in part of technical and professional groups, which cannot be created very rapidly in an industrializing country. A late start frequently means a greater dependence on foreigners and a sharper change in social relations than would have been necessary under an earlier start.

In addition to these economic consequences, there are other major effects of an early or late start for managers or workers. Industrialization at its formative stages in the modern world must now confront, to an extent that was not necessary among earlier starters, the economic and political organization of workers. Institutions as well as technology are borrowed, and they may not be well suited to the problems of countries at the early stages of industrialization. Labor organizations at the earliest stage of industrialization may be associated with a greater degree of industrial strife at the decisive formative stages, with relatively higher levels of wages, with relatively more advanced working rules and with a greater preoccupation with grievances than would have been likely with a historically earlier industrialization. "While in other countries a period of very rapid industrial growth tended to be *followed by* a period of upward adjustments in the standard of living, in Italy the two processes tended to coincide. Had the industrial upsurge in Italy taken place one or two decades earlier, in all likelihood it would have been much less disturbed by industrial strife."[5]

A study of the movement of real wages of industrial workers during the several most critical decades of early industrialization in countries now more advanced economically underscores the magnitude of the undertaking of many newly industrializing countries which promise one generation both industrialization and substantially higher real wages. Real wages may be increased in the sense that agricultural workers, usually with lower living standards, are absorbed into expanding industry at unchanged industrial wages. But some industrializing elites today promise immediate and substantially higher real wages to those already in industry; urban industrial workers are closer to the gains in productivity and are the more active and strategic group politically. But real wage rate increases of 1 per cent a year were a considerable achievement in the critical stages for economies at very much higher levels of development and without a substantial population problem. There was little, if any, rise in real wage rates in England between 1800 and 1830; and in the United States between 1840 and 1860 real wage rates increased less than 10 per cent a decade. The record for Sweden and Germany shows a higher rate in part because of the movement of world prices during the years of critical industrialization. In the Soviet Union after 1928 real wage rates declined.[6]

The role of ILO conventions and resolutions is also a symbol of the change from an earlier period of industrialization. The drive for economic development and against backwardness often includes the adoption of the forms of modern labor legislation and social insurance. The international standards of the ILO stimulate at the outset a full range of advanced labor standards which may impose a heavy burden on capital formation, even granting the difference between legal form and practice.

Any industrialization commenced after 1917, moreover, has had to face, and the more recent industrializing cannot avoid, the historically new problem that emerging workers' organizations may be captured or controlled by the Communists. Industrializing elites must encourage or resist this development. This response is a critical one at the early stages of an industrialization when the form and orientation of labor organizations have not been established.

The Degree of Economic Backwardness. The magnitude of the economic constraints (noted in the previous section) at the time of the industrialization "take off" make a difference in the process of development. The elite which seeks to steer an industrialization course starting from an exceptionally low level of technology and skills, with few developed resources and abnormally high rates of population increase, may be expected to have more difficult problems and perhaps require different methods than one which starts from a materially higher industrial base. Not all pre-industrial societies are equal. In some a political and a commercial revolution precede the industrial revolution, while in others these transformations are telescoped together.

The level of economic performance at which this break occurs may have far-reaching consequences on the process of industrialization that follows. It may be that the lower this initial level, the greater the strain called for by effective industrialization; the greater the burden put on the state in carrying through the necessary transformation; and possibly the pressure exercised by the state or other agents of industrialization upon the existing social institutions to effect the rapid change that is required. On the other hand, the higher the initial economic level, the easier it may be to secure the surplus necessary for facilitating the process of industrialization; the more gradual the transition may be; the less painful the pressures which the active agents of industrialization may be required to exercise upon those institutions and sectors in pre-industrial society that are likely to become less important as a result of the transformation.[7]

The timing of the initial thrust of industrialization and the level of activity (or the degree of economic backwardness) from which a country starts are likely to shape the magnitude of the effort confronting the elite and the policies and decisions adopted to start the journey. The timing of industrialization and the starting level may also influence to a degree the chances of any particular leadership becoming the controlling elite to initiate industrialization (Chapter 10).

Decisions of An Industrializing Elite

Any industrializing elite is required to make a series of major decisions — although the choices are not always conscious — within the economic constraints and the circumstances of the industrialization beginning. All alternatives of economic policy are not equally attainable, and these limitations and facts of history tend to shape in some measure the following basic decisions:

(1) How fast shall the country industrialize? What shall be the pace and speed in the direction of the industrial society, particularly in the earlier stages of the journey?

(2) How shall industrialization be financed? What shall be the source of the funds used for the requisite capital formation?

(3) What shall be the sequence in which industries are developed? What are the relative priorities to be given to heavy industries, social overheads, consumer goods and agriculture?

(4) What pressures are placed upon enterprise management? How is the environment of the enterprise manager arranged?

(5) What are the priorities in education and in the training

of workers and managers? Education may be confined to a few
or designed for the masses; the educational and vocational training system may be narrowly specialized or general; it may stress
the traditional culture or it may be more functionally related to
the culture of industrialism.

(6) What shall be the relation between industrialization in the
one country and other parts of the world? Shall the country
seek a relatively high degree of self-sufficiency or shall it specialize according to comparative advantage and substantially integrate its economy with others?

(7) Shall public policy seek to do anything explicitly about
the rate of increase in population? Are birth rates, death rates
and immigration to come within the purview of policy or to be
treated largely as the result of uninfluenced decisions of households?

Taken as a group, the answers to these questions describe
a program and a time schedule for an industrializing elite. The
answers are not isolated nor independent of each other, and
policies on one set of questions condition the others. Experience
may show an elite that the separate answers are inconsistent, and
the group of answers as a whole may need to be revised. The
aspiration for rapid and immediate industrialization must deal
with the costs of financing, the comparative advantage of raw
materials trade, external demands required for the growth of
many industries, the social costs of industrial expansion, and the
limiting influences of population increases. While these questions
are discussed separately in this section, they must be considered by an elite simultaneously. The choices and answers must
fit together more or less consistently if there is to be industrialization and if the elite is to survive.

Each of these seven major policy issues is considered in a
subsection which also explores the decisions and answers to these
questions provided by each of the ideal type of elites developed in
Chapter 3.

Pace of Industrialization. The central and most fundamental
decision of an industrializing elite concerns the pace of development. A decision on the pace of industrialization resolutely
pursued significantly conditions and predisposes in large measure
the other decisions confronting the elite. A decision on the pace

of development, as on its whole strategy, must be related to the cultural background of the ruling elite and the problems of industrialization as it sees them. The dynastic elite aspires to a pace no faster than essential to preserve itself and its traditional values. The middle class believes that speed should be determined by the individual choice of citizens between consumption and savings and by the decisions of elected governments. The revolutionary intellectuals regard it their mission to attain the very highest possible rate consistent with the endurance of the population and continued control by the elite. The colonial administrator sees the rate of colonial development as a by-product of the needs of the mother country for materials and of other claims for capital on the mother country within the limits essential to preserve his way of life. The nationalist leader promises a rapid rate of industrialization to catch up with advanced nations and to remove the stigma of backwardness.

The later in history industrialization begins, the greater the effort that is likely to be devoted to economic development of the resources available, at least for an initial period. The greater the delay in industrialization, the more economically backward the country and the greater the gap to be narrowed. ". . . the rate of growth in a backward country during the early periods of its industrialization may be assumed to vary directly with the degree of the country's industrial backwardness. The more belated the big industrial upswing, the stronger it is likely to be when it comes."[8] Countries recently starting to industrialize appear to begin from a materially lower pre-industrial base than the earlier starters. The late starters are likely to attempt to travel at a faster rate once they get underway.

Once an industrialization process gets underway, the more generous the resources and the less stringent all the economic limitations, the more rapid the potential rate of economic growth.

The more rapid the pace of development established by an elite, the larger the role of government in the industrialization process. ". . . . in much of Southern Asia and the Middle East governments are impelled by forces largely outside their control to undertake tasks beyond their competence. . . . A government that fails to seize the levers of economic development, or at least to make the attempt, is probably not long for this world."[9] A rapid transfer of resources requires more central direction in an economy, as in wartime. A rapid rate of industrialization necessitates a higher rate of savings and capital formation than the individual members of the community choose to withhold voluntarily from consumption, requiring governmental action to secure promptly the requisite resources for expansion. Workers may not elect the occupations and private managers may not choose the types of output that are consistent with the rapid rate of industrialization, and the labor and product markets may operate too slowly or with too much dislocation, or they may not be sufficiently well established, to achieve the requisite resource reallocation or expansion in the limited time. The more rapid the disruption of the old society, the more extensive the governmental action to contain the dislocations, the opposition, and the resistance to the new industrial order.

The greater the degree of initial economic backwardness, the later the achievement of a self-sustaining growth, the less constrictive the economic limitations to industrialization and the greater the discontent with the old order, the greater will be the pressures on any elite for a higher rate of development. The more rapid the pace of growth in a given setting of economic constraints, the greater the role of government in economic development in the modern world.

Sources of Capital. Economic growth is directly related to an increase in capital relative to population (capital per head). Kuznets' data for Western countries show the ". . . long-term proportion of net domestic capital formation to net national product ranges from about 5 to about 15 per cent," and "the long-term proportion of gross domestic capital formation to gross national product ranges from about 10 to about 25 per cent."[10]

An industrializing elite starting with a net investment no higher than 5 per cent per year of net national income is confronted with the basic problem of how to raise this figure substantially if a cumulative increase in output is to be achieved. The minimum necessary level will depend upon the rate of population increase and the (marginal) capital-output ratio. Thus, if population increases 1.5 per cent a year and the (marginal) capital-output ratio is 3:1, which may be said to approximate conditions in India, then 13.5 per cent of net national income is required as savings to increase net income 3 per cent per year. This rate of increase in real output would require 25 years to double national income and could scarcely be regarded as fast enough to narrow substantially the gap between India and the more advanced countries. A rate of 22.5 per cent of net national income allocated to capital formation would increase net income 5 per cent per year and result in some appreciable narrowing of the gap between a newly industrializing country and the most advanced, under the specified conditions. But a more rapid rate of increase in population than 1.5 per cent a year (and rates of 3.0 per cent a year occur in some underdeveloped countries), would depress the rate of capital formation and the rate of increase of net national income. How is capital formation to be increased from 5 per cent of net income to a higher level such as 13.5 per cent or 22.5 per cent? What are the alternative methods among which an elite must choose?

In general terms the savings for capital formation may be derived from the following sources or achieved through the following mechanisms: (1) domestic savings from a given national income; (2) domestic savings from a larger national income, and (3) international transactions. Domestic savings from a given national income may arise from voluntary reduction of consumption, a change in the distribution of income favorable to high income recipients who save a higher proportion of their income, higher taxes, enterprise savings, reduced imports of consumption goods, and an inflationary process which transfers incomes to savers and restricts consumption among some groups. In addition, savings for capital formation may arise from the higher levels of income created in the course of economic growth such as from the profits of new industries and the development of resources, such as oil. Particular mention should also be made of increases in real output arising from the use of resources previously only partially employed or subject to disguised unemployment as in agriculture; the use of rural populations for road building and irrigation projects which do not require large outlays of capital are also illustrative. International transactions may result in private or public loans or grants; changes in the terms of trade, which result in relatively more favorable movements in export prices than import prices, may be used for capital formation.

Industrializing elites have differed quite widely in their policies regarding sources of capital and their choices among the possibilities. The sources of capital may also vary in the course of economic growth. In some periods, such as 1870–1914, the supply of funds available for foreign economic development has apparently been greater than in more recent periods. Some elites appear to be fortunate in being able to secure capital for economic growth from the development of a few key resources sold in the world markets, such as oil in Iraq and oil and minerals in Venezuela In other cases, the elites have had to rely almost entirely upon domestic savings, as in the case of the Soviet Union.

The sources of capital are closely related to other decisions in the strategy of industrialization adopted by an elite. The more rapid the rate of industrialization, the greater the reliance upon domestic savings and particularly upon various forms of forced reduction in consumption by taxation and inflation. When an elite seeks as much as 25 per cent of net national income for capital formation, voluntary savings cannot be expected to supply such amounts. The larger the amount of capital expected above the levels of voluntary savings, in general, the more stringent the system of controls required to secure the requisite reduction in consumption. The pace of industrialization and the sources of capital are thus related to the means chosen to secure the requisite savings. The more rapid the pace and the greater the reliance on the constriction of domestic consumption, in general, the greater the scope and depth of governmental controls, including the control over the relations of workers and managers.

Among the different ideal types of elites, with internally consistent strategies of industrialization, there are distinctive patterns of the sources of capital formation. The dynastic elite tends to make governmental grants and subsidies for the establishment of new industries which are frequently protected by continuing high tariffs. Taxation and inflation, in which wages lag, is a characteristic source of capital. Agricultural rents may be channeled systematically into industrialization, as in Japan. The system of direct controls is not so rigid as in the case of other elites since the required rate of capital formation is not large unless the military are in the ascendency and are building a modern military machine. The amount of capital available from period to period depends largely upon the fluctuating favors of a paternalistic government.

The industrializing middle class tends to rely upon domestic and foreign capital markets for capital formation; the voluntary choices of individual households between present consumption and a future stream of income, private business profits and savings, supplemented to some degree by taxation, constitute the domestic sources of capital; the foreign sources are determined in relatively free capital markets by the decisions of business leaders seeking private profits. The amounts of capital available from these sources may be expected to vary from period to period, depending on economic conditions.

The revolutionary intellectuals secure capital almost exclusively from the strict control over consumption by an elaborate system of governmental controls. Even when gross product rises with industrialization, consumption tends to be kept at previous levels or increased only slightly in order to use the surplus value of economic growth for further expansion. Foreign sources of capital do not play a role except as governmental grants may be made from other sympathetic elites. The amount of capital available from period to period tends to be relatively less liable to short term variations as the revolutionary elite seeks to devote a relatively constant percentage (and growing absolute amount of national product) to capital formation under a series of long-term plans.

The transitory elite of colonial administrators secures capital largely from the home country for major projects of development, designed to fit into the needs of the home country and for the defense and administration of the colony; other isolated capital formation is secured from the natives by taxation, but no rounded or balanced program of economic development is contemplated. The amount of capital formation from period to period depends on the competing needs and urgencies in the governmental and private budgets of the home country, in the sharp variations in the terms of trade, and there is apt to be a high degree of variability in capital formation under these circumstances.

The nationalist leaders in the early stages of industrializing are likely to be in a particularly difficult position with regard to securing capital. The drive for independence and national prestige may conflict in a variety of ways with the need for capital (and skills) from abroad. Foreign property may be expropriated or nationalized at the very time a promised increase in goods is held out to the masses as the achievement of independence (Indonesia). Foreigners may be less acceptable precisely at the time when the need for them is greatest if industry is to be established. There is a demand for quick results and for a show of national performance. It is hard to squeeze consumption tighter than did the previous colonial administrators or semi-feudal governments, particularly when production may be reduced from the dislocations arising with independence or revolution. There is a great tendency under these circumstances to seek large political and governmental loans from abroad to provide major capital formation and to resort to inflationary fiscal policies. The amount of capital formation from period to period under these circumstances may be expected to go in spurts with loans covering a period or a series of projects followed by a period of uncertainty and decline until new arrangements, if any, can be made.

Priorities by Sector. A decisive question for an industrializing elite is the priority to assign to the development of particular sectors or industries. What industries shall be pushed first? How broad or how concentrated a sector of development should be attempted at one time? Shall the "classical" form be followed of attention first to light industries — textiles, shoes, and other consumer goods — or shall the model of heavy industry first be adopted? What emphasis shall be placed upon industries which provide a military base? How important are industries which yield immediate results in greater food output, foreign exchange, prestige or popular support compared to those which provide a longer period base for broad industrialization such as transport, power, and utilities for urban growth? What priority is to be assigned to housing which can be an enormous consumer of available capital outlays? What expenditures are to go to the development of the educational system? How large an expenditure is to be made on health services, sanitation, and other means of raising efficiency and alleviating sufferings which are also likely to increase population by reducing the death rate?

In more formal terms, what shall be the allocation of capital and other scarce resources at the margin?

The task of assigning priorities among sectors is the more difficult the greater the economic limitations and the less the volume of capital formation, where a little capital confronts large conflicting claims, and where there is danger that a scattering of capital resources and a change of emphasis from year to year may show little cumulative results. The larger the capital melon the easier it is to split.

The assignment of priorities must take into consideration certain technical interrelations among industries and among the skills required of managers and workers. A textile machinery plant generally awaits the growth of an extensive textile industry and an electric motor plant the development of power generating plants. An automobile factory awaits the earlier development of steel and an engineering base.

The view that an advanced industrial plant can only be built upon the base of less complicated plants does not appear to be as valid as it was once thought to be because of the possibility of importing a limited number of technicians. There is apparently no technical reason for industrializing countries now to repeat the sequence of industrial development of the earliest countries — from cotton textiles, to light machinery, to heavy industry. The establishment of an oil refinery appears to pose, even in the least advanced countries, few more serious difficulties than the establishment of a modern textile mill in the same country. In so far as considerably less labor needs to be trained, the more advanced technology may be easier to establish. The availability of transport, power, repair, and financing facilities are the types of external economies, however, which are frequently significant to the priority for the establishment of an industry, and in this sense an industrializing economy may have to go through some of the same stages as the economies which started earlier.

All industrializing elites adopt policies about the priorities in development. Although each must confront the particular economic limitations of its country, the technical interrelations among sectors and the facts of external economies, each of the ideal type of elites faces these issues of priorities consistent with its larger strategy of industrialization.

The dynastic elite tends to preserve the traditional prestige and position of agriculture, and it is likely to be highly protected by tariffs. Industrial development which is particularly significant for a military base tends to receive encouragement, subsidy, and protection. Public works, monuments and shrines, and paternalistic projects including housing receive relatively liberal allocations of capital.

When the middle class directs the industrializing process, the size of the agricultural sector is much more determined by the rigors of international competition, and it tends to be a relatively smaller sector unless it constitutes an industrial agriculture of highly specialized crops. The sequence of industrial growth among sectors depends largely upon the market process and the prospects for private investment opportunities. The pattern of industrial growth tends to proceed from the relatively simple technologies to the more advanced. This sequence may be modified by military considerations. Public works are a relatively less serious claimant for capital resources, and the extent of housing expenditures depends upon the market and the incomes and preferences of households.

The revolutionary intellectual elite stresses a program of intensive capital outlays on basic industries essential for long term growth and a military base. Agricultural manpower is sharply constricted to speed the forced draft industrialization in rural or urban areas, and agricultural produce is procured from farmers at the least favorable terms consistent with requisite production. In keeping with the constriction of consumption, housing receives a very low priority except where absolutely necessary to recruit labor supply.

The elite of colonial administrators seeks to develop first those industries which are expected to be most essential to the mother country for direct consumption or for raw materials, or which furnish needed foreign exchange in the world market. "Foreign capital continues to be strongly attracted to extractive industries. . . ."[11] The range of development tends to be constricted.

The nationalist leaders are primarily concerned to broaden out the economic development of the prior colonial or quasi-feudal administration and to present a full scale and full range of industries. Many industries, such as basic steel, shipbuilding or air transportation are developed for reasons of prestige as well as economic growth. Industries of military significance emerge and capital expenditures for military installations are made where facilities are not taken over from the colonial administrators.

Pressures on Enterprises.   An industrializing elite in arranging its broad policies has a variety of alternatives concerning the pressures to place on industrial enterprises. Shall they operate under great and immediate pressure for output, or shall they feel little direct compulsion to perform? Shall the pressure come predominately from the product market or from governmental bureaucracy? Shall the labor market be used to place pressures on enterprise managers, or shall they be substantially freed, to the extent possible, from such direct pressures? These questions are closely interrelated with the other decisions considered in this chapter. The decision on pace of industrialization is again decisive. The general strategies of the various ideal types of elites create quite different pressures on enterprise managers (Chapters 6 and 7).

The dynastic elite places enterprise managers under little pressure from any source; the pace of industrialization makes no strong demands. The enterprises are organized into cartels, and the domestic product markets transmit no strong demand for efficiency or for production. International competition is often limited by tariffs and quotas, although the quest for international markets may be a pressure making for efficiency in certain enterprises. The labor organizations are not interested or designed to place pressures on enterprise managers for efficiency and productivity. The governmental bureaucracy does not provide quotas or detailed plans, although a patriotic and military-minded elite can generate considerable pressure on enterprise management for modernization and industrial output.

The middle-class elite relies on competitive markets to generate pressures on enterprise managers. The tendency to cartels is curbed, and the test of profits is used to generate pressures on enterprise managers to become more efficient, to expand output, and to develop technical change. Labor organizations are designed to regulate management narrowly at the work place; they press for wage increases and rules at the work place which constrict enterprise managers. This type of society believes that managers squeezed between competitive product markets and labor markets with plant oriented labor organizations will generate under profit incentives the highest standards of performance. Managers produce when placed in a market sweat box. The planned direction of a centralized bureaucracy in this view is unnecessary, inefficient, and violates the general middle-class strategy of industrialization.

The revolutionary intellectuals confronted with the demand for rapid industrialization are compelled to place enterprise managers under very heavy pressure. They use the carrot of premiums and money rewards, but they also rely heavily on the bureaucratic stick. The enterprise is under great pressure to achieve the production plan targets established by the centralized state. The career aspirations of the manager, the party apparatus, the labor organizations, and the ideology all focus upon this objective. Managers produce when placed in this bureaucratic squeeze. The market, domestic or international, plays relatively little role in placing pressure on enterprise managers. Labor organizations do not regulate the managers so much as they are directed towards increasing the productivity of workers.

The elite of the colonial administrators by and large places relatively little pressure on enterprise managers. The enterprise confronts little domestic or international competition; its markets tend to be highly protected. The administrators of the home country are at a great distance, and do not closely supervise the enterprise. No labor organization places significant pressure on managers, although labor shortages and labor turnover may compel attention to labor efficiency if other measures, including forced labor, cannot be found to secure a labor force at low wages.

The nationalist elite faces perplexing problems in organizing the environment of the enterprise manager. The independence movement may have affected the production and efficiency of enterprises under foreign managers. Domestic product markets are not well established, and the nationalist leaders may wish to insulate the new enterprises from the rigors of international markets. Labor organizations arising in the independence movement are not particularly concerned with plant level issues. Moreover, they have high aspirations for rewards. This elite struggles with the problem of how to organize the environment of enterprise managers, but on the whole it places little pressure on these managers.

The Educational System.   An industrializing elite confronts a variety of questions concerning the educational arrangements it shall establish. More issues are involved than the priority to be given to the development of educational institutions. Shall the education be generally available, or shall it be restricted to the few? Shall education be general and liberal or narrowly related and specialized to the technical needs of industrialization? An elite comes to develop an educational policy consistent with its general strategy of industrialization and its other policy decisions.

The dynastic elite in the preservation of tradition provides education for the relative few and for select elite groups. Education stresses the humanities and law and provides only the limited amount of scientific education required for its relatively slow rate of growth. Traditional values and religion are stressed in the educational system at all levels. The universities have little role in the industrialization process. There is little interest in the formal training of workers at the work place or community beyond elementary education and apprenticeship; the family managers receive little specialized education.

The middle-class elite believes in widespread public education. The faculty and students are free to pursue their interests and lines of training and careers suggested by individual tastes, the culture, and the market. Education is general and is not narrowly related to the technical needs of industrialization. The educational arrangements constitute one of the principal means of vertical mobility in the community. Widespread education is essential to the political processes.

The revolutionary intellectuals develop an educational system narrowly specialized to the imperative needs of industrialization. Scientific education receives a high priority, and narrowly specialized training is developed for rapid growth. The established ideology is disseminated in the educational system rather than the traditional values of the dynastic elite or the liberal education of the middle-class elite. The educational system plays a central role in rapid industrialization. Mass education at the level of workers is pushed to eliminate illiteracy and to make a more functional and productive work force.

The colonial administrator largely adopts the educational system of the mother country, except that higher education is often confined to only a small number of indigenous people, and they are often educated in the mother country. Education is confined to the number required to perpetuate and administer the colony.

The nationalist leader seeks to free the educational system from its ties with the previous colonial power and to develop educational forms which reflect prestige to the newly industrializing nation. The choice between using limited resources for mass education and for the development of universities and research organizations for the training of high level manpower is a major dilemma.

Self-Sufficiency or Economic Integration. An industrializing elite must decide the extent to which a country seeks economic self-sufficiency and the extent it shall partake in the world economy through capital and commodity markets and to a lesser extent through labor migration. The same range of alternatives is not open to all elites since the economic limitations, including the size of countries, varies so widely. But at the margin each elite decides on a greater or a lesser degree of a self-sufficient economy.[12]

Before World War II, countries at the early stages of industrialization tended to specialize on the production of primary and raw materials which were exported to the industrially more advanced countries in exchange for finished products for consumption and investment goods. The less developed countries brought three major complaints against this arrangement: in periods of depression the terms of trade moved sharply against the raw materials producers, but in prosperity, as terms of trade reversed, they were frequently unable to secure deliveries of finished goods without great delays, and these delays were accentuated by wartime and periods of crises; the instability of income and the high degree of uncertainty added significantly to the difficulties of economic development and left public and private planning to the mercy of exterior events; and the concentration on raw materials production in accordance with the economic law of comparative advantage hindered economic and political development.

There has developed since the end of World War II a considerable tendency toward a higher degree of self-sufficiency in raw materials among economically advanced countries and a lesser degree of specialization on raw materials by many of the former exporters of raw materials. (This condition is not, of course, incompatible with an expansion of international trade in manufactured goods among industrializing countries.) This development is the consequence of synthetic raw materials and the drive for industrialization among producers of raw materials.

The general strategy of the ideal types of elites with regard to self-sufficiency or economic integration may be characterized as follows: The dynastic elite tends to develop a relatively high degree of self-sufficiency; tariff and subsidy policies are designed to reduce the dependence upon the rest of the world. However, a strong drive toward military strength may lead toward a development of manufacturing export industries with which to procure the foreign exchange to build up an industrial base for the military establishment. Generous loans from allies may accomplish the same purpose without increasing integration to the same degree with the rest of the world.

The middle-class-directed industrialization relies heavily on the market for economic decisions; it tends to create an economy relatively highly integrated with the rest of the world through private commodity and capital transactions. Protectionism is applied on military and "infant industry" grounds, and international competition is seldom allowed quickly to destroy an industry. But the integrated economic world and the common market is the ideal for countries at all stages along this road.

The revolutionary intellectual elite tends to create a highly self-sufficient economic system with a strong military base. Even among allies exchange tends to be sporadic and irregular and the concomitant of political decisions. Trade and exchange are a sign of weakness and self-sufficiency proof of strength and economic development. Imports are concentrated upon strategic materials, equipment and technical items, and exports are only those requisite to purchase strategic imports.

The colonial administrators seek to integrate fully with the mother country, rather than with the rest of the world, as suppliers of raw materials and as a protected market for exports. The range of exports and imports to the rest of the world will be determined largely in relation to the needs of the home country for foreign exchange in world markets.

The nationalist leaders are torn between continuing and expanding specialization in raw materials exports, particularly if terms of trade are favorable to raw materials producers, in order to increase foreign exchange for later economic development and the need to show prompt signs of industrial development by devoting capital resources directly to industry and to an industrial base. A larger stream of resources over time for foreign markets may be sacrificed to immediate self-sufficiency in industrial production. The national leaders are particularly ambivalent to world markets as they balance economic integration with national prestige.

The Response of Population. The decisions of an elite in the area of population policy are not independent of other major questions, although an elite may be less able to affect population than other constraints to industrialization. It may be observed again that the pace of industrialization and the source of capital are particularly dependent upon the response of the population. In considering the strategy of any elite, a distinction should be drawn between policies which are specifically designed to affect the response of population and the indirect effects of a variety of other policies upon the response of population. Within a given framework of economic limitations, the different types of elite seek to influence the response of population to industrialization in the following ways.

The dynastic elite tends to adopt a variety of policies which stimulate population growth, except in the face of gross overpopulation, as in Japan. The family is given a high value; compensation likely includes family allowance payments, and paternalism is the dominant philosophy toward workers. A strong military policy may also seek to encourage the expansion in population. There is little, if any, encouragement of immigration, even in an "empty" country.

The middle class tends to regard population as largely beyond the range of direct public policy, save for immigration. The natural change in population is the consequence of market forces and incomes, including public expenditures on health and sanitation, on birth rates and death rates. An "empty" country is likely to permit widespread immigration possibly restricted to particular ethnic groups.

The revolutionary intellectuals approach population responses more explicitly with their longer view of the industrialization process than other elites. They seek in different ways to hold down the birth rate through less attention to housing, recruitment of women to industry, the rapid contraction of agriculture where birth rates tend to be higher, and with lesser expenditures on public health and social overheads except as they affect directly the efficiency of the work force at the work place. The industrializing process is admittedly more harsh. Immigration is not encouraged and internal movement of the work force is frequently subject to rigid controls.

The colonial administrators are unconcerned with population responses as long as there is a liberal supply of labor at the work place. When there are shortages, various means are adopted, including forced labor, to encourage internal migration or immigration. The different policies of recruitment of males from villages by contract for limited periods, as compared to recruitment by families, and the establishment of company towns and urban communities may have important consequences for the birth rate.

The nationalist leaders, particularly in "crowded" countries, are likely to find the response of population to the beginnings of industrialization to constitute one of the most difficult and perplexing questions about which very little can apparently be done. Industrialization in such a country drops the death rate; the population increases rapidly for a period until birth rates are reduced. But the rise in population in the "crowded" country tends to make the task of industrialization vastly more complex. It is difficult for this elite to encourage emigration. Population responses pose the sternest of problems to the nationalist leader in the "crowded" country.

Implications of Decisions for Workers and Managers

Every elite leading the march to industrialism must confront the group of seven decisions outlined in the preceding section, although the choices are not always conscious. How fast? How finance? What priorities? What pressures on managers? What educational system? Self-sufficient or integrated? What population? Each of the ideal types of industrializing elites develops a body of more or less internally consistent policies incorporating these decisions. The decision on the pace of industrialization is the most fundamental, but the decisions as a group must be internally consistent. These decisions and policies have decisive implications for workers and managers. The set of seven decisions as a group predisposes a distinctive pattern of labor-management-state relations (Chapters 6–9). They narrowly determine, for instance, the extent to which consumption need be curtailed, which groups shall have their consumption constricted and by what methods, how workers shall be made to work harder and faster, the severity of the rules of the work place, how a work force is recruited and moved about, what forms labor organizations take and the functions they exercise, and other features of industrial relations.

The dynastic elite is content with a less strenuous and a slower pace. Less consumption need be diverted to investment out of a given national income, and the prestige position of traditional farmers and landlords means that agricultural arrangements are seldom drastically reorganized to release resources, although technical improvements to increase agricultural output may be stimulated. The requisite constriction of consumption, above voluntary savings, is frequently achieved by price inflation and unbalanced budgets. There is less pressure on workers to develop discipline and a rapid pace of work or to disturb traditional values; there is less need for geographical mobility particularly in a community exalting family and tradition. Recruitment of the work force to industrial activity from the reservation or rural areas is by families rather than by bachelors. Population increases are viewed favorably without regard to narrow economic considerations, except in cases of extreme overpopulation, in line with traditional values and a lesser concern with a rapid pace of industrialization. The slower pace and the views of the dynastic elite tend to create a general body of minimum rules which has little direct impact upon most workers and managers at actual work places. The paternalistic enterprise managers largely establish the rules for the dependent workers.

The middle-class elite is characterized by reliance upon the markets and elected governments to determine the pace of industrialization. Domestic savings reflected in the domestic capital markets and international transactions largely establish the pace, although it may vary a good deal among countries with different economic limitations and with different individual choices reflected in the markets. The reduction of resources in agriculture is a gradual process largely based on the decisions of individuals (landlords, farmers, tenants or laborers) to seek higher incomes in urban employment. Inflation is not an approved method of restricting consumption, save in wartime or in moderate degree. The labor market is relied upon to reallocate the labor force by occupation, industry, and regions. Considerable emphasis is placed upon the pace of work; discipline is highly developed; the principal means of motivating the labor force are resort to monetary incentives and to individualistic ethical values. Original recruitment to the industrial work force is by individuals or families seeking their best opportunities; the population response is left to individual choices without public policy. The reliance upon the market means that the effective web of rules is established at decentralized points between enterprise managers and independent workers.

The revolutionary intellectuals are devoted to the most rapid possible pace of industrialization consistent with continued control. Traditional agriculture is rapidly and drastically reorganized to release resources to urban areas and to industry. The rapid pace also may require constriction of incomes of industrial workers at least for an extended period. The accumulation of industry is to be put back into heavy goods expansion rather than to raise current living standards. The use of stringent direct controls means that inflation is a less essential and generally less effective device to constrict consumption. Labor is recruited and allocated to new occupations, industries, and regions by a combination of monetary incentives and compulsion. The great emphasis upon the pace of work and discipline is stimulated by universal incentive methods of pay and devotion to a rigorous ideology. Where population increases are viewed as an impediment to the pace of industrialization, public policies are adopted to constrict the population response to industrialization. The web of rules is centrally determined by the elite for the dependent class of workers and administered at the work place by managerial, party and labor organization representatives of the elite.

The colonial administrators determine an industrialization pace according to the needs and interests of the home country. This pace may be rapid or slow, and hence workers and enterprise managers confront problems and develop characteristics indicated by the three major elites discussed above. The colonial administrator's concentration upon extractive industries, such as plantation agriculture and mining, tends to create a limited group of occupations in the work force rather than the full range which arises under broader-scale industrialization. The organization of the labor market is a major preoccupation, to provide a surplus of unskilled labor by force if necessary. The colonial administrator reserves certain occupations, particularly in the managerial and supervisory categories, to citizens of the home country. The wage and salary structures reflect accordingly very wide differentials among occupations.

The nationalist leaders confront most serious problems in setting the pace of industrialization. The aspirations of the masses have been stimulated to expect immediate and large results with national independence, while the political uncertainties of a new state and often the loss of confidence by foreign sources of capital make only a much slower pace possible. The national leaders are concerned to expand the scope of industrial activity beyond the extractive industries of the colonial administrators and to open up new occupations to nationals, particularly in technical, administrative, and managerial posts. The wide wage and salary differentials of the colonial-administrators are narrowed. The nationalist leaders find it necessary to control in a variety of ways the organizations of strategic industrial workers in the interest of the national effort to industrialize.

In summary, the process of industrialization constitutes a transformation of society and particularly of the economy. The task of creating the new economic order in a country is shaped very substantially by the economic limitations of the country and the historical facts surrounding the start of the industrial march.

These economic limitations consist of the level of technology, the known natural resources, the levels of skill of the work force — workers, private and public managers, and government administrators — the capacity to secure resources from abroad, and the characteristics of population growth. The essential historical facts concern the timing of the industrializing beginning, which affects the available technology and the response of the emerging industrial work force, and the level of development from which the industrializing start is begun. This economic and historical context is given to any elite seeking to lead a particular country toward industrialism.

Within these given economic and historical limitations, an industrializing elite is required to confront a group of basic decisions on policy issues: (1) How fast shall be the pace? (2) How shall the requisite capital formation be secured? (3) What are the priorities in development? (4) What pressures are to be placed on enterprise managers? (5) What shall be the characteristics of the educational system? (6) How self-sufficient or integrated shall the country be with the world economy? (7) What is to be done, if anything, to affect the population response to industrialization? These are not isolated issues; they are mutually interdependent, and the answers to any one question are more or less directly affected by the answers to the other. Taken together, the set of answers provided by an elite to these issues constitutes its general policies shaping industrialization. The position of the ideal types of elites on each of these basic questions of policy is summarized in the attached chart.

The general strategies of industrialization adopted by an ideal type of elite have decisive consequences for workers and managers and their interrelations. The faster the pace, with given economic limitations, the greater the need to constrict consumption, the more the resort to direct controls, the more drastic the reorganization in agriculture associated with the recruitment of an industrial labor force, the more likely the resort to a rigid ideology and compulsion to motivate the labor force, and the more centralized and severe the web of rules for the work place. The implications of the strategies of each ideal type of elite for workers and managers are summarized in Chart 3.

CHART 3.

A. Summary of policies of elites shaping industrialization.

Basic Decisions	Dynastic	Middle-Class	Revolutionary-Intellectuals	Colonial Administrators	Nationalist Leaders
Pace of Industrialization	No faster than necessary to preserve the traditional elite and its values. Military needs may dictate a more rapid pace.	Pace set by prospects of private gain, individual choices and limited actions of government. Moderate pace.	The fastest possible pace under an extensive set of controls.	Dependent solely upon the advantage of the mother country.	High aspiration and promises but uncertain rate.
Sources of Funds	Paternalistic grants and protection. Agricultural rents may be significant. Continuity of funds depends upon government favors which vary. International sources rarely significant.	Market decisions by voluntary household and business savings, bank credit and international capital market. Continuity depends on uncertainty and variations of the market. International sources sometimes significant.	Forced restriction of consumption by taxation and other means to secure very large proportion of net national income for capital formation. Continuity stable. Largely domestic supply.	Funds from budget of mother country; continuity depends on budget pressures.	Tends to seek large sums from abroad to supplement domestic savings but difficulties great, supply variable and short-term.
Priorities in Development	Preserve and protect agriculture; public works, monuments and paternalistic projects including housing.	Agriculture compressed by international competition. Sequence depends on market, and traditional pattern is from consumers to basic industry. Housing depends on market.	Agriculture compressed by draining manpower and preventing individual agricultural enterprises. Priority to basic industry with a vengeance. Housing compressed.	Industries developed which furnish materials or consumption goods to mother country or supply foreign exchange.	Aspires to a broad industrial base, expands on the range of the previous colonial administrator. Prestige items.

Pressures on Enterprise Managers	Weak pressure: Cartelized product markets and tariffs restrict international competition. Labor organizations have little interest in the plant level.	Strong pressure: competitive product markets domestically and internationally. Labor organizations oriented toward the plant level generate pressure on managers.	Strong pressure: bureaucratically determined production plan targets are supported by party, labor organizations and career interests.	Weak pressure: domestic and international product markets have little impact, and labor organizations are oriented to nationalist interests. Labor shortages may generate some pressure in some cases, but other methods of recruiting cheap labor are likely to be emphasized.	Complex and difficult problem of organizing the environment of the enterprise manager. Little pressure on the whole.
The Educational System	Preserves traditional values; higher education limited to elitists; universities have little role in industrialization; workers have only elementary education.	Liberal education; mass education; educational system a major instrument in vertical mobility for workers and their families.	Education bound to revolutionary ideology; high priority to science and specialized fields; workers receive specialized training.	Education adapted from mother country; higher education limited to few natives and training often only in mother country.	Educational system designed to be independent and to seek prestige. Dilemma of general education vs. training of high level manpower.
Self-sufficiency or Economic Integration	A relatively high degree of self-sufficiency particularly where military considerations important.	The financial and commodity markets tend to create a high degree of international interdependence.	A high degree of self-sufficiency with international economic transactions largely.	Integrate with the mother country.	Conflict between the aspirations for self-sufficiency and the need for integration for development.
The Response of Population	A variety of policies tend indirectly to stimulate growth. No encouragement to immigration.	Population a response to few public policies; largely depends upon market forces, incomes and public expenditures on health which may be indirectly encouraging. Permits immigration.	A variety of policies are designed to constrict the tendency of population to increase in response to industrialization. No immigration.	No concern with population if labor supply adequate. Otherwise recruit labor in the colony or abroad.	Conflict between means to decrease death rate and the impediment of population increases in "crowded" countries.

[128]

CHART 3. (continued)

B. Implications of Policies for Workers and Managers

Implications for Workers and Managers	Dynastic	Middle-Class	Revolutionary-Intellectuals	Colonial Administrators	Nationalist Leaders
Pressure to constrict consumption	Relatively little pressure since slow pace.	Savings arise from voluntary savings and taxes of democratic government.	Stringent constriction of consumption for rapid pace.	Depends on needs of mother country.	High aspirations but pressure difficult to apply.
Methods of restricting consumption	Inflation.	Private savings.	Direct controls on a broad front.	Direct controls on a few items, particularly imports.	Inflation.
Policies toward agriculture	Minor structural dislocation except to increase efficiency for export surplus to cities.	Contraction by market forces alone.	Sweeping reorganization to release resources and increase output.	Develop in specialized directions for mother country.	Tendency to neglect in program for industrial development.
Methods of allocation of labor	Family and community ties limit mobility of labor and make for greater need for mobility of capital.	Reliance upon the labor market and public training.	Direct allocation and training with emphasis upon monetary incentives.	Direct allocation of native labor and importation of high-level skills.	Training of nationals to replace foreigners.
Methods of motivating labor force	Loyalty to tradition, family and church.	The personal ethic of hard work and money rewards.	An ideological compulsion and money rewards.	Limited compulsion, limited acceptance into ruling group in a few cases.	Nationalism as an ideal.

PART II

THE MANAGERS AND THE MANAGED:
STRUCTURING THE LABOR FORCE

The central theme of the four chapters which comprise Part II is an examination of the uniformities and diversities in industrialization as they shape the power, position, and policies of enterprise managers, give a structure to the industrial labor force, and influence the relationships between managers and the managed. Managers of enterprises, both private and public, are in short supply in every industrializing country, and the development of managerial resources is a central need everywhere (Chapter 6). Industrialization changes the access to managerial positions, the internal authority structure of management, and the power of managers over workers — all toward professionally oriented, decentralized and "constitutional" management. These basic tendencies are associated with diversities occasioned by the stage and pace of economic development and the character of the industrializing elite.

Managers also play a decisive role in developing the industrial work force: in recruiting workers for growing industry, in getting them to be committed to industrial employment with the demands it makes on workers, in developing raw recruits into productive members of the industrial work force, and in adapting the work force to ever changing conditions (Chapter 7). These labor problems are largely management problems because the competence of managers of enterprises, more than any other group, determines how successfully an industrial work force is established. The development of a labor force is a common feature of all instances of industrialization. The methods used by management, however, will vary with the strategies of the various industrializing elites.

The impact of industrialization upon the emerging work force creates a response of protest in various forms: absenteeism, labor turnover, sabotage, withholding of effort, and organized protection and action through labor organizations (Chapter 8). Protest in most industrializing societies peaks early in the process of development; as industrialization proceeds it becomes organized, channeled, and moderated. The strategies of the industrializing elites and the pace of development play a determining role in the way in which protest is handled.

This process merges into the development of industrial relations systems in which workers and their organizations, managers, and government agencies organize their relationships (Chapter 9). These industrial relations systems not only define the relative duties and responsibilities of labor organizations, managements, and government agencies, but they help control the responses of workers to industrialization and establish a body of rules, practices, and regulations which govern the work place and the community. This is the essential process for providing a structure for the labor force of any industrial society.

CHAPTER 6

MANAGERS OF ENTERPRISES:
THEIR POWER, POSITION, AND POLICIES

The managers of enterprises, public and private, and their technical and professional associates are part of every industrializing
elite. They are crucial to the success of any industrialization effort. Their policies and practices have far-flung influence in shaping the labor problems which emerge in industrializing societies.
The role of management of enterprises, in contrast to earlier periods, now generally enjoys prestige in the economically developing countries.

The term "management" is difficult to define; it means different
things to different people. Some identify it with functions performed by entrepreneurs, managers, or supervisors. Others think
of it as a particular group of persons. To workers, management is
synonymous with the exercise of authority over their working lives.
Some social scientists view management as a class with definable status and power in a society. Management, indeed, is all of
these things and perhaps more. It has economic, social, and political dimensions.

Management may be analyzed from different perspectives.
First, it may be looked upon as an economic resource or factor
of production. In this respect it is analogous to capital, labor,
or natural resources, and it is combined with them in varying factor proportions in productive processes. The generation and development of managerial resources, like the accumulation of capital, is one of the central tasks confronting every industrializing
society. Second, management is a class into which access is limited. In any industrializing society, the members of management
are a small, but active minority, and they enjoy a measure of prestige, privilege, and power as part of the elite. Third, management may be analyzed as an internal system of authority. Within

the managerial hierarchy there are lines of command and patterns
of authority at all levels of decision-making and administration.
Fourth, and finally, management can be viewed as a rule-making authority over the managed. In this role, it seeks to establish,
to bolster and to make legitimate its prerogatives to determine
the conditions under which the industrial working forces labor.

Management is a hierarchy of functions and people. It includes
entrepreneurs, managers, administrators, engineers, and professional specialists who hold the top positions in an enterprise.[1] In
this hierarchy the organization builder plays a critical role. He
may be the owner of the business, a professional private manager
or a government official. He is the keystone in the arch of management; he cannot be separated from his organization, but is fused
with it. His function is to establish the conditions under which
the other members of management perform their jobs. The tone
of the organization is usually sounded by its top executive, and
the success of the enterprise may well depend upon whether he
infuses the whole hierarchy with energy and vision or whether,
through ineptness or neglect, he allows the organization to stag-
nate. The most important enterprise managers in an industrial
society are those organization builders who occupy the top command posts in their managerial hierarchies.

Management as an Economic Resource

As an economic resource, management is similar in many respects to capital. A growing economy must be able to accumulate capital and invest it in productive activity. It must likewise accumulate managerial resources and utilize them effectively
in public or private enterprises. Management, indeed, is a form
of human capital which is indispensable for successful industrial
development.

Pre-industrial societies, characteristically, require comparatively
little capital or management. But, as a country industrializes,
larger amounts of both capital and management are required. As
a country develops industrially, it uses management more inten-
sively — the proportion of managerial resources in the labor force
inevitably increases. There are several reasons for this development.

First, as enterprises become larger and more complex, they require greater numbers of highly trained people. Pre-industrial societies are characterized by the ubiquitous small handicraft and trading shops. Customarily they are run by individuals or by families. The same is true of small loan enterprises or individual money lenders. Although they may require an "enterprising spirit" and a good deal of shrewdness, they certainly do not call for much integrative or managerial skill. But, as a country industrializes, it begins to develop sizeable wholesale trading organizations, financial institutions, railways, ports, public utilities, and factories. These require much larger and more complex managerial hierarchies that ordinarily cannot be operated just by individuals or families. The advanced industrial society has large and complicated banking institutions, far-flung industrial enterprises and large governmental bureaus. Here a great many more managers, professional specialists, and administrators are required.

Second, as markets grow wider, enterprises become more complicated. The local market, which is characteristic of the less developed economies, is a relatively simple institution. Buyers and sellers all congregate in a single location and clear the market through direct dealings. By contrast, nationwide and international markets, which are characteristic of the advanced industrialization, are more complicated. They require a wide range of detailed information at frequent intervals. The price and quality of products have many dimensions and often require technical specification. In far-flung and dynamic markets, the costs of wrong judgments may be very high. Thus, enterprises tend to make large investments in market research departments, sales forces, and economic analysis, as well as in accounting, costing, and budgeting. Such activities call for considerable expansion of specialized personnel in the managerial hierarchy.

Third, as production processes become more capital-intensive, they also tend to become more management-intensive. Large investments in machinery and processes in themselves require more and better trained managerial resources. If, as is usually the case, the machinery and processes are complicated, engineers, chemists, or other technical staff specialists are required. Labor-saving machinery usually requires greater investment in personnel who specialize in planning, production scheduling, engineering, and

"control" of all kinds. Thus an additional cost involved in investment in labor-saving machinery is that of procuring and developing the managerial resources necessary to utilize it effectively.
When a business organization employs technicians to supervise
and control more complicated processes, there is also need for
more experienced top management to coordinate their activities
and to plan for future developments. The technological revolution
requires more management, not less.

Fourth, as the external political and social environment of enterprises becomes more complex, staffs of specialists are necessary
to deal with external problems. The large-scale enterprise, in developing as well as advanced industrial countries, must have tax
experts, lawyers, management association representatives, labor relations specialists, and those with political and governmental contacts. The managerial hierarchy is thus widened by these pressures from the external environment.

Fifth, and finally, as the pace of innovation increases, the utilization of high-level manpower resources expands. The classic individual inventor, who developed a new process or product in his
isolated workshop or laboratory, is increasingly being replaced in
advanced industrial countries by the industrial research laboratory, which represents a substantial investment in highly trained
chemists, physicists, engineers, and other technically trained manpower resources. As industrialization reaches an advanced state,
the enterprise emerges as an organization of high-talent managerial resources, with product development specialists, production
engineers, and planning departments, all coordinated and directed
by divisional and top managers.

There is clear evidence of the relationship between investment
in high-level human resources and innovation in the United
States. An examination of the changing employment structure in
fifty American companies since World War II showed very clearly
that the greatest proportional increase in technical, professional,
administrative, and managerial personnel took place in the firms
which were investing most heavily in change.[2] Those which made
the greatest changes in processes, machinery, products, and
methods of distribution showed by far the highest increase in
utilization of high-level human resources, while those which were
innovating the least showed almost no increase in intensity of

utilization of managerial resources. The same relationship between innovation and the utilization of high-level manpower is evident in other industrial countries.

Thus, in relatively advanced economies the greater complexity of enterprises, wider markets, more extensive use of complicated machinery and processes, the pressures of the larger community, and a quicker pace of innovation, all demand larger investments in management. Industrialization is achieved by a substitution of both capital and management for labor. By the same reasoning, the productivity of labor in an industrializing society is dependent upon management as well as upon the capital invested in machinery and processes. At any given level of capital investment, management is the principal determinant of the productivity of labor.

The skills and qualities of the working forces depend more upon what management does than on any innate characteristics of the workers themselves. Most, though not all, skills of manual labor and even clerical employees are acquired on the job. Management develops and stimulates the incentives for work. It is also responsible for proper layout of machinery and processes, work study, breakdown of jobs in order to economize on use of critical skills, safety programs, systems for appraising performance and discovering talent, and many other related policies. These techniques are not easily applied. They require the employment of specialized personnel and investment of time on the part of members of the line organization. Even more important, they require relatively high levels of education, experience, and training among the members of the managerial organization; and they require a high degree of coordination.

In some respects, of course, the efficiency of labor resources may be independent of management. The more important factors here may be levels of education, conditions of health and nutrition, ideological orientation, and general experience and attitudes toward work. Management, however, is able to influence some of these factors at least in part. Attitudes toward work can be molded by supervision; companies can provide medical services and adequate diets for employees; and some firms in underdeveloped countries even provide facilities for general education of members of the labor force. In the industrially advanced countries, of course, the laboring population may be generally more efficient because of long tradition and previous experience with industrial enterprises, and thus the development of high labor productivity in an economically underdeveloped society may be particularly dependent upon managerial initiative and skill.

As the skills of the working forces are increased, moreover, the need for management of higher quality becomes greater. This reinforces the general conclusion that, as societies move from earlier to later stages of industrialization, they must invest ever more heavily in the building of managerial resources, private or public.

The Generation of Managerial Resources

In all industrializing societies, the process of accumulation of managerial resources is of critical importance. Dams, power plants, and factories can be built in a few years, but it may take decades to develop domestically the engineers, scientists, administrators, and managers to operate them. Managerial resources, in short, require a long period of gestation, and in all industrializing societies substantial investments must be made to develop them.

Management manpower may be accumulated in different ways. In some cases the first industrialists may be drawn from the ranks of the handicraftsmen; small traders and moneylenders have often been a recruiting ground for management; and the wealthy merchant capitalists may take the initiative in establishing industrial enterprises. In other cases, as, for example, in Japan, a dynastic elite may be induced by the state to build the nation's basic industries. In some countries the government civil service is a source of technical and administrative manpower. And in many of the newly industrializing countries, such as Egypt, army officers with technical and organizational training have been assigned to the management of the larger and more complicated enterprises.

Most industrializing countries have at one time or another imported managerial talent from the more advanced countries. For example, the United States relied on British and European managerial resources during the nineteenth century. And today, the newly industrializing countries make extensive use of managers, engineers, and technicians from the United States, Britain, the Western European countries, and the Soviet Union. In many cases these expatriate managers are brought in by joint ventures undertaken by various interests in the advanced and newly developing countries. In any case, they are often the "seed-corn" for subsequent development of indigenous managerial talent, for they help train the latter.

The late comers to industrialization may also send persons to the more advanced countries for general education, technical training, and industrial experience. For example, in 1958 and 1959, India alone sent several hundred engineers to the Soviet Union, Germany, and the United States for technical and managerial training in steel mill operations. Indeed, in modern times far more than in earlier periods, the training of managerial resources in foreign countries is a widely accepted method of developing high-talent manpower. The greater the differences in levels of technology, the greater the resort to such training.

Yet, no country is likely to progress very far along the road to industrialism by exclusive reliance on encouragement of joint ventures with foreign interests, the temporary hiring of foreign managers, or sending its own nationals abroad for training. The modern industrializing nation requires engineering universities and technological institutes; it needs specialized programs for development of administrators for its governmental services and managers for its industrial enterprises. This means heavy investment in institutions of higher learning and priority for education which is functionally oriented to the needs of the industrial process. And the institutions of higher learning must be built upon a base of extensive primary and secondary education, which in turn requires orientation to the needs of an industrializing society.

The pace of industrialization in a country is dependent upon its ability to accumulate capital and to invest it productively. It is likewise related to its ability to generate highly trained human resources and to employ them effectively in the productive processes. The accumulation of capital without a corresponding generation of highly trained manpower will not bring about satisfactory economic growth. In the newly industrializing countries, the accumulation of capital and the generation of managerial manpower involve difficult choices, long-range planning, and consciously coordinated effort.[3]

Access to the Managerial Class

Only a few gain access to the ranks of management. Some families or family groups may control important segments of industry, as in Japan in the late nineteenth century or in India at the present time. In the Soviet Union, the government, and more particularly the Communist Party, may designate the factory manager, although technical training is also usually a prerequisite. Education is increasingly an important entrance requirement in many other societies, and a degree from one of the status universities, such as Tokyo Imperial University in Japan and similar universities in other countries, may be the best assurance of entry. Professional training and experience in management becomes an avenue to higher managerial positions.

Incumbents in the managerial hierarchy seek as new recruits those they can rely upon and trust. They demand that the new-comers be loyal, that they accept authority (of the family, the government, or the professional superior, as the case may be), and that they conform to a prescribed pattern of behavior. In any enterprise, therefore, management is an identifiable high-status minority, just as in an army the officer group is a clearly identifiable class. And, of course, the orientation and outlook of the managerial group in an enterprise and also within an industrializing society as a whole usually reflect the criteria which govern admittance to it.

Access to management may depend upon family relationships, political connections, technical competence, or various combinations of these criteria. For analytical purposes, it is useful to consider three ideal types of management: patrimonial, political, and professional.[4]

Patrimonial management is management in which ownership, major policy-making positions, and a significant proportion of other top jobs in the hierarchy are held by members of an extended family. The effective decision-making authority is centered in the family, and the goals of the enterprise are oriented toward the interests and the aspirations of the family.

Patrimonial management is a common first stage in a country's economic development. The early merchant-capitalists in England were heads of family enterprises. In the early stages of industrialization the family enterprise is a simple and logical instrument of business activity. Loyalty and trust within the hierarchy are assured. Often the forces of tradition and religion support the essential integrity of the family dynasty. The enterprise provides the means for safeguarding the security and the reputation of the family.

In a society where trained skills are scarce and the sons of the wealthy have much of the training, nepotism may be relatively costless. And, if the key members of the family dynasty are competent, well-educated, and diligent, patrimonial management can be quite dynamic. This is well illustrated by some of the patrimonially oriented enterprises in Germany where the typical family-type industrialist is usually himself a man with extensive technical or professional education. He frequently exerts great pressure upon his sons or sons-in-law to prepare themselves for the responsibilities they will be "called" to assume. Thus, when motivated by a creed of hard work and determination to acquire or maintain a position of power, the family enterprise can be an effective agent of industrialization.

However, the key members of the family dynasties are often incapable, either by training or psychological inclination, of sustaining the progress toward industrialization. France and Italy, for example, provide some mid-twentieth-century documentation of the family firm's preference for vegetating instead of expanding. The typical French family firm has been described as placing ". . . inordinate stress on safety and security. It fears change and is unwilling to borrow for fear that the lender, whether individual or bank, will gain a foothold in the enterprise. As a result, the firm prefers to enjoy its own little market. . . ."[5] Traditionally, Italian capitalism has remained family-capitalist, and this has been a major factor retarding industrial growth.

The family enterprise is usually most effective in small and relatively simple organizations such as retail and wholesale trade, craft industries, and small or medium-sized industrial plants. In such cases it is relatively easy for the family, particularly in the extended form, to recruit and generate from within most of the capital and managerial resources it needs. However, in large-scale and complex enterprises the family is eventually forced to bring in outsiders, whose qualifications are mainly professional training and competence.

When the family enterprise expands, its patrimonial form is undermined. To find technicians, engineers, and administrators with the requisite knowledge, training, and skill, it must go beyond blood relatives. As the number of professionals in the patrimonial enterprise expands, the members of the family find it increasingly difficult to maintain their control. There comes a point where the interests of the family are better promoted by turning over the operation of the enterprise to competent professional managerial careerists. This is what happened in the case of hundreds of family enterprises in the United States, and the same trend is apparent in the larger enterprises in England, Germany, and even France and Italy today. In the most advanced economies, therefore, the family enterprise, though still important in petty trade or small-scale industry, no longer plays an influential role in large industrial establishments. The proprietory capitalist, who used to own and control the large business houses, tends to disappear as a power in advanced industrializing societies.

Political management is less common, and like patrimonial management, its chances for survival are slim in modern industrializing societies. Political management exists where ownership, major policy-making positions, and key administrative posts are held by persons on the basis of political affiliation and loyalties. Access is thus dominated by political considerations, and the orientation and interests of management are colored throughout by political goals. However, just as patrimonial management may hire professionals to work under its direction, so political management may enlist the services of professionally trained managers and technicians.

Political management is often commonly associated with government-owned and operated enterprises. Sometimes, as in the case of postmasters in principal cities in the United States, political managerial appointments are regarded as a reward for the politically faithful. Some of the nationalized enterprises in India were at first headed by managing directors whose principal qualifications appeared to be their government connections rather than their proven ability as managers. The Egyptian National Railways had for many years managements which were essentially political in nature. Indeed, a danger in all socialized industries is that managerial appointments may be made at the outset on the basis of political connections rather than professional competence.

As in the case of patrimonial management, however, there may be an element of loyalty and trust involved in managerial appointments to public enterprises. When a new revolutionary elite seizes power, as it did in Russia, for example, it may have good reason to doubt the loyalty of the old managerial cadre. Political management in the sense of loyalty to the new regime may therefore become a necessity in the eyes of the ruling group. In the Soviet Union, warnings about the necessity for political loyalty in state enterprise management appeared in the late 1920's, and there were official notices of reprimand and discipline in the early 1930's. The "kill the Kulaks in management" period occurred approximately five years after its application to agriculture. The general purges of 1937–1938 coincided with the more specific elimination of the politically-questionable from managerial authority. Caught between pressures for maximum output and the fear of sedition, therefore, the Kremlin demonstrated an extreme example of political management. Not only were party members appointed to managerial positions, but in many cases, these managers and others were checked by political commissars or representatives with power equal to the technical managers in each enterprise. Some of those managers, sharing the commitment to revolutionary goals, accomplished remarkable feats of production. Eventually, however, the inefficiency of this system resulted in the establishment of "one-man management" in the factories, although Party membership and loyalty was still an important criterion.[6] This coincided with political stability of the regime, and in post-Stalin Russia, professional competence clearly is the primary standard for managerial appointments among party members.

Political management, however, is simply incapable of coping successfully with the intricate tasks which must be performed in modern, large-scale industry. In this respect, it is even less viable than patrimonial management. But this does not imply that management is likely to be free of political influence even in the most advanced societies. For example, when the protection of the enterprise is dependent upon receiving favors or special treatment from the government or from the political party in power, it may be important to have someone in the managerial ranks who is close to the seat of power and who can "get things done." In most countries, "political connections" are indispensable both to patrimonial and professional management.

There is a basic similarity between patrimonial and the forms of political management: the importance of finding managers whom a ruling elite can trust and who will be loyal and obedient. But the prime movers in industrialization gradually find that the stress on loyalty and obedience may not lead to efficiency. It becomes increasingly evident that they must rely on competence rather than merely on connections as the standard for access to managerial positions. Moreover, the test of loyalty may be less decisive when the society has developed a high degree of consensus. The logic of the industrialization process requires managerial competence.

Professional management is enterprise management in which major policy-making positions and nearly all other positions in the hierarchy are held by persons on the basis of claimed or demonstrated technical qualifications. In professional management, technical ability, experience, education, knowledge of the organization, and ability to impress people who make decisions are more important than relationships to a family or a political regime.

This definition does not imply, however, that management *per se* is a "profession" in the sense that law, medicine, chemical engineering, or teaching are professions. To be sure, within the ranks of management there are members of professions such as engineers, chemists, and lawyers. They are sometimes engaged in the work of their respective professions, but they also may hold administrative posts quite unrelated to their prior professional training. Administration, however, is not strictly a profession, nor is organization building. But administrators and organization builders may be careerists, and they are oriented more professionally than patrimonially or politically. Professional managers are a distinct group, access to which is secured by training, experience and performance.

Professional management is most prevalent in advanced industrializing societies. It is found in large and complicated enterprises which operate in nation-wide or international markets. The need for professional management is as great in a state-enterprise economy as it is in a capitalistic society. In both the United States and the Soviet Union, for example, professional management holds the reins of power within large and strategic enterprises. The professionals are likewise now dominant in the industrial empires of Japan and Germany, in the state-owned enterprises of France and Italy, and even in many of the emerging large-scale enterprises in the newly developing countries. In the logic of industrialization, with its increasing emphasis on technological complexity and large-scale organization, the professionals are bound to sweep aside both political and paternal management.

The professionals, however, do not take over without a struggle. In the intermediate stages of industrialization, they are only the hired subordinates of the proprietory capitalists, the family patriarchs, or the political commissars. In this capacity they may feel indignant at taking orders from persons they deem to be technically incompetent, and they may resent the ceilings which arbitrarily restrict their upward movement into the top echelons of the managerial hierarchy. But as industrialization advances, the numbers of professionals in management swell. The owners of the large enterprises become increasingly dependent upon professional skills. As more authority is necessarily delegated to the professionals, they demand appointment to the top command posts and become the organization builders.

Although professional management is destined to sweep aside its political or patrimonial predecessors, it seldom becomes a ruling elite in any society. In other words, the state does not become the property of the professional managers, as James Burnham envisioned in his "managerial revolution."[7] Rather the managers may be as much servants as masters of the state, as much subordinates as controllers of the market. The managers are a part of the ruling elite, but they are not *the* elite. In the Soviet Union, for example, the industrial managers are clearly subservient to the political and governmental elite. In Japan the heads of the great *zaibatsu* were always conscious of their prior obligation to serve nationalist objectives and the interests of the state. The German industrialists became the willing instruments of Hitler. In the United States, the professional managers argue that the market is really the supreme master of their destiny. Some markets are an exacting taskmaster while others contain such extensive monopoly elements that they are a lenient and even lax governor. If management were to claim to be the dominant elite in the United States, it would be rebuffed, investigated, and shackled with further legislation designed to protect the public interest. In the modern industrializing society, it appears, management can be supreme only within the orbit of the enterprise, and even here it must share its authority with others who demand and obtain a share in the making of the web of rules which governs industrializing man.

The process of industrialization universally tends to change management from patrimonial and political to professional, but the patterns of change in management vary with the ideal type elites. In the dynastic and middle-class-led societies, the change is from patrimonial to professional; under the revolutionary intellectuals and nationalist leaders, the change is from political to professional. The colonial administrators are pressed to move from foreign managers of various types through native political managers to native professional managers.

Management as an Internal System of Authority

An abundance of high-talent manpower and the development of a managerial class do not necessarily result in effective management, for management is more than the mere sum of its members. It is an integrated hierarchy of people with differentiated functions whose activites must be coordinated to achieve specific objectives. The direction of an organization and the coordination of internal activity are dependent upon the system of authority.

The most primitive system of authority in enterprise management is the sovereign rule by a single person or a single family. One-man or one-family management is common, especially in small and medium-sized enterprises. But large organizations, too, may try to cling to this kind of rule. In the United States Henry Ford and Sewell Avery ran their enterprises for many years as virtual dictators. Some of the German owner-managers are still convinced that they are born to rule their enterprises and that their authority is based upon a kind of natural law rather than upon their function in the organization. French and Italian patrimonial management has a similar outlook. The following description of Egyptian enterprise is typical of management in many newly industrializing countries:

Here the manager is a dominant individual who extends his personal control over all phases of the business. There is no charted plan of organization, no formalized procedures for selection and development of managerial personnel, no publicized system of wage and salary classifications. The status of individuals in the managerial hierarchy is based not so much upon function as upon the nature of their relations with the owner-manager.[8]

The sovereign ruler in management thinks of himself as holding the combined portfolios of chief engineer, head salesman, general production manager, personnel man, and time keeper, as well as proprietor. He is invariably suspicious of his subordinates and complains that people in the organization lack initiative, imagination, or just plain common sense. This kind of manager cultivates the art of making himself indispensable. The one-man ruler delegates too little, does too much himself, and thus has little time for effective organization-building or for forward planning. This type of management breathes only at the top, and when the top disappears, the organization either collapses or the leadership group must be completely rebuilt.

At the other extreme is management by participation. Authority is based upon individual initiative, consent, persuasion, and self-direction. This type of management implies a substantial revision in the conventional relationship between a senior and subordinate. The control devices conventionally used to enforce "authority over" the subordinate are given to the subordinate himself, and the job of the superior becomes more "assistance to" and "development of" those under him in the managerial hierarchy. In management by participation, the essential task is to arrange organizational conditions so that people can achieve their own goals by directing their own efforts toward organizational objectives. The emphasis is on self-control and self-direction rather than on direction and control imposed from above.

Between the extremes of top-side sovereign rule and management by participation are the systems which show various blends of decentralized administration with centralized control. The General Motors Corporation is often cited as an outstanding example of decentralization and delegation of administrative authority and responsibility to its operating divisions; General Electric is a more recent apostle of this concept. Similar examples can be cited in other countries: Imperial Chemical Industries and Unilever in Great Britain, and the Indian managing agency, Tata, Ltd.

In decentralizing and delegating authority to subordinate managers, top management does not give up all its authority; indeed, the logic of the situation is that it cannot do so. It must retain some control over the limits within which subordinates can make decisions. Hence, top management must determine objectives and policies, establish some sort of centralized reporting and control mechanisms to inform itself on how divisional objectives are being met, and if they are not, why. The final responsibility for the errors of subordinates still rests with the superior, even to the point of taking corrective action. This is a major paradox of delegation.

The subordinate managers in a decentralized management structure may be under considerable pressure from their superiors to show results, to cut costs, and to adhere to established company policies. Staff-line conflicts frequently arise because high-level staff men, reporting to the top management, perform a control function as well as an advisory one. In the organizations studied in various countries, these conflicts are just as likely to occur in enterprises in India or in Egypt as in Sweden, Great Britain, or the United States. But despite the dilemmas and the difficulties, administrative decentralization gives subordinate managers a greater opportunity to make specific decisions and to develop managerial competence than is possible under the sovereign rule system.

The logic of industrial development calls for increasing managerial decentralization as enterprises grow in size and complexity. The sovereign rule of a single man or family is not appropriate except for small establishments. The proportionate number of persons in management tends to increase as industrialization proceeds. As membership in management expands, it becomes

humanly impossible for one man to control everything and every-
body. Therefore, if sovereign rule persists as the prevailing
system of managerial authority in a society, it will retard and in-
hibit successful industrialization. Conversely, industrial development may be significantly accelerated if the appropriate means
are found to delegate authority and decentralize administration in
the management of enterprises.

Rule-Making Authority over the Managed

A primary concern of management, in its relationship to workers,
is to establish, to make legitimate, and to maintain its authority.
The logic of industrialization impels management to covet the
role of rule-maker. It seeks control over any of the factors which
must be coordinated in the planning-production-selling process.
The specialization of functions which industrialization demands
also requires that the work force accept tasks whose nature, time,
and method of accomplishment are to be determined by management in its role of planner and order-giver.

Acceptance by workers of this role for management typically
means a substitution of one authority for another in the transition
to industrialization. Management of the enterprise tends to displace the head of the village family, the tribal chief, or the communal leader as the authority which prescribes the duties, obligations, rewards, and punishments of workers at the work place.
If management is completely free to make the rules at the industrial work place, without interference from other contenders
such as labor organizations or government, its philosophy or approach toward workers may be either (1) dictatorial, or (2)
paternalistic. But if various pressures, including labor organizations and governments, force management to share its authority
and modify its philosophies and approaches, the new managerial
approaches may be characterized as (3) constitutional, or (4)
consultative and participative.

Dictatorial or Authoritarian Management. This characterizes
the manager who arbitrarily and often ruthlessly compels workers
to accept his unquestioned authority, with very little concern for
their dignity as human beings and with virtually no feeling
of responsibility for their welfare on or off the job. According

to this philosophy, the worker must never question the authority of the manager; indeed, to do so is cause for immediate discharge. In the manager's eyes, the worker should have no recourse if for any reason his services are no longer required.

A humanitarian concern for workers may precede or follow an attitude of dictatorial indifference, but at some point early in the industrialization process, the imperatives of rapid capital formation may result in ruthless exploitation of industrial workers. This was the case in nineteenth-century Russia,[9] and in England in the early nineteenth century the rising entrepreneurial class refused to accept the earlier notion that their claim to authority over their workers created reciprocal responsibility to look after their welfare. Although there were striking exceptions to this attitude, certainly more common was the conviction that a person could by hard work and diligence do well in the world, and that in any case the employer's responsibility was filled by buying labor services and providing employment.

While there are still instances among management of dictatorial or authoritarian treatment of workers, this approach is seldom a stable one over time in the absence of police or military support. It may be able to achieve subordination of labor, but it usually fails to develop loyalty and productivity. Industrial workers sooner or later everywhere rebel against or resist such unmitigated exercise of authority.

Paternalistic Management. This philosophy carries forward the traditions of responsibility and subordination of the master-servant relationship; it often serves to smooth the major dislocations which an industrial way of life forces on the newly recruited workers. Paternalism reflects the feudal tradition in which the lord of the manor has responsibility for the welfare of his subordinates in return for faithful service. The manager may provide housing, food, medical care, and social services for him. In turn the worker is expected to be grateful, and also productive. The worker is regarded as dependent on the manager for security and welfare. Here the image of the industrial *pater* takes the place of the head of the family, tribe, or primary group in pre-industrial society.

In the early stages of industrial development in many societies, the paternalistic approach is quite consistent with the prevailing social order. In small establishments, where the proprietor may hire his relatives as workers, it affords an ideal rationale for maintaining the security and integrity of the family. It is a logical first step in some countries, Germany and Japan, for example, where the members of the preexisting dynastic elites become the agents of industrialization. Thus:

Patriarchal management in Japan retained the socially responsible characteristics of the traditional kinship system. Although it gave little encouragement to individualists and indeed individualism was frowned upon if not actually punished, each member of the organization was regarded as an integral and important cog in the functioning of the whole enterprise. Conformity to the purpose of the unit rested upon fostering and structuring the situation to achieve complete identification between superior and subordinate. The reward was life-long security within the group and full acceptance of one's functional role.[10]

In India today there are examples of this "benevolent paternalism," based on an apparent willingness of the employee to accept a dependent status and of the employer to play the role of a wise father. An indication of this is suggested by the words of the founder of an important family group of Indian enterprises:

At first . . . I found that if workers got a few annas more, they were absent more often; they didn't know how to live properly. So I had to show them how to live better, to keep their houses clean. I started various games and recreation centers. I had to provide these outside interests to soothe the workers' minds.[11]

Managerial paternalism, moreover, has not been confined to the early stages of industrial development. In the United States the present personnel policies of International Business Machines, Eastman Kodak, and the Hershey Chocolate Corporation, for example, seem to reflect a considerable paternal concern for the employees' welfare which is bound up with management's expressed conviction that such programs are sound investments in long-run employee productivity.

Managements may also find it necessary to provide many services for employees for reasons which have little connection with a sense of moral obligation. Malnutrition may force managements to provide free lunches in the interest of higher productivity. Other services or payments in kind may be required in enterprises which operate in areas remote from centers of population. The oil-producing companies in Saudi Arabia, Iraq, and Kuwait are good examples, as are the sugar plantations and mills in the sparsely inhabited coastal deserts of Peru or the copper mines of Rhodesia.

Paternalistic management, with all its overtones and variations, tends to be most stable (1) when the preexisting culture and social structure are congenial to this type of superior-subordinate relationship, as in Japan, India, France, and Italy; (2) when strong labor organizations do not challenge management's decisions at the work place concerning what should be done for employees; and (3) when the community does not provide housing, schools, medical, and other services.

Pressures on Management for a Different Approach. In the advanced industrializing societies such as the United States, Great Britain, Sweden, and Germany, managers are forced increasingly to abandon many of their authoritarian and paternalistic practices. They do this reluctantly since the desire of managements to be rule-maker and the dispenser of favors, for which gratitude, loyalty and good work are expected, is very strong indeed. But in most countries pressures operate on managers to change as industrialization advances. The more important of these pressures are the following:

First, there are the social values of a society, and they are not static. If the society places high value, through its educational system or its religious ethic, on the freedom of the individual to have a voice in determining his own present and future, it will be increasingly difficult to maintain autocracy or even paternalism in industry. Changing social values may impel a different approach by managers to workers.

Second, there are pressures from individual workers. A worker may protest against managerial authority by being absent from work, restricting output, rebelling against discipline, or quitting. Pressure of this kind, of course, is greatest where some types of labor are relatively scarce. In the course of industrialization, workers tend to acquire more skill, higher education, and more knowledge of alternative conditions which influence their relations to management.

Third, there is the pressure of government legislation, often influenced by international comparisons and conventions of the ILO. Increasingly, the unilateral authority of the manager is restricted by government intervention in the labor-management relationship. In most industrial countries, the government restricts the right of the manager to discharge or lay off workers; in many it sets minimum wages; in some it prescribes mandatory benefits in the form of housing, medical care, vacations, or sickness allowances. In nearly all countries the government prescribes minimum working conditions and safety precautions. Thus, in the area subject to government regulation, the manager exercises his rights only within legally determined limits.

Fourth, there is pressure from labor organizations. The growth of strong labor organizations in advanced industrializing countries and their emergence in various forms and under various auspices in the less-developed economics likewise brings varying pressure on management to share rule-making authority.

Fifth, there is pressure from other managements. The individual manager may be significantly influenced by the actions and policies of other enterprises, and particularly by management associations, business schools, "staff colleges," and other institutions which tend to disseminate less paternal and less authoritarian concepts of managerial organization and managerial policies.

Sixth, in some economies the pressure of competition from other enterprises forces managers to become more efficient. Greater efficiency is achieved, in part, through improving relationships with employees, motivating them to work more effectively, and increasing their pace of work in conjunction with better methods and equipment. When cartels, tariffs, and other market-sharing of "live and let live" practices prevail, competitive pressures will be less than in an economy where price and product competition or centralized direction is more prevalent.

Seventh, and finally, the pace of economic development itself puts pressures on management to change its policies. A faster pace generated by governments under economic planning may temporarily enhance the authority of enterprise managers over workers by instituting controls over labor which protect managerial power. But often the other pressures discussed above work in the direction of limiting managerial authority over workers, possibly at the expense of a faster pace of economic growth.

Thus, in industrializing societies managers are often no longer free to adhere consistently to pure authoritarian or paternalistic policies. Enterprise managers must share their authority over workers with other contenders, and they are continuously influenced, even though indirectly, by outside forces. Their policies are the result of accommodations, and their philosophy at any one period is likely to be a rationalization of the cumulative impact of the pressures on management. As these pressures mount in the modern world, the managerial approach tends to become "constitutional" rather than dictatorial or paternalistic.

Constitutional Management. This term is used to characterize management which governs its working forces according to procedures and policies which have evolved from the intervention of outside forces in the rule-making process. Here the rule-making power of managers is shared in a constitutional manner with other agencies. Wages and working conditions may become subject to determination by collective bargaining or various forms of governmental determination, and jointly negotiated agreements or governmental regulations may establish a constitutional framework within which management exercises its functions. In some countries, such as the United States, these agreements are more frequently company-wide in scope; in others, such as Sweden, national agreements between industry-wide unions and employers' federations establish the constitutional limits within which the manager deals with his workers.

In some cases, labor organizations and their political allies may be the driving force behind passage of labor legislation to regulate managerial authority over the work force. This pattern is more typical in the newly-industrializing countries today, where the labor organizations are so weak at the level of the enterprise that they exert little direct pressure for "constitutional" management, and, as a consequence, government is the principal contender for sharing rule-making authority with enterprise management (Chapter 9).

Most managers probably would not choose of their own free will the constitutional approach to dealing with their working forces. But they alone do not make the choice. They learn to accommodate themselves to limitations imposed by others on their unilateral authority to prescribe the rules.

Democratic or Participative Management. Finally, pressures can lead under some circumstances to a fourth type of philosophy and approach, which may be called democratic or participative. This type is very rare.

The democratic-participative philosophy grows out of the conclusion that people respond best in an organization when they can participate in the process of decision-making on matters that directly affect them. Here, management is not leaderless. It takes the initiative in enlisting genuine participation, as in consultation beforehand to get reactions to proposed courses of action before management makes decisions. The organizational structure itself may be changed by enlarging the jobs of people at subordinate levels to give them more responsibility and the information to act on that responsibility. Sometimes this involves decentralization of management's internal system of authority. Or, at the shop level, it may involve something like the "Scanlon Plan" of labor-management cooperation or, as in Great Britain and Sweden, some forms of joint consultation on production problems, with production committees to act upon suggestions submitted directly and not through suggestion boxes.[12] The works councils of Yugoslavia and other countries are in some respects another illustration. The essence of democratic-participative management is the assumption that people are not lazy, do not have to be pushed to do a good day's work, and are not simply interested in more money. Instead, they are eager to work "for the good of the order" if they are given a real chance to share at all levels in formulating the conditions under which they shall labor and the criteria by which they will be rewarded. The managers who hold to this philosophy are indeed true believers in industrial democracy.

Using the typology outlined above, it is possible to characterize the prevailing managerial philosophy of relations with workers in many countries today, recognizing that there are variations within each country and that no country conforms fully to any ideal type. In Japan, for example, the leading industrialists follow a policy of paternalism. Because industrialization was originally sparked by a dynastic elite, the idea of paternalistic concern for the welfare of subordinates is strongly rooted in Japanese management. Although the government has intervened to regulate the manager in the field of labor relations, it has nevertheless given strong encouragement to the paternalistic approach. Until recently, the labor organizations have been fairly weak at the enterprise level, and they have made only minor inroads into the area of managerial authority. The paternalistic tradition is strong also in France and Italy, but here the inroads by both the government and labor organizations upon management's monopoly of rule-making power have been greater.

In Sweden and England, on the other hand, the middle-class tradition does not provide as fertile a soil for paternalism. The manager who once might have been an advocate of authoritarian policies has been forced to share the rule-making authority in the enterprise with strong unions. Management accepts unionization as a permanent and even a desirable institution in a society where all kinds of rule-making are jointly shared by many groups in a pluralistic arrangement and where every manager is to some extent a rather confident politician, adjusting to the pressures around him. In the United States, the extent of paternalism has been substantially reduced in large-scale industry. The high cost of labor, the emergence of strong unions, and the lessons of the Great Depression have made American management aware of both the rights and the aspirations of workers, who have a strong sense of independence. The American employer simply cannot afford to be indifferent to the welfare of the labor force, and he recognizes that wages and working conditions must be established with consultation or consent of the workers. Thus, managers are constrained by constitutional limitations established by labor organizations and the government.

In the Soviet Union, the authority of industrial management is rigorously circumscribed by the party, the government, and to a lesser degree by the trade unions. In some respects, the workers may circumvent the manager by appealing directly to the party functionaries. As in other societies, the workers are subordinated to management, but their ultimate master is the state. Soviet enterprise management, therefore, has reason to be cautious in its handling of workers, but as industrialization becomes more dominant in the society, the managers apparently have been able to increase the areas of authority over their working forces. The Soviet manager can never be indifferent to labor's welfare, and there is little reason for him to be paternalistic. Indeed, within the limits of his authority, he is much more likely to operate as a kind of "constitutional" manager, although the checks to his authority in the plant are quite different from those in other societies and he may be able to be authoritarian in some areas. The position of the Soviet manager thus reflects the broader power and authority of the country's rulers. On the surface, at least, the role of management in Yugoslavia is different from that in the Soviet Union. Here apparently in very wide areas within the enterprise management shares decision-making authority with representatives of the workers through the workers' councils.

Finally, in the industrializing countries with nationalist leaders, there may be many varieties of managerial approaches to labor problems. There are instances of callous indifference to, as well as paternalistic concern for, labor's welfare. Labor organizations for the most part are weak, and labor is often plentiful. The only strong pressure on management's rule-making authority is the government. In Egypt and India, the government has moved with deliberation and force into the field of labor relations, thus compelling rather drastic accommodations by management.

The logic of industrialization is particularly powerful in its impact on the rule-making authority of management. Management evolves from authoritarian and paternalistic types to constitutional management. The resistances to this development vary among the ideal types of elites. In the dynastic-led society the resistance is from paternalism; among the revolutionary intellectuals it is from the state and the necessities of the rapid pace of industrialization; in the middle class society there are least obstacles; the nationalist leaders find resistances in the state and the older culture; the colonial administrators find a deep contradiction in the pressures for constitutional management and their alien character.

Elements of Unity in Management Development

In looking at management as an economic resource, as a class, as an internal system of authority, and as a rule-making authority over workers, various tendencies have been described and analyzed. These may now be summarized and designated as the elements of unity in the development of management in the course of economic growth.

As industrialization proceeds, the number of persons in management increases both absolutely and relatively in the economy. This is the inevitable consequence of larger capital outlay, the pace of innovation, the use of more modern machinery and processes, the growth of markets, and the increasing complexity of the advancing industrial societies. In this process, enterprise organizations become more complicated as they grow larger, and the effectiveness of management becomes increasingly dependent upon administrative skill in reducing the inherent frictions and inefficiencies of complicated human organizations.

In the early stages of industrialization, the management class may be drawn from family dynasties, from a new middle class, from political parties or the government service. But in the march toward industrialism, technical and organizational forces tend to favor careerist rather than political or patrimonial management. Increasingly larger numbers of trained engineers, technologists, and administrators are required. And, as the managerial class becomes larger, it also becomes less exclusive since of necessity the avenues of access to its ranks must become broader. In its logical development, therefore, management at all levels becomes more of a profession than a preordained calling. As an industrializing society continues to lay stress upon scientific discovery, technological innovation, and economic growth, patrimonial and political managers tend to be displaced by the professionals.

Industrial growth forces enterprise managements to develop means of delegating administrative authority within a framework of centralized controls. Management by sovereign rule is not viable except in small-scale operations, and thus it tends to disappear in large-scale enterprises, in the more advanced countries. At the other extreme, management-by-participation is such a radical departure from traditional systems of authority that it is seldom realized in practice. Between these extremes is a broad range of possible combinations of decentralized administration with centralized policy control. Large and even medium-sized enter-

prises in all industrial societies, through conscious planning or
trial and error, are continuously searching for some kind of balance in this area. Almost never do they find a perfect or permanent solution, but some are more successful than others in
finding arrangements which substantially reduce organizational
frictions.

As all industrial societies advance, management becomes less
authoritarian in its attitude and policy toward workers. Management, of course, tries to preserve its prerogatives as the rule-
maker over the workers. But others also seek and gain a voice
in the rule-making and rule-enforcing process. Among the principal contenders are the state and labor organizations. They tend
to limit, to regulate, or sometimes to displace the unilateral authority of management. As industrialization proceeds, management
is forced to share its rule-making power with one or more of these
contenders. Governments by legislation or labor organizations by
collective action limit or circumscribe management's freedom
unilaterally to exercise its prerogatives. As a consequence, dictatorial or paternalistic direction usually gives way to a kind of
"constitutional" management in which wages and conditions of
employment are based upon laws, regulations, decisions of government, collective contracts, or procedural agreements. And in
rare cases, a system of industrial relations may be established in
which management and labor not only share in the rule-making
process but also cooperate in improving efficiency and increasing output.

The outlays for technical and managerial education become
enormous as industrialization follows its inherent logic. The advanced industrializing economy must have a fully developed system of general education, and at the same time its basic educational institutions must become more functionally oriented
to the training of skilled technicians, engineers, scientists, and
administrators. But it also requires the lowering of arbitrary non-
educational barriers to entry into the managerial hierarchy as
well as some vertical and horizontal mobility within the managerial class itself. In some societies the processes of generation
of managerial manpower have been spearheaded by the state, in
others by private initiative. As industrialization advances and even
as it is being started in the presently underdeveloped countries,

however, the means of generating and accumulating managerial resources is increasingly a matter for careful planning, judicious investment, and conscious effort. High-talent manpower does not grow wild; it requires careful seeding and meticulous cultivation.

Finally, although the professional management class is destined to grow in size in all industrializing societies, it has neither the capacity nor the will alone to become the dominant ruling elite. Being preoccupied with the internal affairs of the enterprise, which become ever more complex, the members of the managerial class are prone to become conformists rather than leaders in the larger affairs of society. Modern organization builders, unlike the old-style proprietary capitalists who are being swept aside in the march toward industrialism, do not own the means of production. In an increasing number of cases, they are more characteristically the agents of stockholders, state bureaucracies, or in some cases, workers' councils. In the logic of industrialization, management plays a vital and indispensable role. But it serves rather than dominates the society of which it is a part.

Diversities in the Development of Management

Although management develops in a common direction, it does so from quite different initial positions. Particularly in the early stages of industrialization, the orientation of management in various societies may be quite diverse, reflecting the influence of the different initiating elites. The following diversities among the ideal types of elites are to be noted.

Under the leadership of a dynastic elite, family connections tend to control access to the managerial class. Careerist managers and technicians are employed, but they are kept subordinate to the members of the owner families. Patrimonial management is most likely to be paternalistic in its relationship with the industrial working classes. Owner-managers of enterprise legitimatize their position on the basis of a predestination or "calling" for industrial leadership. Their authority is rationalized more by divine right than by the specific functions performed in enterprises. The dynastic elite favors the idea of education of a chosen minority, often in a status university, which by virtue of its position in society has both the opportunity and the obligation to be trained to direct the affairs of business enterprises. Since the members of this minority are "born to manage," they scorn tasks which might dirty their hands, and they resist as long as possible the introduction of rational or impersonal procedures to govern relationships within the managerial hierarchy.

The middle class tends to favor access to the ranks of management on the basis of individual initiative and competence. This facilitates an earlier and more rapid development of a professional managerial class. Imbued with the idea that workers should be self-reliant rather than dependent upon the manager for their well-being, management is quicker to move toward the "constitutional" approach in agreeing to rules and procedures for the governing of the working forces. Managerial authority is rationalized by the functional positions which persons hold rather than by family connections or by calling. A society in which the middle class is the leading elite emphasizes education for the masses rather than for a chosen few. Without centralized design, institutions of higher learning may adapt themselves to the needs of the society for engineers, technicians, and managers. In this kind of society, management moves more easily and painlessly along its evolutionary course.

The revolutionary intellectuals try at the outset to promote political management, and to make party loyalty and service the gateway to the managerial hierarchy. Managers perform a legitimate role only as the servants of the party and the state. The revolutionary intellectuals press for a functionally oriented system of education giving the highest priority to development of technical skills required in an industrializing society as well as to the ideological indoctrination according to the prescribed dialectic. In this society change also takes place toward professionalization of management. And in the relations with workers, subsequently, the authority of management is usually circumscribed by party functionaries, plans prescribed by a central bureaucracy, and also by pressures brought to bear by labor organizations or workers' councils. In this society, management is likely to become more "constitutional."

The colonial administrators reserve for themselves the controlling positions in the managerial hierarchies both in government and in industry. They train the local nationals to perform the lesser jobs in management, but place ceilings on their upward advancement. The authority of management is rationalized on the basis of the superior technological, educational and cultural position of the people of the home country. Management is likely to be either dictatorial, or, if it is relatively progressive, paternalistic in its relations with the workers. The colonial administrators favor an educational system which trains a relatively small number of nationals to assume minor positions in government, and they are reluctant to establish institutions of higher learning to develop engineers, managers, or highly skilled technicians. Advanced education is largely reserved to the home country. Indeed, the colonial administrator attempts to prevent rather than to promote the emergence of an indigenous class of top-level industrial managers.

The nationalist leaders, in their rush to embark upon industrialization, tend to encourage development of political or professional management, and they may also rely temporarily on foreign management. A managerial class is accepted as an indispensable instrument for industrial development and economic growth. The relationship with the working masses will vary according to types of management. Nationalist leaders usually press for universal general education and also for functionally oriented institutions of higher learning, and they lean heavily on the more advanced countries for assistance and capital to develop technical colleges and industrial management training programs. In most cases, they follow in various intermediate combinations the routes taken by the middle class in the market economies and the revolutionary intellectuals in the totalitarian states.

Chart 4 summarizes the approaches of each of the ideal types of industrializing elites to the development of management. The different approaches are most distinguishable in the early stages of industrialization. In practice the hybrid character of the elites in an evolving society imparts a blended coloration to its managerial class at any intermediate stage of development. As the society reaches the more advanced stages of industrialization, management is likely to have the universal common markings which have been described in the previous section. As industrialization proceeds, the elements of unity tend to overshadow the elements of diversity in the development of management.

CHART 4.

Management and the industrializing elites.

Industrializing Elite	Dynastic	Middle-Class	Revolutionary-Intellectuals	Colonial Administrators	Nationalist Leaders
Access to management	Access based upon the family with professionals subordinated to the authority of the family.	Access to management on basis of initiative and competence--early development of professional management.	At first, access on basis of political affiliations, later on professional standards.	Top positions reserved for nationals of the home country.	Various, with emphasis on political and professional qualifications.
Character of managerial authority over workers	Paternalistic concern for the "dependent" worker.	Constitutional or occasionally democratic.	Dictatorial and authoritarian, later becoming constitutional to a limited degree.	Dictatorial or paternalistic.	Various, depending on nature of managerial class.
Basis for managerial authority	Concept that certain families are "called" to manage. Personal rather than functional organization.	Authority of managers based upon functions they perform.	Managers as servants of party and state.	Superiority of nationals of the home country.	Managerial resources looked upon as necessary instruments for industrial development.
The education and development of managerial resources.	Education of a small, elitist minority.	Education of the masses, and functional education in technology and management.	High priority to functional education at all levels.	Very limited educational development of the nationals of the colony.	Education of the masses, and priority given to higher education.

The industrial world has witnessed the increasing acceptance of the managerial function in enterprises, private or public. Industrializing countries today are demanding more competent management; the role of management is no longer on the defensive as it was in an earlier stage of industrial history. Modern management is no longer the "alien minority" which it was in the more traditional societies resisting industrialization.

One of the universals of the industrialization process is that management of enterprises becomes professionalized rather quickly. But the characteristics and strategies of the different industrializing elites relate to the early development of management by influencing the access to managerial positions and the authority system of management. Cultural factors, and particularly family, class, and race, also have an early impact, but eventually the universal imperative — the need for competent, professionalized management — prevails. While both the stage and pace of industrialization affect the position and policies of enterprise management, the similarities of enterprise management in all advanced industrializing societies are far greater than their differences.

All enterprise managements face the task of building and developing an industrial labor force. The problems and alternatives are discussed in the next chapter.

CHAPTER 7

DEVELOPING THE INDUSTRIAL LABOR FORCE

Industrializing elites, and more specifically the managers of enterprises, are required to recruit, to build, to maintain, and to direct a large and diversified industrial labor force. The members of this working force must learn to accept the authority of managers in place of the family, tribe, or village. They must conform to a pace of work established by the dictates of new masters rather than by their own inclinations or traditional standards. Industrialization involves the setting up of a new body of rules governing relationships between those who give and those who take orders; and this requires a new system of rewards and punishments to mobilize and to direct the brawn and brains utilized in the new productive process. Industrializing society also requires the development of labor market mechanisms to recruit, sort out, distribute, and redistribute workers into a myriad of occupations and jobs requiring varying degrees of skill, and rewarded at different rates of compensation.

There is, of course, no precise dividing line between the managerial group and the industrial labor force. Those in the lower echelons of the managerial hierarchy may differ in only minor respects from the more highly skilled members of the working forces. In some cases foremen are members of management; in others they are the highest ranking members of the laboring class. The demarkation between the managers and the managed is more like a gradient than a cliff. With this qualification, the working force may be said to include the following: manual labor of all skill levels, clerical workers, group leaders and straw bosses. First-line supervisors and the lower grades of technicians constitute a middle group which for some purposes and in some countries may be classified as management and for others as workers, whereas administrators, professional employees, engineers, and scientists are clearly in the managerial category.

This chapter is concerned with the processes of development of an industrial labor force as well as with the broader problems of the general supply of human resources for development. At various stages of industrialization, the problems encountered by the industrializing elites with similar resource constraints may be fairly similar, but their policies and approaches to the common task of developing an industrial labor force are likely to be quite diverse. These similar problems as well as the diverse policies and approaches are treated in the final two sections of this chapter.

Building the Industrial Labor Force

Most countries have human resources which are available for industrial employment, but no country is endowed with a full-blown industrial labor force. Industrial man is a product not of a particular climate or ancestry but rather of persistent development and specific policies. In the development of an industrial labor force, there are four interrelated processes: (1) recruitment, (2) commitment, (3) advancement, and (4) maintenance. These processes may overlap each other in the course of time.

Recruitment is the first step in developing the industrial labor force. It is the process of selecting, hiring, and assigning persons to jobs. This process may be repeated many times with the same individual. Commitment is a longer and more intricate process. It consists of achieving the workers' permanent attachment to and acceptance of industrial employment as a way of life. Advancement is the process of building the skills, the work habits and the incentives for productive employment. It involves the training and the energizing of the working force. Maintenance includes the various arrangements which may be needed to provide security both on and off the job for committed workers.

The sections which immediately follow identify the various methods and stages of recruitment, commitment, advancement, and maintenance of the labor force in the industrialization process.

The Recruitment Process. In the history of industrialization, compulsory as well as voluntary means of recruitment have been used separately and in combination. Among the more common methods of compulsion are the following: recruits may be forced into industrial employment by outright enslavement, by various kinds of indenture, by the imposition of "labor dues," by the levying of taxes payable only in money, or simply by forcing people to move from the land and to seek other means of earning a living. The agents of such recruitment may be tribal chiefs, colonial administrators, labor contractors, or private or public industrial enterprises.

Slavery as a formal institution of labor force recruitment is practically extinct today, although it once played an important role in the recruitment of labor for industrial employment, particularly in the initial development of extractive industries[1] and industrial agriculture. Common peonage and long-term indenture systems with penal sanctions still exist today, but these are generally found only in industrialized agriculture where it is necessary to recruit workers in distant places and transport them at considerable expense to their place of employment.

The use of forced labor by some of the early colonial rulers in Africa followed the form of tribal practices, where it was customary for each able-bodied male to contribute a certain number of days of work per year for such community tasks as clearing bush, making new paths, or assisting the chief. The colonial administrators, working through the tribal chiefs, attempted to use the same device, but without the traditional safeguards which were inherent in the native systems.[2] The French system of labor dues, or "prestations," used in Equatorial Africa (imported from Metropolitan France) obligated all able-bodied males to work a certain number of days each year (theoretically about 15) on public works. These workers were sometimes assigned to the operators of mines and factories, or conscripted for temporary projects such as road repair and porterage.[3]

In modern times, forced labor has been used in the Soviet Union, but for reasons quite different from those in Africa. In part it grew out of a need to make productive use of large numbers of political prisoners, but in the main it stemmed from an attempt to stabilize the labor force and allocate it to high-priority users.[4] But in all societies compulsory methods generally have proved to be unreliable as a permanent means of building an industrial labor force. The Africans quickly developed a desire for things which only money could buy, and thus wage employment has supplanted the older systems of forced labor; and in the Soviet Union positive incentives have proven to be superior to direction as a means of allocating the labor force. It is true that "labor contractors" in countries such as Egypt and India have often used methods of exploitation which at times have approached forced labor, but abuses of this kind are on their way to being eliminated by protective legislation and changes in the labor market.

In some countries labor has been "pushed" into industrial employment by being forced out of agriculture. The enclosure acts in Great Britain and the development of collective farms in the Soviet Union had this effect. The enclosure of common meadows and pastures in England created a body of transient workers without land, who generally migrated to the then developing urban areas and were available for industrial employment. The measures taken in the Soviet Union in modern times were even more drastic. For example, from 1928 to 1932 about eight and a half million workers entered the labor force the majority of whom had been evicted from their lands and refused to work on the collective farms.[5]

For the most part, however, labor is attracted into industrial employment largely because of the opportunities afforded. People seek jobs in factories because of relatively high wages, availability of housing, aspirations for a higher standard of living, greater social prestige, or simply because they prefer the kind of work offered. Workers may appear at the plant gates seeking employment. They may learn about jobs from friends or relatives. Employers may send recruiters about the country to find workers. Or, in some cases, recruitment may be channeled through public or private employment exchanges or through labor contractors. Such procedures of recruitment may be haphazard or systematic; they may involve careful selection, interviewing, and testing; or they may be entirely indiscriminate.

The managers of enterprise normally have some choice in recruitment. Selection may be based purely on whim or fancy, on physical fitness and health, on aptitude, or on the basis of nepotism and favoritism. In some cases, certain categories of persons are excluded from particular kinds of employment. Thus, in the Union of South Africa, the Mines and Works Act of 1926 ex-

cluded black Africans from specified skilled and semiskilled occupations in the mines, and subsequent attempts have been made
to reserve certain jobs in other industries "for whites only." In
some parts of the United States, Negroes are excluded from all
"white" occupations. In India and Ceylon it is virtually impossible to employ members of particular castes for certain kinds of
work. In the Middle East the oil companies, in accordance with
their concession agreements, are required to give preference to
nationals in all types and levels of work for which they are qualified. And, in the more advanced countries there are legislative
restrictions on the employment of women, children, handicapped
workers, aliens, and other specialized categories of people.

Of all the processes of labor force development, recruitment
is the easiest to handle. Managers generally are able by one means
or another to recruit the number of bodies they need. As industrialization advances, compulsory methods of recruitment are
abandoned in favor of measures designed to make industrial employment more attractive. And along with the greater emphasis
on voluntary recruitment, managers are prone to become much
more selective in hiring new recruits. From a social standpoint,
therefore, discrimination in recruitment is more likely to cause
trouble than the inability to get recruits. The mere recruitment of
workers is in most cases the simplest process in the building of an
industrial labor force.

Of course, in some countries or areas there may be an initial
scarcity of human resources for industrial development. In the
Middle East, petroleum was discovered in unpopulated areas,
and consequently the oil companies had to import labor from
distant areas. The same problem has confronted mining companies in many parts of the world, rubber plantations in Liberia,
and the sugar haciendas and factories in Peru. At times, moreover,
entire countries have been short of labor. The United States for
many years had to import workers from Europe to man its steel
mills, mines, and fast-growing manufacturing enterprises. More
recently, Belgium has tried to staff its collieries with workers from
Italy and other southern European countries. The Soviet Union
was short of industrial labor in the 1920's until it was able to
draw people from the rural areas into the industrial centers.

Yet, even in sparsely populated areas or regions, the general shortage of human resources for industrial development is likely to be mitigated in a relatively short time. Enterprises located in isolated areas can induce workers to move long distances if appropriate wages, housing, and community facilities are provided. Where living accomodations are provided for families as well as for workers, local labor supplies can be generated within a few decades. Likewise, when workers and their families are transplanted from agricultural to urban areas or from one country to another, they sink their roots in the new environment and soon generate a supply of labor. Where labor is scarce at the outset of industrialization, moreover, wages are higher and enterprise managers are forced to invest more time and resources in the proper recruitment, commitment, and advancement of human resources. As a consequence, labor may become more productive in a shorter period of time. Likewise, measures are adopted earlier to replace men with machines. Thus, even in sparsely populated areas, industrialization tends in one way or another to generate the labor resources it requires.

Commitment. The commitment of workers to industrial employment is a more complicated process than recruitment. Hiring workers may be relatively easy, but keeping them consistently at work tends to be more difficult. A committed worker is one who stays on the job, and who has severed his major connections with the land. He is a permanent member of the industrial working force, receiving wages and being dependent for making a living on enterprise managements which offer him work and direct his activities at the work place.

In the commitment of workers to industrial employment, it is useful to distinguish four stages or points on the continuum of behavioral change which mark the transition of the worker from a traditional society into adherence to an industrial way of life. These stages are as follows: the uncommitted worker, the partially or semicommitted worker, the generally committed worker, and the specifically committed worker.

The uncommitted worker has no intention of entering industrial employment on any continuing basis. His is a temporary sojourn for an immediate purpose — perhaps to get a needed sum of money to liquidate tax obligations, or to buy a bride, or to tide over his family during a period of famine, price decline, or other emergency. Although the length of the initial sojourn may be determined by the immediate need for income from industrial employment, it does constitute a break with the rural tribal background, and it may be a first step toward further migrations to industrial work and even to more permanent commitment as time goes on. The "target worker" in the South African gold mine is a good example. He may accept work in the mines for a specified period of a year or two, return to the land for a time, and then seek different industrial employment again. In a number of the newly industrializing countries uncommitted workers constitute a major proportion of the industrial labor force.

The semicommitted worker is a man at the margin of two ways of life. He works more or less regularly in industry but maintains his connections with the land, the tribe, or the village. His periods of industrial employment may be no longer than those of the uncommitted workers; the primary difference is that he contemplates spending a major part of his adult life shifting between agricultural and industrial employment, while the uncommitted worker regards industrial employment as only temporary. In many cases, the wife and family remain on the tribal land where she supports herself and the children. The industrial "bachelor," as in Kenya, will send her small amounts of money and return home periodically. Thus the semicommitted worker gets cash and perhaps a more interesting life from his industrial employment without giving up the security connected with the land or the tribe. For example, in some areas of Africa, about half of the national work force may alternate between tribal and industrial areas. The semicommitted workers generally show high turnover rates; they belong neither to the tribe nor to industrial or urban life.[6]

The generally committed worker is one who has completely severed his connection with the village to become a permanent member of an urban or industrial work force. This involves more than just being an urban dweller; it requires an adjustment to all the institutional aspects of urban living and industrial employment. The security of the generally committed worker is geared to the availability of industrial employment, for he no longer has strong ties to the rural or tribal society. He may be a textile worker, a steel worker, a dock worker, or a truck driver, and in some societies he may have tried his hand at different occupations in a variety of industries. He may be committed to a craft, occupation or profession through an apprenticeship or education. But whatever his occupation, he must sell his labor to maintain himself and his family. All advanced economies depend mainly on this kind of committed labor, or on the more specifically committed worker described below.

The specifically committed worker is one who is permanently attached not only to the industrial way of life, but to a particular employer and often to a particular occupation as well. He is a member not just of the industrial labor force but rather of a small and closely prescribed segment of it. He is committed to a particular enterprise by virtue of work experience, specific training, seniority rules, welfare programs, pension rights, or personal obligation. He is immobile, and inextricably rooted in the culture of a particular establishment. In Japan, for example, industrial employment commonly has involved a life commitment to a single firm. Indeed, the nontemporary Japanese worker has been as bound by custom to his employer as if he were in the closed circle of a preindustrial tribe. He would not think of seeking alternate employment, nor would his employer ever try to dismiss him. He has had permanent membership in the enterprise. This relationship has been expressed as follows in a speech by a Japanese executive to his workers:

Not only is there the fact that our life's work is our employment in our company, but I feel that as people in this situation we have two occasions that can be called "a birth." The first is when we are born into the world as mewling infants. The second is when we all receive our commissions of adoption into the company. This is an event that has the same importance as our crying birth.[7]

Japan is not the only society in which specific commitment is common. It exists in Germany, Italy, France, and England, and it is becoming increasingly prevalent in the United States as a result of greater occupational specialization and the growth of seniority and pension systems without vesting provisions.[8] In many countries, moreover, legislative restrictions on the enterprise manager's freedom to discharge or lay off have tied the worker to particular establishments almost as tightly as his Japanese counterpart.

In general, the degree of commitment is related to the stage
of industrial development. In the very early stages of industrialization, the working forces may consist largely of uncommitted
and semicommitted workers. Labor turnover and absenteeism
are usually high. The managers make very little effort to build a
settled labor force. Indeed, in some cases, as in parts of South
Africa, the large enterprises may prefer an uncommitted or a
semicommitted labor force which expects to receive only part of
its subsistence from industrial employment. The preference for
uncommitted and semicommitted workers, who migrate only
temporarily to the industrial areas and who leave their families
on the land, is usually strongest where community facilities are
inadequate, where the demand for labor is seasonal, where the
managers seek to employ large numbers of unskilled laborers at
low wages, where the managers wish an "unspoiled" labor force,
or where the better jobs are reserved for a class or race.

As industrialization proceeds, the enterprise managers become
more interested in permanently committed working forces. High
rates of turnover, absenteeism and low levels of skill become
burdensome. Efforts are made to move the families along with the
breadwinners to the industrial areas. Or, if the factories are located
in urban areas where there are adequate supplies of labor, attempts
are made to select and retain the more stable workers. The managers devise systems of rewards and punishments to reduce turnover and absenteeism. And in the more remote areas, enterprises
provide housing and other amenities for workers and their
families. Managers are most likely to make an investment in building a committed labor force where expensive machinery and
processes are utilized, where the skill requirements of labor are
relatively high, where quality as well as quantity of production is
important, and where the work load is distributed fairly
evenly throughout the year. These conditions are likely to prevail
in newly industrializing countries which are placing heavy emphasis on new factories with modern technology.

A characteristic feature of all advanced industrializing societies is the existence of a fully committed industrial work force.
Workers are permanently attached not only to industrial employment, but often specifically committed to particular enterprises and occupations as well. Absenteeism, except for unavoid-

able reasons such as illness, ceases to be a problem, and turnover is reduced to the very minimum. Managers are characteristically as much concerned with the problem of discharging or laying off the workers they find undesirable or unnecessary as with attracting and holding new recruits. Tied to particular occupations because of specialized skills and to particular enterprises because of seniority, pensions, or sheer tradition, the worker's chance to change his employment is closely circumscribed. Being thus "over-committed" to his enterprise and his occupation, the industrial worker in the advanced economies tends to demand shorter hours of work and a greater opportunity to seek fulfillment in activities unconnected with his job.

Environmental factors, of course, may speed or retard the process of commitment. In large urban areas, commitment is more easily achieved than in more isolated communities. Cultural factors, such as religious and ethical valuations, the family system, class and race, all have a bearing on commitment. But, in one way or another, workers are uprooted from the old order and relatively soon become generally or specifically committed to the new. The new order of society overpowers the holding power of the old. The transition is even quicker if the old order is already disintegrating, for in this case it is a rejecting rather than a holding force. In the modern world, the new spreading culture is an industrial one, and the future into which the laboring masses are going is much more determinative of what happens than the past from which they are drawn. They must and will conform to the logic of industrialization.

Advancement. Of all the processes of development of industrial working forces, the advancement of human resources is the most critical. It involves investment of time, energy, and money in the education, training, motivation, and rational utilization of labor. Commitment alone is not sufficient to create effective industrial workers. They need to have pride of workmanship, specific skills, and general industrial "know-how," and they must be energized to do a good job. The pace of work must attain a high and sustained standard. The advancement of workers involves building into the labor force the knowledge, skills, and attitudes appropriate for efficient industrial production. It calls for a "rational" system of organization of the work force; it requires

varying degrees of training; and it necessitates a conditioning of
the minds of men to the needs and goals of the enterprise.

The starting points of advancement vary from country to country. In some, for example, even the use of a long-handled broom
may be a totally new experience for a manual worker; in the
Middle East, bedouins employed by the oil companies may have
to be shown how a door knob works. In most underdeveloped
countries, new recruits can neither read nor write. In the more
advanced societies, on the other hand, levels of education and
experience are higher, but extensive new training or retraining
may be required to develop needed skills. Cultural factors often
place obstacles in the way of effective advancement. The desire for
security of employment sometimes stifles the incentive for personal advancement. Or there may be a preference in the society
for commercial positions which makes training for mechanized
jobs less attractive. Advancement may be hindered by negative attitudes toward heavy or dirty work, or by established traditions.
But, in the end, industrial workers must have a strong desire to
work and to produce. They must be propelled, therefore, by some
ethic or ideology which places high value on hard work and
achievement. This is an integral part of the development process.

Human resources may be upgraded for industrial employment in three ways. Workers may advance themselves. They may
be provided with education by the community or the state. And
they may be trained by enterprise managers. In most cases, advancement is the result of all three processes. For purposes of
analysis, however, each can be scrutinized separately.

In some cases, the worker advances himself by his own efforts
without much help either from management or from formal education. In many situations, the young worker is simply assigned
to an older worker who is supposed to teach him the required
skills. But the older worker himself may be apathetic and poorly
trained; and he may be unwilling to teach the new recruit for fear
that the youth will replace him. Managers who expect workers to
train themselves invariably complain about the lack of understanding and motivation on the part of the workers, and use
this as a justification for low wages, arguing that workers are not
as productive. On their own initiative, workers can do a lot to

develop skills and "an industrial consciousness." But, industrialization in modern times can no longer rely primarily on this kind of self-upgrading.

A more prevalent notion is that the community, the state, or society is responsible for the advancement of human resources. Those holding this view stress the importance of education in general and vocational education in particular. Here the assumption is that the lack of industrial aptitude is largely attributable to the preemployment conditioning of workers, and that the deficiency may be overcome by the proper investment in compulsory general education and enlarged vocational training programs. This is particularly true in most Western countries, and it is given great emphasis in Communist societies such as the Soviet Union, Yugoslavia, and China. There is considerable truth in this assumption. Certainly the elimination of mass illiteracy makes a contribution to the development of higher-capacity workers, and trade schools are helpful in "breaking in" potential recruits for the industrial labor force.

The larger part of a worker's advancement usually takes place on the job, and thus the really critical factor in development of human resources for industry is management. The enterprise managers, if they are so motivated, are in a position to make the most vital contribution to the advancement process. They can provide the organization of work, the training on the job, and the incentives which make the difference between a mediocre and a highly efficient work force. Within limits, good managers are able to build a well-adjusted and reasonably contented force instead of an unadjusted and discontented one. And poor managers may create an inefficient labor force even in countries with high levels of general and vocational education. Thus, to a large extent, working force efficiency is dependent upon the time, energy, and resources that management invests in the advancement of human resources within a country's enterprises.

In the initial stages of industrialization, neither the state nor the managers pay much attention to the building of an efficient labor force. School systems are designed primarily to turn out civil servants for the government bureaucracies. The universities, if they exist at all, concentrate attention on philosophy, the arts, religion, the law and medicine. The managerial resources for incipient industries are drawn largely from the more advanced industrial countries. And the managers are interested primarily in hiring docile rather than educated manpower. The managers want above all else a well-subordinated work force. They are prone to hire and retain the kind of workers who will not "talk back," and they will insist upon the right to discharge any persons who question in any way the authority of their superiors. At this stage workers are largely responsible for their own advancement, and as a consequence the working forces consist largely of poorly trained, partially committed, and mostly apathetic workers who have very little incentive to produce efficiently.

As the drive toward industrialism becomes more serious, the state invests more heavily in vocational and technical schools. As an attempt is made to eliminate illiteracy, the younger members of the work force have had at least some formal education. Scientific, engineering, and other technical faculties are added to the universities. The enterprise managers become interested in building stable and loyal rather than merely docile working forces. They want workers who can understand as well as take orders. More determined efforts are made to give workers systematic training on the job. The managers become convinced that a smaller, higher paid, and better directed work force is cheaper than a larger mass of illiterate laborers living on a bare subsistence wage. In this stage of industrialization, workers are advanced as much by their managers and by society as by themselves.

In the more advanced stages of industrialization, all workers have considerable formal education. Vocational schools and technical institutions are extensively developed. The universities are equipped to turn out not only scientists and engineers, but persons with some knowledge of administration and management as well. The enterprise managers concentrate primarily on building efficient working forces. They rely upon more carefully designed incentives to energize the workers; they invest more heavily in selection and development of competent supervision; they institute formal programs for skill training at all levels; and through attitude surveys and other forms of personnel research, they seek to discover the means for motivating men to produce at high efficiency. At this stage, society and the industrial managers are perhaps more responsible for advancement than the workers. As the productivity of workers becomes as important as the productivity of machines, there is widespread recognition of the value of conscious investment in the development of enterprise managers and workers.

In modern times, a newly industrializing society, if it so chooses, may speed up the industrialization process by making the required investments in the advancement of human resources at a comparatively early stage of its development. By studying the course of industrialization in more advanced countries, it can anticipate its requirements for trained manpower. It can purchase the latest equipment and machinery for its factories in the advanced countries. And it can likewise adapt the appropriate parts of educational systems, on-the-job training techniques, and modern methods of manpower management.

The foreign oil companies in the Middle East have demonstrated strikingly the applicability of modern methods of education and management to primitive working groups. They have taught illiterate bedouins to weld pipe and drive trucks in a matter of months, developed all-around craftsmen in a few years, trained numbers of clerical workers and technicians, and promoted local nationals into the lower supervisory positions. Within the past decade, the Egyptians have succeeded in upgrading workers to perform practically all the tasks involved in the operation of oil refineries, textile mills and steel-processing factories, chemical plants, and the Suez Canal. The same holds true for many other newly industrializing countries.

The advancement of the labor force depends, in part, upon where the line is drawn in determining eligibility for positions in the industrial hierarchy. Thus, for example, in the Union of South Africa, most skilled jobs are reserved for whites, and this is conveniently rationalized into a widely held conviction that the blacks do not have the innate capacity for development beyond unskilled or semiskilled labor. In Kenya and Natal, the Indians form a layer of craftsmen and merchants into which the Africans find it difficult to penetrate. In the Belgian Congo there is less of a color bar in occupations within the industrial labor category, but executive positions have been reserved for the experienced and the educated, who are mostly Europeans.

There are, of course, instances where workers may not wish to acquire skills: some tribal customs or taboos discourage individual self-development and in some respects education may even reduce commitment to industrial employment. Knowledge has such a high prestige value that a worker who learns to read and write may get the idea that he is above industrial work and thus seek employment in government or civil service.[9] Unfortunately, the training in the vocational schools in many instances is not specifically related to the more precise requirements of industrial employment, and in some cases, students may be taught things which they must "unlearn" if they are to make good production workers. Thus, formal education can dampen as well as create incentives for future productive employment.

Yet, in the end, the conclusion is valid that the capacity for advancement bears no relationship whatsoever to race, creed, color, or nationality. To be sure, the development of the required attitudes and skills for industrial employment takes time. But even more important than time is the proper emphasis on investments in man consistent with the logic of industrialization.

Maintenance. The final step in building the industrial labor force is the provision for the maintenance of the general welfare and security of its members. Unemployment insurance, accident compensation, old age annuities, and other forms of social security, as well as schemes of sickness benefits, dismissal compensation and pensions, are instruments for the maintenance of working forces. And included also in this category are measures designed to regulate the layoff and discharge of workers. These various measures are important results of various kinds of management-labor-state relationships, and will be discussed in more detail in Chapter 9.

In the very early stages of industrialization neither the state nor the managers make provision for the maintenance of the working forces. The worker is thrown back upon his family if he becomes injured, ill, unemployed, or too old to work. In effect, therefore, the family is his only available system of social security. In Egypt, the father of the family is traditionally cared for in his old age by his sons, and thus it behooves him to have large numbers of children to insure his support. In India, the members of the extended family expect to be supported by the family unit. The family system of "social security," of course, is consistent with and perhaps a cause for the lack of permanent commitment of many workers to industrial employment and to urban life.

As industrialization progresses, however, wider family ties may be broken. Committed workers demand that the state and the enterprise share some responsibility for their maintenance. The scarcity of jobs in industry in relation to the number of persons seeking to get and hold them leads workers to attach tremendous importance to tenure of employment. Their interest centers naturally on rights to jobs, restriction of discharge, control over labor-saving improvements, unemployment compensation, dismissal pay, and other measures designed to promote employee security. In Japan, the forces of tradition and chronic underemployment have induced employers and workers alike to perpetuate a system of life membership for permanent employees in industrial establishments. In newly industrializing countries such as Egypt, Brazil, Chile, Argentina, and Peru, there are networks of laws designed to protect the specific commitment of workers to their establishments and to restrict the freedom of management to discharge or lay off labor which has been engaged beyond a probationary period. Social, legislative, and trade union pressures operate toward the same end in India, France, and Italy. And even the sheiks in the deserts of the Middle East are demanding that the foreign oil companies provide more jobs for Arab labor as well as guarantees of employment for those already in the working forces.

Advanced industrializing societies characteristically have formal programs of accident compensation, sickness benefits, unemployment insurance, and old age pensions for industrial workers. There is general recognition that neither the individual nor his family should assume the major responsibility for the hazards involved in being a permanent member of the industrial working force. The mature industrializing society, in other words, is called upon to maintain persons who cannot work for reasons beyond their control as well as those who are engaged in productive activity. In the logic of industrialization, the responsibility for guaranteeing the minimum welfare and security of industrial man rests in large measure upon his managers and his government. This completes the severance of his dependence, both materially and emotionally, on kinship and family ties.

The transition from family to institutional systems of maintenance can be quite rapid in the newly industrializing countries. These latecomers borrow modern technology, educational methods, and systems of management from the advanced countries. In like manner, as a result of the conventions and resolutions of the ILO and the demonstration effect of highly industrialized societies, they adopt elaborate systems of social security for their industrial working forces. In some cases, however, as in Chile, they move too far and too fast in this direction by instituting measures which are too costly for their stage of development and too difficult for their governments to administer. Indeed, they often are induced to give priority to maintenance before completing the more fundamental processes of recruitment, commitment, and advancement of their human resources. A major explanation for this, as explained in the next section, is the surplus of available labor for industrial employment in many of the newly developing countries.

The Problem of Labor Surpluses

Today, many of the economically underdeveloped countries have rapidly increasing populations, and characteristically they are plagued with an overabundance rather than a scarcity of labor resources. India, Egypt, Indonesia, Pakistan, and Ceylon, for example, have surplus unskilled labor in nearly every sector of their economies. Except in isolated areas, the South American countries appear to have more than enough recruits for industry. The same even holds true in Nigeria which is not overpopulated as a country but which is experiencing large-scale migration from rural to urban areas. Industrial labor redundancy is, or will become, a persistent problem in many of these countries. The major reasons for the abundance of available industrial labor are as follows:

First, industry by itself employs a relatively small number of workers. In countries such as India, Egypt, China, and Indonesia, for example, the proportion of the total labor force employed in the modern industrial sector probably does not exceed 5 per cent, and in the less developed countries it is much lower. Since the compensation of industrial labor is nearly always higher than that in agriculture, handicraft shops, or petty trade, the small numbers of workers needed are easily attracted to the larger factories.

Second, in most of the newly industrializing countries, a population explosion usually precedes rather than follows large-scale industrial development.[10] In modern times economically underdeveloped countries are able to reduce death rates far below birth rates long before any substantial industrialization occurs. India, Egypt, and China are prime examples, and it appears that the same trend may be starting in the presently pre-industrial economies of Africa.

Third, the bulk of industrial growth takes place in urban areas, and large urban populations are likely to build up prior to industrialization in those areas.[11] As a consequence, cities such as Cairo, Bombay, Calcutta, Bagdad, and Lima all have a mass of unemployed or underemployed workers, and similar tendencies in this direction are already evident in Accra, Ibadan, and other growing African cities.

Finally, as industrialization gains momentum, the productivity of factory labor tends to rise sharply, and this limits the expansion of demand for general industrial labor. As the skill levels associated with more modern technology increase, the need for masses of manual and clerical workers declines.

For all these reasons, the development of new industries and modern factories is likely to afford employment for only a fraction of the labor resources which are available. In Egypt, for example, there are large surpluses of unemployed or underemployed agricultural labor located fairly close to most of the factories. In addition, there is a vast and expanding pool of unemployed persons in the major cities. The number of persons entering the labor market each year greatly exceeds any conceivable requirement over the next few decades for new workers in the expanding industrial sector. Yet despite the existence of abundant and cheap labor, the large Egyptian factories continue to introduce new labor-saving machinery and processes wherever possible. If this trend continues in the future, it is likely that industrial production may be doubled in five years with little, if any, corresponding increase in factory employment. In India, the same problem is illustrated by the "rationalization" of the textile and jute mills. India's jute mills in recent years have increased their production and reduced total employment from 300,000 to 220,000 workers.

The large sugar haciendas in Peru have done the same thing. Here in recent years production of sugar and related products has been increasing sharply, while the number of agricultural and factory workers needed on the haciendas continues to decline. In this case the problem is even more serious because the original workers and their families were imported from distant locations and housed in company communities. As the children of these workers have grown up, the labor force has greatly expanded in the face of an ever-shrinking number of available opportunities in the area.

Surplus labor and redundancy is thus a common problem in most of the underdeveloped countries which are still in the early stages of industrial development. This is a problem which industrialization of relatively empty countries such as the United States, Canada, or Australia never faced. How, then, may the industrializing elites cope with the social and economic consequences of the underutilization of human resources?

One means is to make the industrialization process as labor-intensive as possible. Logically, this would suggest relatively heavy reliance on handicraft or cottage industries together with the use of comparatively simple and inexpensive machinery in industrial plants. But for a number of reasons most of the newly industrializing countries are likely to reject this approach in favor of reliance on factories using the most modern technology. Countries such as Egypt, India, and Indonesia cannot be persuaded to invest in antiquated steel mills, fertilizer plants, textile mills, and metal-processing factories. In terms of both quality and long-run costs of production, the modern technology is deemed to be more efficient. And aside from considerations of efficiency, many of the underdeveloped countries are tempted to favor modern factories purely for reasons of prestige. If modern plants are built, of course, measures may be taken to force enterprise managers to use more labor than they need. This can be achieved by restricting discharges and preventing managers from reducing working forces; and legislation in many countries is

purposely designed to induce enterprises to retain surplus labor
in industrial establishments. Logically, it is shortsighted to attempt to reduce redundancy by employing unneeded persons
to do little or no work in modern factories, but this method
has been widely used in industrializing countries with surpluses
of industrial workers.

If the surplus workers cannot be used within the plants, they
then become a charge on the community. Some may find employment in petty trade, in local government services, in construction, or as domestic servants. Here, however, opportunities are
likely to be limited unless incomes and services in the community
are expanding fairly rapidly. As already indicated, however,
the migration of persons from rural to urban areas is likely to
precede rather than follow the expansion of economic opportunities in the cities. In the cities of most underdeveloped
countries one can see masses of unemployed and underemployed
persons crowded into dreadfully inadequate quarters. The
maintenance of such persons on public relief is usually beyond
the means of the community. Quite rightly, therefore, the governments of these countries are alarmed about the social and
political consequences of "storing" unneeded labor in already
overcrowded and overburdened areas.

Another alternative may be to hold the surplus human resources on the land. Theoretically, excess labor may best be kept
in the agricultural areas. But, in many countries, the rural areas
are already overcrowded and there is considerable disguised
unemployment. Indeed, in some countries, it is evident that total
agricultural output could be increased if fewer people were living
on the land and the size of agricultural units was increased.
Thus, surplus labor in the rural areas in most cases is no asset
and in some cases is definitely a liability for increasing agricultural output.

A further alternative is to utilize surplus labor in massive programs of public works. Of all the alternatives, this offers perhaps
the most promising method of soaking up surplus human resources. The community development projects in India have utilized labor on a limited scale in the villages for building schools,
digging irrigation canals, and improving roads. The mainland
Chinese have gone further by mobilizing masses of people for

work on dams, roads, irrigation systems, and other large construction projects in all parts of the country. The employment of labor on public works, however, requires a considerable amount of capital and a great deal of organization, requiring in many cases the diversion of scarce financial resources and high level manpower from other development projects.

Clearly, therefore, industrialization by itself is not likely soon to solve the problem of surplus labor in most of today's underdeveloped countries. The superabundance of labor is a consequence of overpopulation. In most underdeveloped countries death rates are falling while birth rates remain high. Birth rates may decline if standards of living can be raised substantially, but increases in the standard of living require greatly increased levels of capital formation and investment over long periods of time. If raising the standard of living is a prerequisite for reducing the birth rate, therefore, the problem of surplus population and surplus labor is likely to persist for many years in most of the underdeveloped countries. Industrializing elites will resort to the range of policies outlined above to ameliorate or control unemployment.

Some Common Themes of Labor Force Development

In practically all countries, human resources are available for industrialization. In sparsely populated areas or countries, requirements may be fulfilled initially by the movement of people to the industrial areas and by immigration. As these people become settled, they tend to generate in a few decades sufficient new manpower to meet the needs of expanding industry. In densely populated areas or countries — which is characteristic today of many of the underdeveloped countries — there is already a superabundance of human resources for industrial development, and the problem is clearly one of coping with a general redundancy rather than with a scarcity of labor. In nearly all countries, of course, skilled labor and most kinds of high-level manpower are in critical short supply. But this does not stem from a general shortage of human resources. It is an indication that insufficient effort and investment have been made in the recruitment, commitment, and advancement of particular kinds of human resources. Many underdeveloped countries today have a twofold problem. They are faced with a general surplus of labor as a consequence of the growing pressure of population, and at the same time they suffer from a shortage of skills and highly trained personnel because of the underdevelopment of institutions for the effective advancement of manpower.

It may be argued that the more rapid the process of industrialization, the more painful it is likely to be. Certainly, rapid industrial development normally requires high rates of savings which must be achieved in most cases largely by holding down levels of consumption. If people must be uprooted from rural backgrounds, a rapid transition under some circumstances may result in greater stress and tension than a slow one. And, if compulsory measures are to be used to recruit workers, the adjustment can be extremely painful. In addition, poor living conditions, ineffective upgrading, and arbitrary use of managerial authority may add to the strains of workers entering the industrial labor force. Any kind of shift from one culture to another is apt to cause distress and dissatisfaction, and the problems of adjustment in some cases may well be aggravated by rapid change.

On the other hand, there is also reason to believe that in modern times rapid industrialization may be less painful in some respects than gradual industrialization. In overpopulated countries with disguised unemployment on the land and overcrowded conditions in the urban areas, rapid industrialization coupled with rapid development in other sectors of the economy may alleviate the miseries of unemployment. In modern times, moreover, the managers of enterprises may use enlightened measures to recruit, commit, and advance workers. Education, in itself, may make the transition easier. Indeed, education raises the expectations of people, makes them less satisfied with traditional ways of life, and thus creates a desire for almost immediate change to the industrial way of life. At the same time, of course, there is the possibility that failure to realize these expectations may accentuate the transition difficulties. The central problem in too many countries already is too many people with too high expectations.

The underlying problem in the transition from a traditional to an industrial society is not the adaptability of man. His capacity and eagerness for change is infinitely greater than is commonly recognized. The more fundamental factor is the suitability and adaptability of institutions. The transition from the old to the new order can be managed well or managed poorly. Newly industrializing societies need not repeat the mistakes made by the presently advanced countries. Population pressures, which are building up now in advance of economic growth, put industrialization in a new and different light. The underdeveloped countries do not by tradition resist industrialization but instead seek to achieve it. In so far as the development of industrial working forces is concerned, a speedy rather than a gradual transition may well turn out to be less painful and most acceptable for most of the peoples of the modern world.

The Diversity of the Industrializing Elites

The common problems of development of the industrial working forces have been set forth above, and the general approaches associated with the various stages of industrialization have been suggested. Within limits, however, the various ideal types of industrializing elites may be inclined to emphasize different tactics in effecting labor force development. These may now be traced briefly.

The dynastic elite is likely to rely as long as possible on recruitment of labor through family and tribal connections; it will likewise favor docile and loyal employees rather than necessarily the most productive workers. The dynastic elite holds in high esteem paternalistic devices to tie the worker to the enterprise, and at the same time it expects the manager to assume responsibility for the well-being of his dependent workers. Unless under pressure, it is the least concerned with skill development, and it shows comparatively little interest in general education for the masses. At the same time, it is most likely to tolerate a slow pace of work so long as labor remains loyal. The dynastic elite is most likely to place the obligation of maintenance of workers on the paternalistic manager. The manager, moreover, is expected to provide jobs for all permanent members of the working force, but is not to concern himself with employment problems beyond the factory gates or with jobs for the temporary work force.

The middle class is more likely to rely on the labor market

for workers. It is more interested in productive than in loyal workers. It assumes that there will always be a relatively large supply of workers committed to industrial employment who will be seeking jobs in the labor market. For this reason, the middle class is not so much concerned as the dynastic elite with paternalistic measures to tie workers to a particular establishment, although it may favor limited private benefit plans. The middle class tends to emphasize skill development within the plant, and supports the idea of public responsibility for general education of the masses. It relies on incentives of various kinds to quicken the pace of work and to increase productivity. At the same time, this type of society thinks that self-reliant workers should be responsible for their own maintenance, with a minimum of assistance by the community, and thus it accepts somewhat reluctantly government social security measures. The middle class assumes no direct managerial responsibility for unemployment, since it argues that a free market and a free economy can be relied upon to provide jobs in the long run. Indeed, it accepts some unemployment as both normal and necessary in a market economy, although it may advocate limited programs of accident insurance, unemployment compensation, and old age pensions.

The revolutionary intellectuals are likely to direct the flow of labor to priority employment, using both compulsion and positive incentives. They are also more likely to favor recruitment of women for industrial as well as for agricultural work. They get commitment of workers by ideological appeals, direction of employment, and differential incentives. The revolutionary intellectuals stress training on the job, and give high priority to education, particularly along vocational lines. At the same time, pressure is put on workers to be productive through compulsion, ideological indoctrination, and payment by results. In the totalitarian regime, the revolutionary intellectuals favor broad systems of social security, usually administered by the state and by labor organizations. Finally, they either refuse to admit the existence of unemployment, or mobilize a redundant labor force on labor intensive projects such as road building, irrigation ditches, dams, and other large-scale public works.

The colonial administrators, like the dynastic elite, are more likely to favor docile workers. At the early stages they may resort to forced labor of one kind of another, and they often rely heavily on tribal and family recruitment. For the managerial and high level positions, they usually bring in nationals of the home country. They often use paternalistic measures to get skilled workers committed to an industrial work force, but they are of all the elites the least interested in getting permanent commitment of unskilled and semiskilled labor. The colonial administrators are apt to provide only a minimum of training on the job, and show relatively little interest in general education. They are prone to accept as unavoidable a slow pace of work. For the most part, the colonial administrators are opposed to government-sponsored social security measures, since they rely upon the native economy, through tribal, village, or family organizations, to maintain those who for one reason or another are displaced from industry.

The nationalist leaders, in their drive to press rapid industrialization, may use any and all means of labor recruitment. And they will resort to nationalist appeals, differential incentives, and even direction of employment to build a committed labor force. They are interested also in a highly productive labor force, and they emphasize skill development within the enterprise and press for rapid expansion of general and vocational education. All these things they do in a hurried and often spotty manner. They are also prone to introduce at an early stage ambitious social security schemes patterned after those in the very advanced industrializing societies. Finally, the nationalist leaders see in industrialization a solution to problems of unemployment and expanding population, and for this reason they may attempt to overburden the new factories with surplus labor and resort to other questionable measures for maximizing employment.

The dynastic elite and the colonial administrators are most likely to favor those approaches which are characteristic of the early stages of industrialization. For this reason, they usually tend to retard rather than to accelerate the effective development of industrial working forces in accordance with the logic of industrialization. The revolutionary intellectuals are likely to adopt earlier those measures which are consistent with rapid industrialization. The middle class uses the market and those measures which are most consistent with gradual rather than rapid transformation. And the nationalist leaders may adopt almost any approach which economic and political pressures are likely to dictate. The approaches likely to be emphasized by these ideal types of elites are summarized in Chart 5.

As the industrial labor force is developed, there is latent protest against the harshness of the rule-making processes inherent in industrialization. Some protest is by individual workers, but more often protest is expressed through labor organizations. The next chapter is concerned with this aspect of the relations between the managers and managed.

CHART 5.

Diverse emphases in building the industrial working forces.

Industrial-izing Elite	Dynastic	Middle-Class	Revolutionary-Intellectuals	Colonial Administrators	Nationalist Leaders
Recruit-ment	Relies for longest period on family or tribal recruitment. Insists on hiring docile workers.	Relies on the labor market. More interested in productivity of labor than in its loyalty.	Direct flow of labor to priority employment by both compulsion and positive incentives.	Try to recruit docile workers. Occasional use of forced labor. Rely on family or tribal recruitment.	Use all means of recruitment to speed industrial development. Inclined to develop mechanisms for central direction of recruitment.
Commit-ment	Relies on paternalistic devices (housing, company communities, etc.) to command the loyalty of working forces.	Assumes large supply of generally committed workers. Sometimes develops enterprise pension and welfare plans.	Use combination of ideological appeal, direction of employment, and differential incentives to get effective commitment.	Sometimes use paternalistic devices to tie workers to the enterprise. Least interested in permanent commitment, particularly of unskilled and semi-skilled labor.	Use combinations of nationalist appeal, differential incentives, and occasionally direction of employment.
Advance-ment	Least concerned with skill development and with general educational policy -- accepts slow pace of work.	Provides extensive training or the job. Supports idea of public responsibility for general and vocational education. Uses incentives to motivate workers.	Emphasize training on job, and also vocational training in schools. Encourage workers to be productive through ideological education, differential rewards, and compulsion.	Some emphasis on training within the enterprise; little interest in general education. Put ceilings on levels of jobs for which "natives" are trained. More interested in control than in productivity.	Emphasize training within the enterprise, and rapid expansion of general and vocational education. Interested in increasing productivity of workers and pace of work.

CHART 5. (continued)

Industrializing Elite	Dynastic	Middle-Class	Revolutionary-Intellectuals	Colonial Administrators	Nationalist Leaders
Maintenance	Requires enterprises to accept obligation to maintain permanent workers for life as they remain loyal. Takes no responsibility for temporary workers.	Tends to disregard problem of maintenance, or develops enterprise benefits schemes. Reluctant acceptance of government social security.	Establish formal systems of social security, administered by the state and controlled labor organizations.	Either disregard problem, or follow policy similar to dynastic elite. Depend upon tribes or villages as the traditional social security mechanism.	Attempt to introduce social security systems similar to those in advanced countries.
Unemployment	Accepts obligation to maintain employment for those with jobs. Less interest in providing or creating jobs.	Accepts little responsibility for redundancy. Assumes that free market will in long run provide jobs. Considers some degree of unemployment as normal and necessary, and advocates limited social security measures.	Either refuse to admit existence of unemployment, or mobilize entire work force on labor-intensive projects such as road-building, irrigation projects, and other forms of public works.	Little concerned with problems of unemployment or with creation of jobs for the natives.	See in industrialization a "solution" to problems of unemployment and surplus population. May overburden factories with surplus labor.

CHAPTER 8

THE WORKERS: IMPACT AND RESPONSE

Industrialization characteristically redesigns and reshapes its human raw materials, whatever the source. It transforms urban
populations of old commercial cities; it transplants peasants,
farmers, and tribal groups to mines, factories, and offices, and
it imports labor into empty regions and countries. The development of an industrial work force necessarily involves the destruction of old ways of life and work and the acceptance of the new
imperatives of the industrial work place and work community.
The drastic changes in human beings and their relationships
required to achieve a settled industrial work force have been
made only with significant reactions from the workers-in-process.
While the work force has in the end been malleable, the metamorphosis has ordinarily involved considerable stress and tension
and even violence.

The impact of industrialization on the work force and its
response has been a persistent theme since the early days of the
classic British case which so concerned economists, social historians, legislative investigators, novelists, and reformers. The
following excerpts refer to the early British experience:

A new sense of time was one of the outstanding psychological features
of the industrial revolution. . . .[1] The discipline of the early factories
was like the discipline of a prison. Small children were often cruelly
treated to keep them awake during the long hours, which shortened
their lives or undermined their health. . . .[2] But to all the evils from
which the domestic worker had suffered, the Industrial Revolution
added discipline, and the discipline of a power driven by a competition
that seemed as inhuman as the machine that thundered in factory and
shed. . . . if he broke one of a long series of minute regulations he was
fined. . . .[3] All I wish to prove is that the discovery and use of machinery
may be . . . injurious to the labouring class, as some of their numbers
will be thrown out of employment. . . .[4] The operative is condemned

to let his physical and mental powers decay in this utter monotony, it is his mission to be bored every day and all day long from his eighth year.[5]

The work force in process of industrialization is not entirely passive or inert and responds in a variety of ways to the impacts of the new civilization. A few references also from the early British experience are illustrative:

There were others who — whether from inertia, conservatism, or an understandable wish to control their own lives — refused to conform to the new order. . . .[6] There is actual evidence of the rise of one of the oldest of the existing Trade Unions out of a gathering of journeymen to take a social pint of porter together. More often it is a tumultous strike, out of which grows a permanent organization. Elsewhere . . . the workers meet to petition the House of Commons, and reassemble from time to time to carry on their agitation for the enactment of some new regulation, or the enforcement of an existing law. In other instances we shall find the journeymen of a particular trade frequenting certain public-houses, at which they hear of situations vacant, and the "house of call" becomes thus the nucleus of an organization. . . .[7] The frame-breakers called themselves Luddites, and signed their proclamations Ned Ludd, sometimes adding Sherwood Forest. The original Ned Ludd . . . was a boy apprenticed to learn frame-work knitting. . . . Being averse to confinement or work, he refused to exert himself, whereupon his master complained to a magistrate, who ordered a whipping. Ned in answer took a hammer and demolished the hated frame.[8]

The response of the new workers may be a suppressed withdrawal of effort or overt action by isolated individuals or groups, and concerted action may be a temporary flurry or involve continuing organization. The total of these negative reactions and responses to the impact of industrialization on the work force is drawn together under the term "worker protest."

The Secular Decline of Protest

Continuing industrialization and its spread throughout the world might suggest that worker protest was on the increase. But the dominant fact about protest is its secular decline.

The significance of protest has declined primarily on account

of the greater positive attractions of industrialization, despite the
dislocations and readjustments for emerging workers. Industrialization has become a prime objective of nationalist movements and political parties; it is requisite to national survival.
The potential benefits to the individual worker everywhere appear to transcend the negative consequences of industrialization.
This is not a moral judgment, but a description of the dominance
of the demands for modern goods: clothing, transport, movies,
education, health, and so on. The dislocations of industrialization appear less onerous in comparison to its potentialities for real
income. Moreover, the rewards to industrial workers in the
earlier stages are often substantially greater than for other producer groups; the industrial workers are often a preferred group.

A century ago the range of alternatives for the organization
of society that appealed to new industrial workers as means to
confront rising industrialization were very great. These included
the programs of the anarchists, utopians, communal groups designed to escape the wages system, producer cooperatives, the
socialists, and others. A century of experience has narrowed
the practical alternatives. The level of protest has declined, since
programs to escape, to avoid, or to overthrow the industrial
order have lost any appeal. The choices for workers are seen to be
more limited: how to accommodate, to participate in the industrial order, and to share in the gains. Experience has tempered
visionary aspirations, sobered expectations, thereby constrained
worker protest.

Governments in newly industrializing countries have copied
advanced labor standards, such as many standards of the ILO
which have been adopted in legislation or are recognized as
desirable norms. Some larger-scale enterprises and their managers
have adopted modern personnel practices. Industrialization has
in several cases been less harsh than a century ago, but where it
has been raw and cruel the instruments of control or even re-
pression over the work force by management or government have
been more efficient and have constrained most of the outward
signs of protest. Industrializing elites and enterprise managers
have more experience on which to rely and are more skilled in
the control of protest.

The secular decline in the outward signs of protest does

not mean that the reactions of workers to the constraints, frustrations, and readjustments of industrialization have disappeared. The manifestations of protest operate beneath the surface in new factories and industrial communities, erupting at times into violence, riots, demonstrations, and passive resistance when the pressures can no longer be contained or when they are ignited by national crises. Moreover, in the course of an industrialization the forms of group protest become more disciplined and tend to be more prolonged. There are fewer spontaneous outbursts, chance disturbances, and impulsive melees. The forms of group protest are better organized, with formal leadership, conscious tactics and strategies.

In industrializing societies there is keen sensitivity to the importance of the power to control, to organize and to select the targets for latent protest when it erupts. Among the contenders for power to control and direct latent protest are managements, labor organizations, political parties, and nationalist movements. The resort to strikes and riots in the independence movements in India and Indonesia illustrates the control and manipulation of tensions and frustrations of workers by a nationalist movement. A disturbance or violence in a foreign-owned plant may be part of the same pattern. The general strikes and demonstrations in Egypt in 1954 in support of Nasser and against Naguib and in 1956 in support of the government's position in the Suez crisis illustrate the manipulation of protest for wider political purposes. The Peronista strikes in Argentina were of the same sort. "Often the protest tends to become generalized, starting as a demonstration against a decision of the employers or the Administration and ending as a protest against the Administration proper. In the Conakry strike of September-November 1953, for example, the union leaders asked all Africans to avoid the Armistice Day ceremonies and festivities, a request that was remarkably effective."[9] But instances of spontaneous outbreaks, small group violence, wildcat strikes, and emotional mob action may persist into the more advanced stages of industrialization in some communities and under special provocation, or they may on occasion break through strong repressive measures, as in the case of a coal stoppage in Spain or Yugoslavia.

The present chapter considers in turn the universal impact of industrialization on workers, the universal response of workers, the diverse characteristics of protest arising from different policies of the various elites and their different speeds of industrialization, and the diverse response of workers including different forms of labor organizations.

Universal Impact of Industrialization on the Labor Force

The industrialization process has certain uniformities in its impact on the labor force. These universals are operative at the immediate work place, in the community and home, and in the larger national community. The following points explore briefly some of the more significant common consequences of industrial growth in shaping the responses of workers.

Destruction of Old Trades and Creation of New Skills. The skilled occupations of agrarian or traditional societies are typically broken down into a series of operations, often performed largely by semiskilled workers. The experience of the cordwainers, tailors, and the skilled trades in glass-making are classic illustrations. Generally the old skills facilitate the learning of new jobs, while on occasion the old habits are an impediment:

The problem of security arises especially with the loss of skills involved in the shifting of handicraft workers into the factory. . . . little effort has been made in recruitment and initial placement to utilize these skills already developed in the pre industrial economy . . . it may be guessed that this circumstance has led to considerable frustration and loss of confidence on the part of the worker. . . .[10] To begin with, these are people whose skills relate to old technologies or demands, and who cannot adjust to changing conditions. . . . Since each of us is likely to suffer from change, in our capacity as producers, economic growth makes as many enemies as friends.[11]

The industrial order requires many new skills and everchanging skills. The industrializing society has a chronic shortage of skilled labor, at least a relative scarcity. The levels of skill are gradually rising. The inducements to acquire new skills and the methods of training new workers or upgrading the existing work force were shown in Chapter 7 to be central problems of industrializing societies. The ever-changing demands for skill — abandoning traditional occupations and creating higher-skilled and more specialized workers — constitute a universal impact on the labor force. The uncertainty and real cost of these changes, particularly for older workers, is a source of tension.

The Web of Rules. There is a popular image of primitive society pervaded by customs, rites, and rituals for securing a livelihood at the workaday world of agriculture and in the household arts which is sharply contrasted with the *laissez faire* of modern society. But industrializing societies at the work place and work community are in fact characterized by a vast network of detailed rules, regulations, and norms. The highly complex and interdependent technology and scale of modern industry with its endless contingencies cannot function without rules prescribing conduct and expected performance for managers and the managed. The web of rules is a universal of industrialization, and the content of many rules at the work place is closely related to technology and market or budget restraints, and accordingly, many rules are similar in different countries, despite wide differences in political and economic institutions. Thus, many of the same rules operate in a technologically comparable textile mill, railroad, construction site or coal mine regardless of the country, economic system, or legal form of the rules.

The complexity of the rules in early New England textile towns has been described as follows: "The factory and boardinghouse regulations were innumerable, and covered every smallest corner of the operatives' lives. . . . The operatives were told when, where, how, and how much they must work; when and where they were to eat and sleep. They were ordered to attend church, for which they had to pay pew rent. They were discharged for immoral conduct, for bad language, for disrespect, for attending dancing classes, or for any cause that the agent or overseers thought sufficient."[12] The factory system was depicted by Engels in these terms: "Here ends all freedom in law and fact. The operative must be in the mill at half-past five in the morning: if he comes a couple of minutes too late, he is fined; if he comes ten minutes too late, he is not let in until breakfast is over, and a quarter of the day's wages is withheld, though he loses only two and one-half hours' work out of twelve."[13]

The web of rules becomes more explicit and formally constituted in the course of industrialization. At the very early stages, the very notion of a rule may be alien, and individual incidents are confronted without regard to their more general implications. The continuing experience of the same work place, the growth in its size, the same workers, and the emergence of managerial staff tend to result in customs and traditions which begin to codify past practices. Eventually these may be reduced to writing in general form. Some rules may later emerge which anticipate problems rather than merely summarize past decisions. The statement of the rule then becomes more formal and elegant, particularly as specialists are developed in rule-making and administration. The process of industrialization thus brings more and more detailed rules and a larger body of explicit rules. Industrialization proliferates rules. A few rules become many, simple rules become complex, and a small document expands. Changing technology and markets produce new situations, higher compensation takes new forms; organizations of workers and managers develop new interests; a general rule invites loopholes and exceptions. The imagination of workers and managers, and the talents of their professionals in emerging organizations of increasing size, help to create the growing complex of rules. While there may be periodic codification and simplification, the dominant tendency is toward a larger complex of rules.

The two most significant groups of rules in their impact upon an emerging industrial work force are those relating to discipline and to the pace or tempo of work operations. Chapter 7 noted that all managers require a subordinated work force, that is, one that recognizes the authority of management, is reliably responsive to its orders and directions, is malleable in accordance with a system of rewards and punishments, or in a word is a disciplined work force. It was also observed that as industrialization proceeds, all types of managers become increasingly concerned beyond subordination with the efficiency, skill, and pace of the work force. The quality of the work force is often related to the rules of discipline, since below-standard performance is subject to penalties.

Levasseur observed of employers and workers in the United States in the 1890's: "As an employer he expects his men to work, and he rids himself without hesitation of those who are unsatisfactory in this particular; as a workman he is exacting in many respects, but realizes that he should work hard during working-hours. . . ."[14] In reference to Meiji Japan, "Two supplements to *Shokko Jijyo* give details of these brutal punishments, which were meted out not only to runaways but also to girls whose work was not up to required standards of efficiency. . . ."[15] "An extreme type of labor indiscipline is illustrated by physical assaults on managerial staff by workers. In eight months during 1946, for example, 75 assaults were reported in Bombay cotton textile mills, on managers and other higher staff, clerks and timekeepers."[16]

Discipline and pace are not only embodied in a complex of formal rules of the work place, but industrializing societies also develop a set of values or an ideology to reinforce these rules from within managers and the managed. "In Western civilization, work, whether seen as curse or as blessing, has always stood at the center of moral consciousness."[17] The detailed rules on discipline and pace may be reinforced by the protestant ethic, the communist ideal or dedication to a nationalist mission, but some moral sanction underlies the rules of the work place on discipline and pace in each industrializing society. "Do you imagine that sloth will afford you more comfort than Labour? No, for as Poor Richard says, trouble springs from idleness, and grievous toil from needless Ease . . . " "The prospect before us," said Nehru, "is work, hard labor. This generation is sentenced to hard labor . . . ."[18] "The main religion of new China is work. Only through hard work can a good Communist reach his paradise."[19] Even though industrialization is an affirmative good for workers in economically underdeveloped areas today, the universal impact of the rules, in particular relating to discipline and pace, is so potentially disruptive in the first instance that a basis for these rules is always sought in an ethic, national ideal, or ideology.

The Industrial Community. While the city antedates industrial activity, the process of industrialization creates new towns and cities and transforms older metropolitan areas. The new life at the work place is associated with a new life in the family and in the community. The urbanization process has a variety of impacts on the emerging industrial community. The urban slums are a symptom of a society in transition toward industrialism as any tourist in Bombay, Osaka, Kirkuk, or Brazzaville can report.

Capital cities in industrializing countries reflect the same features even more vividly as rural population flocks to old capi-
tals. The worker is uprooted from the larger family and the village. The immediate family, at least for a period, has been left in
the village. These dislocations are accompanied frequently with a
new position and status for women, many of whom may also
come to be wage workers in factories or service employment. New
relationships based upon employment or occupation come to replace the larger family and village attachments. New methods
of communication among city dwellers — newspapers and radio
— replace those of the village. The security and loyalty of the extended family disintegrate and in their place is imposed the government of the city and nationalist state. The impersonal regulations of the city replace the more personal relations and customs of the village. The simple response to the immediate need,
to nature, and to impulse in the village gives way to the variety,
perplexity, and indecision of the industrial community. These
transformations to the industrial community are inevitably associated with new frustrations, confusion, complexity, and resentments.

The new industrial towns in the early nineteenth century in
Great Britain have been described as follows: "They were not
so much towns as barracks: not the refuge of a civilization but the
barracks of an industry. . . . They were settlements of great masses
of people collected in a particular place because their fingers or
their muscles were needed on the brink of a stream here or at
the mouth of a furnace there. . . ."[20] In the contemporary world,
"It is not the noise or soot in the city which corrodes the nerve
of the worker. . . . but rather the 'absence of neighborhood' —
the anonymity and impersonality of life in a big city. These factors go far to explain the high absentee rate, the high rate of
turnover, and the low standard of performance of many industrial
workers in underdeveloped countries."[21]

The industrializing cities are comprised of populations with
great diversity in their development. They magnify contrasts.
There are rich and poor, the employed and the unemployed, the
settled city dweller and the newcomer, racial, language and
tribal mixtures, the isolated individual and the established system,
the literate and the illiterate. The city shows the mass of have-

nots what they might have. The diversity and contrasts of the industrializing city excite discontent and stimulate unrest and reform. The urban community breeds and distributes new ideas which undermine traditional values. The constraints and authority of established religion is weakened, and the eternal battle between the generations is sharpened as contrasts and frictions between father and son are magnified. The city rather than the countryside, peasant rebellions being the exception, has been the locus of revolt even prior to industrialization. "In the rise and fall of societies, the urban mob has always played its part, impelled partly by instinct, and partly by instigation."[22]

The emphasis upon the destruction of old trades and the creation of new skills, the impact of the web of rules including those relating to discipline and pace, and the turmoil of the emerging industrial community is not intended to detail the full range of the universal impacts of industrialization on the labor force. There are effects upon health, literacy and education, and standards of living. But the features of the impact of industrialization here stressed are those decisive to the responses of the labor force which constitute worker protest.

Universal Responses of Workers

The wrenching from the old and the groping for the new in the industrializing community create a variety of frustrations, fears, uncertainties, resentments, aggressions, pressures, new threats and risks, new problems, demands and expectations upon workers-in-process, their families and work groups. The emerging industrial work community, locality, or nation is no less in ferment. This is not to say that the industrializing community is in constant revolt or always in overt conflict. On the contrary, the surface may be quiet by virtue of strong controls, dedication to a national dream or an ideology, a sense of futility or resignation or on account of hopes spurred by small tangible evidences of improvements. But beneath the exterior is always latent protest, seething and simmering, to erupt in violence or to overflow in indolence in times of crisis or tension.

One of the classic analyses of labor protest, that of the Wheatland, California, riots of 1913, states: "Resistance by the worker to an employer's labor policy takes one of two forms: either an open and formal revolt such as a strike; or an instinctive and often unconscious exercise of the 'strike in detail' — simply drifting off the job."[23] The distinction between the spontaneous responses of individual workers or small groups and the planned and coordinated reactions of workers, particularly in large-scale organizations, continues to be insightful.

Individual or Small Group Responses. The response of workers to industrialization typically reflects the extent of their attachment or the stage of their commitment (see Chapter 7) to the industrial work place and community. Recruits to industrial employment secured by labor contractors, the attraction of factory jobs or a push off the land and the recent arrivals in urban areas in the early stages of industrialization all reflect a high degree of absenteeism in industrial employment. Thus, 71 per cent of Bombay textile workers in 1953–1954 visited their villages at least once a year. They went to escape the city and factory routine, on account of homesickness, to visit kinfolk, for religious festivals, to help with the harvest, and to attend to personal business.[24] It is probably impossible to separate in these high rates of absenteeism the relative roles of the dissatisfaction and frustrations arising from the new industrial and urban work place from the ties to the old village and extended family. The high absenteeism of the uncommitted and the semicommitted worker often reflects both a form of individual protest against the impact of industrialization as well as attraction to the pre-industrial society. The accommodation to the new work place and work community is evidenced by a significant drop in absentee rates as industrialization proceeds, although wide differences may remain among industries and types of workers.

The "strike in detail" may take the form of turnover rather than irregular attendance of one job. Turnover is apt to be lower where there is a substantial labor surplus relative to available jobs and where enterprises are more lenient with absenteeism, as in India. Turnover rates tend to be higher, depending upon whether recruitment involves single workers or married workers, whether it involves a transfer of residence for workers-in-process from their villages and whether it envisages temporary periods of industrial work or a permanent commitment to urban and industrial life.

"High labor turnover is. . . . endemic wherever modern economic enterprise relies on the native social structure to provide the worker's security, or has at least not offered sufficient inducement to capture the worker's whole loyalty."[25]

The "strike in detail" also takes the form of withdrawal of effort on the job and a lack of attention, application, cooperation, and morale compared to workers in more advanced industrial communities. It may take more violent expression in fighting, spontaneous flare-ups, and work stoppage by small groups, machine or parts breakage, and even sabotage to the production process. The chafing of the rules of discipline and pace, the lack of industrial experience, the absence of motivations geared to the industrial community and poor physical health may combine to produce lethargy, poor workmanship, indiscipline, theft, vice, and violence. "Indeed opium smoking, the use of other narcotics, and alcoholism are commonly associated with the worker's sense of frustration and dissatisfaction."[26] The outward forms of indiscipline tend to disappear as the work force becomes fully committed to industrialization, but morale and its effects upon productivity and output remain a major problem even in advanced industrial communities.[27] The large gap between the potential and the actual performance of workers in modern industry is the basis for continuing experiments in many countries with incentive methods of payments and worker participation in management processes at various levels of responsibility from the managing directors to the first level of supervision.

Organized Responses. The responses of workers to industrialization are not confined to isolated individual or spontaneous small group reactions; they are congealed into informal group activities and into the programs of complex organizations. The responses of industrial workers tend to become formally organized, although the process, speed, forms, and programmes of these organizations may vary widely among societies and although these organizations may in time develop functions remote from their origins in protest. Moreover, in industrializing societies the control over protest is critical to the industrialization process and to the dominant elite. In industrializing communities groups of workers have strategic economic power to affect vital production in the short period and the rate of economic development over the long term. Industrial workers and their organizations are further a key element and concern in the political processes of any industrializing nation. Industrial workers constitute an urban group; they are relatively better off and more literate than villagers; and they may seek to transfer strategic economic power into the political arena. Thus, the organizations of industrial workers are of decisive concern to every industrializing elite, and in a community with competing elements seeking to control and to shape the industrialization process, workers' organizations come to be the subject of keen competition for dominance and for alliances.

The following account describes the evolution of labor organizations over the course of a decade in the Northern Rhodesian copper mines:

As a result of the recommendations by the Foster Commission the system of consultation between the mine managements and African tribal elders, established at some of the mines prior to 1940, was developed in 1942 and 1943 into a general system of Tribal Representatives. In 1943 "Boss Boys' Committees" were formed at individual mines. The Tribal Representative system continued to deal with domestic matters, living conditions, etc., exclusive of industrial matters, until it was terminated in 1953. In 1947 and 1948, from the "Boss Boys' Committees" were evolved "Works Committees" representative of African workers in all departments, and during the year 1948 those committees were finally replaced by four African Mineworkers' Unions established at the four major mines with the assistance of a Labour Officer with trade union experience. In May 1949, those four separate Unions were amalgamated to form the Northern Rhodesian Africa Mineworkers' Trade Union. . . .[28]

This experience illustrates both the waning influence of the traditional society in the form of the tribal representatives and the gradual adoption of the organizational form of labor unions from Western industrial societies.

The response of organization among industrial workers is associated with the development of an explicit and distinctive ideology defining the role of workers in industrialization and the relations of their organizations to the rest of the society in transition. A number of ideologies may be identified. The Marxian ideas

(Chapter 1) have afforded the most widely influential body of doctrine in its pristine form or in various revisions and versions ranging from revolutionist to mildly reformist among organizations of industrial workers. The labor organization in the orthodox Marxian view is subservient to the guiding direction of the Communist party. "The spontaneous labor movement is able to create (and inevitably will create) only trade unionism. . . ."[29] At the other extreme of the socialist spectrum has been the Fabian program of reform in Great Britain or social democracy in Scandinavia. A competing body of ideas is represented by the Papal encyclicals as developed by Catholic labor organizations, particularly in France, Italy, and the Netherlands. The body of ideas developed by Gompers and the American Federation of Labor after the rejection of socialization of the means of production in the 1890's is distinctive to the industrial scene of the United States. The ideas of a dominant dynastic elite as in Spain were reflected in their labor organizations. In the newly industrializing countries the nationalist ideas have pervaded the emerging labor movements.

The response of workers in groups also consists of various forms of spontaneous and ordered conflict. There is a tendency for industrial conflict at the early stages of industrialization to consist of short-lived incidents and to involve fights, riots, demonstrations, directed action, violence, and mob action. As organizations of workers develop, the forms of conflict tend to become more disciplined and of longer duration. At the early stages the provocation for conflict, or the center of protest, as frequently concerns complaints in the community as at the work places. Issues of transportation, housing, return to the village and extended family, and racial, nationalist, and religious diversity within the work force, and protests against the racial and nationalist character of supervision tend to ignite and precipitate conflict.

In a major work stoppage in Basrah, Iraq, in December 1953, for instance, the initial demands of oil workers included a requirement for the company to provide a school, transport for shopping, and a dispensary for workers compelled to live in company houses in Zubair, and to cease discharges on unsupported complaints of American engineers.[30] In Qatar the following are among the incidents reported in 1955: A deputation purporting to represent all Qatari mooring launch crews at Umm Said demanded the removal of a mooring master. A two-day strike developed over the dislike of two Pakistani traffic clerks; in the strike, roaming gangs at Dukhan and Umm Said took very threatening attitudes. Forty employees from Umm Bab camp commandeered two trucks and drove to Dukhan for lunch (thereby missing most of their afternoon's work) on the grounds that they had been served cauliflower on the previous day which they did not like. The May 1958 strike at Jamshedpar, India, has been described as follows: "The ensuing week of violence saw police firings, mob destruction of property, looting, arson, prohibition of all meetings, scores of arrests, and the imposition of a curfew, and the movement of federal troops into the city. . . ."[31] These recent episodes from newly industrializing communities have their counterparts in the earlier history of the United States and other more advanced industrial countries: the looting and riots in July 1877 which destroyed the Pittsburgh round house and shops of the Pennsylvania railroad and killed scores; the Molly Maguires in mining communities; the bitter and violent strikes in mining at Broken Hill, Australia, in 1892 and 1909; the Swedish general strike of 1909; and the clashes and violence in Italy in the first decade of this century.

In the course of economic development a sharper division tends to arise in the issues of industrial conflict between the work place and the larger community. The forms of organized protest tend to divide between those directed toward enterprise management and the industry and those directed toward the community and political authority.

The following list summarizes the forms of protest which are characteristically related to the stages of commitment of workers to the industrial work place and urban industrial community. Just as the process of commitment is a gradual process and a continuum, so is the transformation of the forms of worker protest. The dominant forms of protest are largely individual and small group responses for uncommitted and semicommitted workers, while they are largely organized responses for committed and specifically committed workers. Some forms of individual protest and informal group actions continue to be evident among some committed workers.

Stage of Commitment	Characteristic Forms of Protest
Uncommitted workers	Turnover Absenteeism Fighting Theft and sabotage
Semicommitted workers	Spontaneous stoppages Demonstrations and guerilla strikes
Committed workers	Plant and industry strikes Political protests and activity
Specifically committed workers	Grievance machinery, labor courts, and disputes settlement machinery largely without stoppages Political party and organizational alliances

The Natural History of Protest

The course of worker protest during the transition to the industrial society has been a persistent problem in the analysis of capitalism and industrialization. Marx saw the intensity of protest and discontent rising as capitalist production expanded, as skills were destroyed, with falling rates of profit and increased misery of the working class and increasingly severe crises until protest reached the crescendo of the revolution under the communists. The reconstituted society would eliminate the bases for protest; the classless communist society would confront no worker protest problem (Chapter 1). The view that worker protest increases in the course of industrialization under capitalist direction was also held by Veblen and Schumpeter, although a violent revolution does not play the same role. The views of Tannenbaum and Mayo appear to hold that the dislocations of status created by industrialization are gradually restored in the new industrial society and the curve of protest reflects a gradual rise and then gradual decline in the course of industrialization. Perlman seems to have suggested that left to themselves, without the interference of intellectuals, manual workers would show no significant variation in protest in the course of capitalist development.

The conclusion of the present study is that worker protest in the course of industrialization tends to peak relatively early and

to decline in intensity thereafter.[32] The critical period of industrialization is during the early stages. It is the current generation which is decisive in the newly industrializing countries. At
the early stages, the break with the traditional society is sharpest;
the labor force is making the more basic and difficult adjustments
to the discipline and pace of industry; the plant and work community are at the most formative stages; nationalist and social
revolutions are also likely to be occurring in addition to the introduction of modern industry; the reactions of workers are more
direct and violent; the appeal of utopias and grandiose schemes
for transforming society is likely to be greatest in such periods.

The extent of latent protest at the early stages is related directly related to the extent to which the new industrial order
ative to resources, and the harsher and quicker the adjustments
required of the work force, the greater the potential protest, and
the greater the technical need for controls over the work force,
labor organizations, and the labor market, if latent protest is not
to be explosive.

The extent of latent protest at the early stages is also directly related to the extent to which the new industrial order
adapts or destroys the institutions of the traditional society. The
course of protest in Denmark was significantly affected by the
gradual growth of industry, and the legacy of the guilds early
disposed both workers and employers toward organization. In
Japan the role of the old order in promoting industry and in
constraining manifestations of worker protest through paternalistic enterprises and the state tended to create an atypical pattern
of little protest.

As time passes, formal organizations of workers emerge, and,
as has been observed, the forms of overt protest become more
disciplined and less spontaneous. The organizations gradually become centralized, formalized, legitimatized, and viable. The industrializing elite develops its strategies and means of controlling,
limiting, or directing worker protest. Protest expressions are
stripped of the inchoate and volatile character of the early stages.
Sporadic riots, violence, explosive outbursts are replaced by an
industrial relations system for establishing and administering the
rules of the work place. Spontaneous strikes give way in some
industrial relations systems to the enlightened, orderly and bu-

reaucratic strike, almost chivalrous in its tactics and cold-blooded in its calculatedness.[33] Leaders of the worker organizations become concerned with survival and perpetuation, with finances, and internal discipline and stability. These labor organizations take on new and expanded functions.

The ideologies of the early period seem dated, and the old slogans lose their meaning and their appeal. The 1959 programs of the German Social Democratic party now declare for "free competition in a free economy" and denounce a "totalitarian controlled economy." The old Socialist demand for socialization of the means of production has been changed to "effective public controls" to prevent the "misuse of economy by the powerful."[34]

While forms of individual protest remain, with some absenteeism, turnover, and withdrawal of the full potential of effort, the industrializing societies universally come to contain, to control, and to redirect the responses of industrial workers to the transformation of society.

Worker Protest and the Elites

The facts of worker protest confront each ideal type of industrializing elite with fundamental problems and opportunities. The universal responses of individual workers and the inherent tendency toward the formation of labor organizations with potential economic power, political strength and with an explicit ideology pose basic issues of strategy for each elite directing the development of industrialism. Is the elite able to influence or explicitly to mold the form, policies, and ideology of worker organizations? How do alternative policies of the elites affect the forms of worker protest? Can organization of workers be successfully suppressed, and for what period and with what means? Can worker organizations be guided and controlled? Can they make a contribution rather than constitute an impediment to the transformation of the community and work force? Can they be used to increase output, skill, and discipline, or must they be disruptive of the productive process? Can worker organizations be used to support the power and prestige of the elite, indeed, can they constitute an element of the ruling elite?

The policies of an elite toward worker protest must fit into and

be consistent with its grand strategy of the industrialization process (see Chapter 3). These issues are the more difficult when a
dominant industrializing elite is confronted by competitors. The
groups competing for control of industrialization strategies tend
to fan the protest of workers; the expression of protest may become exaggerated above its natural level for the stage of development, and the leaders of labor organizations are often split in
the contest for power.

The pace of industrialization, which has been shown to be a
central decision facing every elite (see Chapter 5), has a significant impact on the response of the emerging industrial work
force. The faster the pace, other factors being the same, the
more sudden the transformations required of workers-in-process,
the greater the impact of discipline and pace at the work place,
the greater the limitations on consumption, and the greater the
dislocations in the community. The faster the rate of industrialization, with comparable resources, cultural settings and historical periods, the greater the degree of latent worker protest.
The faster the pace of industrialization in comparable settings,
and the greater the pressures upon the managements of enterprises from the market, budgets, or directly from the elite, the
greater the derived pressures and protest from the emerging
work force.

Similarly, the more drastic the methods used to structure the
labor force (see Chapter 7), and the greater the adaptations required in the arrangements to recruit, hire, allocate, and train
the labor force, the greater the latent protest in any period. Or,
the greater the resistance of the traditional culture to industrialization and the more virile that pre-industrial culture (Chapter 4), the greater the stresses and the latent protest involved in
the industrial transformation.

These analytical propositions do not readily lend themselves
to the direct test of historical experience, since two industrializing efforts are seldom, if ever, fully comparable. Moreover, the
historical experience only reveals the actual forms of protest which
reflect not merely latent or potential protest but the measures
used by an elite to channel, control, or suppress the outward
forms of individual and organized protest. Further, the character
of protest, as was developed in the last section, changes signifi-

cantly in the course of industrialization. But there should be
general assent to the propositions that protest is distinctively
shaped by the strategies of the particular elite, and further that
the measures adopted to control or contain the universal fact of
worker protest are distinctive to a particular elite and reflect the
diversity of their basic strategies.

Protest Organized around Some Principle. The principles
around which protest congeals vary with each of the ideal type
of elites and their programs for the transition from the pre-industrial society. In the society led by the dynastic elite, protest tends
to crystallize around the principle of class consciousness. The traditional elite and the new industrial workers do not arise at the
same time; they do not have a common origin in the industrialization process. The elite is fundamentally bent on the preservation of the old order. The frustrations and the tensions of the new
industrial workers tend to be organized on the principle of class
consciousness and conflict. A drastic transformation of the old
order is the objective of the working class. This is not the design of the dynastic elite with its paternal view of the community,
but the gulf is so wide, social contacts on the basis of equals so
infrequent, and vertical mobility so rare that worker protest is
congealed around antagonism to the old order and its representatives in the work place.

Job control has tended to be the principle around which protest is organized in the middle-class community.[35] The tensions
of the work place focus attention of workers upon control over
the job and job conditions. It is not so much the objective of the
drastic transformation of the whole social system which emerges
from protest as the desire for control over the job by a variety of
means. The worker is not so much against society as against specific features of the job and work community. The pluralism
and social mobility of the society led by the middle-class elite
preclude the class consciousness of the more rigid dynastic elite.

The revolutionary intellectual elite tolerates no overt forms of
group protest in the society it leads toward industrialism. But
it provides for a carefully controlled channel for organizing
and directing the inevitable worker protest, the principle of self-
criticism. The chafings and tensions from rapid industrialization
are turned largely inward. Protest is pointed toward the workers

themselves and carefully contained and absorbed within the ruling party rather than directed against the ruling class of the old order or toward control over the job and work community. Protest may also be directed against foreign enemies or rivals of the elite.

In the colonial community protest by indigenous workers is organized around the principle of anticolonialism and independence and turned against the mother country and its representatives. Worker protest in the newly independent nation is organized around removing the vestiges of colonialism, including the elimination of control by foreigners and toward "progress." The ideal of the new nation may also be used to constrain organized protest, to diffuse it away from the nationalist elite, and to rationalize the gap between aspiration and reality.

Attitudes of Elites toward Conflict. The dynastic elite looks upon industrial conflict and strife as inconsistent with its paternalistic view of the traditional society. It is a negation of the basic presumptions of the ruling elite to cast doubts both upon the integrity of the elite and the loyalty of workers to the ideals of the established order.

The society led by the middle-class elite treats a degree of conflict — in the form of the strike or lockout — as no more than an extension of the market and the necessary corollary of voluntary associations. If buyers and sellers are to be free to refuse to buy or sell under terms regarded as unsatisfactory, then a strike or lockout is a logical extension of the market. This is the only elite to tolerate in its strategy of the industrializing process a degree of industrial conflict and to assert for strife even a degree of positive value.

Revolutionary intellectuals look upon group conflict as entirely inconsistent with its ideology. This requires that there can be no basic conflict in interests between the managers and the managed. Strife is viewed as a failure of the principle of self-criticism, and as a practical matter a stoppage of production is a detriment to the goal of rapid industrialization.

The colonial elite regards industrial strife as inconsistent with the ideals of the relations of the colony to the mother country. As a practical matter conflict is abhorred as a breeding ground of independence movements and a stimulus to direct action in the political area. The nationalist leaders also abhor industrial conflict. It interferes with both the national dream and the practical objectives of increasing production and economic development.

Forms of Group Protest. Protest takes a variety of distinctive forms in the communities led by the various ideal types of elites. These forms arise partly out of the diverse attitudes toward conflict just surveyed and partly out of the characteristics of worker organizations to be surveyed in the next section of this chapter. While the fact of organized protest is a universal of industrialization, protest takes on distinctive forms in the societies led by the various ideal types of elites. While protest changes in the course of an industrialization, the present discussion focuses attention upon the character of protest inherent in the strategies of the prime movers of industrialization.

In the dynastic-led society, demonstrations of a relatively short duration and political strikes constitute the overt form of group protest. The following description is illustrative of this general response to a sense of grievance. "The traditional manner for the Italian people, from the *Renaissance* on, to express dissatisfaction with their lot is to mill around in the central squares of their cities, making and listening to fiery speeches. These demonstrations last from several hours to several days, during which time there may be no casualties. The whole affair is often quite disorganized and generally constitutes no real threat (no clear and present danger) to the government."[36] In other cases the demonstrations have been more violent and a serious threat to the dynastic elite.

The organized economic strike is the form of group protest in the community of the middle-class elite. The strike is essentially nonviolent, disciplined, and may be of considerable duration.

The revolutionary intellectuals diffuse or channel protest into other forms, and they suppress conflict or industrial strife if necessary. Only occasional and isolated instances of overt group strife or demonstrations are encountered. Industrial strife is viewed as incipient revolt against the regime.

The colonial elite confronts the demonstration, strike, and political strife organized for the purpose of independence and nationalist purposes. The experiences of India, Ghana, Egypt, and

Indonesia before independence and the unsuccessful Hungarian revolt are replete with the mobilization of workers for nationalist purposes and political freedom.

The nationalist elite encounters demonstrations which tend to be more peaceful and less violent than before independence. They are likely to be more organized and, in the early years of independence, to be constrained by nationalist fervor and to be directed against foreign scapegoats. Labor strife and demonstrations may also reflect and be used in contests for power where the elite faces serious competition.

The discussion of worker protest and the ideal types of elites of this section is summarized in Chart 6.

Worker Organizations and the Elites

In the community led by each ideal type of industrializing elite distinctive worker organizations develop in conformity to the elite's grand strategy of the great transition and reinforcing its other policies. Industrialization everywhere creates organizations of workers, but they differ widely in their functions, structure, leadership, and ideology. Indeed, the term "labor organizations" is used here rather than "labor unions" to emphasize more generality and to avoid implications of forms and functions peculiar to the middle-class ideal type.

The general relationship between each of the ideal types of elites and the labor organizations which arise in the societies they seek to industrialize may be briefly characterized at the outset. The dominant labor organizations in the dynastic-led society remain foreign to the elite; they do not fit nor do they readily conform to the paternal view of the elite. The labor organizations of the middle-class elite conform and are consonant with the market. In the industrialization program of the revolutionary intellectuals the labor organizations are consistent with and conform to the state. The labor organizations of the colonial elite are not congenial to the dominant elite; they tend to be nationalist and press for independence. They are foreign to the colonialist vision of industrialization. The labor organizations under the nationalist elite are beset by a deep dilemma and divided loyalties in shaping their policies, as is developed in a later section of this

CHART 6.

Worker protest and the elites.

Industrializing Elite	Dynastic	Middle-Class	Revolutionary-Intellectuals	Colonial Administrators	Nationalist Leaders
Organizing principle of group protest	Class consciousness.	Job control.	Self-criticism.	Anti-Colonialism.	Nationalism.
Forms of group protest	Demonstrations and political strikes.	Organized economic strikes.	Diffused and suppressed, except for occasional outburst.	Demonstrations for independence, often violent.	Demonstrations, ordinarily peaceful.
Attitudes of elites toward conflict	Inconsistent with paternal society.	Affirmative role for limited conflict.	Inconsistent with ideology and rapid industrialization.	Inconsistent with role of mother country.	Inconsistent with nationalist ideal and economic development.

chapter. These general relationships between the ideal types of elites and their labor organizations suggest that greatest conflict and tension would characterize the dynastic and colonial-led industrialization.

This section describes in turn the labor organizations which arise under each of the ideal type of elites. The labor organizations are described in terms of a list of seven features: (1) the view workers take of managers,[37] (2) the functions of labor organizations, (3) the extent of competition among labor organizations, (4) the structure of these organizations, (5) their sources of funds, (6) the sources of leadership, and (7) their ideology. Chart 7 summarizes the characteristics of labor organizations arising under the various ideal types of industrializing elites.

The Dynastic Elite.   The dynastic community is characterized by workers personally dependent upon the enterprise manager. The worker looks to the paternal manager for guidance in personal, economic and social problems; community affairs are not properly his concern, but the province of the paternal elite.

The dynastic elite does not in principle encourage labor organizations. At the plant level, organizations of workers supplement and help to administer the paternal activities of the managers and the state, but they provide little effective constraint on the decisions of management. At the industry level they provide a broad form of minimum regulation which the enterprise managers often find congenial to the support of cartels or associations. These standards have little relevance to actual plant conditions, and there is little connection between the plant level and the industry level of workers' organizations. In the society led by the dynastic elite, political organizations of workers emerge which often have only indirect connections with the plant and industry levels of workers' organizations, and they seek detailed government regulation of compensation and working conditions to offset plant and industry-level weaknesses and division of workers. These political organizations also seek to challenge the established elite and conduct political demonstrations.

In the traditional society led by the dynastic elite there are frequently deep social distinctions, religious, racial, nationalist, linguistic, and political party divisions among workers. There tends to be multiple representation of workers at the plant level,

CHART 7.

Worker organizations and the elites.

Industrializing Elite	Dynastic	Middle-Class	Revolutionary-Intellectuals	Colonials	Nationalists
View toward workers	Personally dependent upon managers in time of need.	Independent workers.	Class of dependent workers.	Dependent upon foreigners.	Partners in the new nation.
Functions of workers' organizations	Social functions at plant level; little constraint upon management. Provides minimum industry conditions by legislation. Political activity challenges the elite.	Regulates management at the local and industry level. Independent political activity accepted. Does not challenge the elite.	Instrument of party to educate, lead workers and to stimulate production. No political activity except through the party.	Largely a part of the independence and nationalist movement.	Confronts the conflicting objectives of economic development and protection of workers.
Competition among workers' organizations	Limited rivalry at the plant level and the distribution of functions between the local and industry levels. No exclusive representation.	Exclusive representation and keen competition. Some rivalry between plant and industry levels over allocation of functions.	No rivalry or competition allowed.	Divided by ideological, tactical, regional and personal leadership factions.	Tendency for consolidation among organizations recognized as loyal by nationalistic elite. Advantage over those not so recognized.
Structure of worker organizations	Relatively large number of industrial unions. Centralized confederation often limited by rival confederations. Unions perform narrow range of functions.	A variety of structural forms. Confederations not so centralized. Organizations perform a wide range of functions.	A few industrial unions. Centralized confederation. Organizations perform a narrow range of functions.	A wide variety of structures. Organizations not well developed, often personal.	Tendency toward industrial unions with one confederation acceptable to elite.

CHART 7. (continued)

Industrial-izing Elite	Dynastic	Middle-Class	Revolutionary-Intellectuals	Colonials	Nationalists
Sources of funds	Meager resources from irregular dues payments and indirect government allowances. Financial success not highly regarded by workers' organizations.	Substantial resources secured by regular dues; regulatory functions require administrative organizations and large budgets.	Substantial resources secured by assessment of all workers; financial resources present no problem with support of regime.	Meager funds often raised outside workers' organizations.	Funds often secured indirectly from government in addition to meager dues. Officers receive other salaries.
Sources of leadership	Intellectuals and those ideologically oriented toward political activity. The leaders income position is often insecure.	The ranks through lower levels of workers' organizations. They have an established career.	Reliable party leaders with experience in worker organizations. They have an established career.	Nationalist and independence leaders. Intellectuals with a personal following.	National leaders and intellectuals except where confined to manual workers.
Ideology	Class-conscious and revolutionary except for a minority.	Reformist.	Preserve the true revolution.	Independence.	Nationalism.

as in workers' councils, and at the industry level, as in negotiations for agreements signed by several overlapping workers' organizations. Among these organizations at the plant and industry level, and in political activities, there may be keen rivalry and competition. In the absence of exclusive jurisdiction or exclusive representation for the majority organization, the rivalry is limited since it need not end in extinction for any of the competitors. Majority rule does not apply with the winner-take-all. Changing conditions lead to relative shifts in workers' support, but the existence of the organizations is not endangered. There may also be keen competition between organizations at the plant level and at the national level over the distribution of functions. Any competition among workers' organizations is lamented; it is tolerated as an unavoided consequence of historical divisions in the traditional society.

The dynastic elite tends to build organizations which provide minimum regulation on an industry basis, without a direct line of control to the plant level. The labor organization is constricted on the one hand by work-level groups, such as workers' councils, over which it has little, if any, control, and the political organs which seek regulative legislation. The labor organization operates in a relatively narrow corridor between plant groups and the political parties. There is strong internal confederation control which may be further limited by rival confederations.

The operations of labor organizations, as any other, are much influenced by the funds at their disposal and the source of their finances. Under the dynastic elite labor organizations tend to be relatively poorly financed. There are a variety of competitors for support by the workers — work-level organizations, national level groups, and political parties — and their access to workers for funds is not often coordinated. The paternal characteristics of the system are not congenial to large dues payments. The focus of the society around the family, state, and religion is not congenial to the financial support of vigorous voluntary associations. Labor organizations do not place a high preference upon building strong financial positions in view of their major activities. Labor organizations are a movement, and movements are not primarily concerned with finances. At times the government may provide some resources in the form of buildings, a subsidy for the operation of labor exchanges, or social insurance services, or pay the salaries of some leaders who may fill some nominal public function in exchange for loyalty.

Leadership of labor organizations may be drawn from the ranks or from intellectuals outside the organizations or be imposed from a party or subject to government approval. The leadership of labor organizations in the country under the dynastic elite tends to be drawn from those ideologically oriented toward political activities and from intellectuals. The activities of the labor organizations, as opposed to works councils and enterprise or plant bodies, are primarily at the industry and national level. The emphasis upon social policy and law places a relative premium upon learning. The absence of plant level problems as a concern in these organizations decreases the need for leadership more familiar with the actual work processes. The income of such leaders may not always depend solely upon the labor organization, but may be based also upon political activity, legal practice, journalism, and other activities. It should not be inferred that leaders do not arise from the ranks, but the dynastic arrangements tend to favor the intellectual type for labor leadership.

The labor organizations which emerge in the course of industrialization under each ideal type of elite tend to develop a distinctive ideology or view of their place in the community. Under the dynastic elite the dominant labor organizations tend to be class-conscious and revolutionary; they advocate the drastic overhaul of the traditional society. There may also be labor organizations, particularly organized along religious lines, which are more loyal to the traditional society.

The Middle-Class Elite. The middle-class case is characterized by the independent worker. While the worker is required to follow the directions of management at the work place, as are workers everywhere, his personal affairs are his own concern within a system of rules, and in community life his vote is the equal of the manager's.

The middle-class elite is more readily reconciled to the principle of workers' organizations than the dynastic elite and supports the principle of their affirmative public value. At the plant and industry level the organizations regulate relationships with

managements. There is closer coordination and often direct lines
of authority in these workers' organizations between the industry and the plant level; in some cases this authority extends to a
single national center, as in Sweden, at least on some questions.
The political organization of workers is less concerned with detailed regulation of managements and more preoccupied with
community issues. The middle-class elite regards such organized
political activity as legitimate, and the workers' political organizations are less dedicated to challenge or to displace the industrializing elite.

In the society led by the middle class there is typically supposed to be one workers' organization for each type of worker
by craft or industry. The scope of labor organizations often conforms to the contour of the market. There tends to be competition among contending organizations since the triumph of one
means the loss of recognition to the rivals among a particular
group of workers, at least for a period. A degree of competition
among workers' organizations, moreover, is regarded as an affirmative good to stimulate more responsiveness to the wishes of
the workers. There is relatively little overt competition, however,
between organizations over the distribution of functions at the
plant and industry levels, although there is internal tension in
workers' organizations over the extent of centralization and decentralization of functions.

The labor organizations under the middle-class-led industrialization tend to build a variety of unions: craft, industrial, and general. The range of functions is broad, not constricted by other
forms of worker organizations. The diversity in structure represents a response to a gradual historical development, to a lesser
degree of confederation centralization, and to a greater responsiveness to the preferences of particular sectors and groups of
workers. It also reflects an economy with more reliance upon
the market mechanism under which the pattern of union growth
may have had to conform to market constraints to survive. The
powers of the confederation often tend to be lesser than in the
other ideal types; the principles of decentralization and autonomy are highly regarded values.

The country led by the middle-class elite develops labor organizations that tend to be relatively well financed by dues regu-

larly collected from the membership. The labor organizations
seek to build strong financial positions, partly to provide more
effective services to the members and partly to provide security
in case of struggle with managements. The labor organizations
typically receive little, if any, support or subsidy from the government (save in a few cases related to social services). Financial
independence from government is a cherished value. The emphasis upon regulatory functions, in constraining management
through rules at the work place, operates to create modern administrative organizations which require large-scale budgets.

The leadership of labor organizations in the middle-class-led
country tends to be drawn almost exclusively from the ranks of
workers. The predominate concern with rules constricting enterprise managers and the direct interest in the immediate work
place necessarily place a premium upon leadership seasoned in
the practical operating problems of enterprises. The intellectual
would be out of place. The more direct organizational tie between plant and industry or confederation levels of workers' organizations creates more of a ladder on which leadership starts at
the bottom. Full-time officers arise who regard the labor organizations as a career; they are in a sense professionals or bureaucrats
of the labor organizations with a primary concern for administering and negotiating agreements with professionals in management.

The middle-class elite leads a society in which labor organizations are bargaining institutions primarily; they are mildly reformist in their ideology and attitudes toward the larger community.

The Revolutionary Intellectual. This elite regards workers as a
dependent class. Industrial workers as a group are subject to
managerial direction which is regarded as an expression of the
elite leadership. The personal conditions of individual workers
are not the concern of managers, and workers do not look to them
personally, as with the dynastic elite, but the rules of the work
place are paternal rather than market oriented. In community
affairs the worker is to look to the leadership of the party.

The revolutionary intellectual elite regards organizations of
workers at the plant or industry level as its own preserve. The
purpose of the workers' organizations is less to constrain managements than to educate, to stimulate production, and to lead the

industrial workers on behalf of the ruling elite. They are agents of the state to insure industrial production. Independent political organization or activity is precluded except through and under the direction of the party.

In the society led by the revolutionary intellectuals there is no room for competition between contending labor organizations at the plant level, nor is there any contention over functions to be performed by rival workers' organizations. Since the organization of workers is an instrument of the ruling party to educate and to lead workers, discordant tones serve no purpose and are not tolerated. Labor organizations are agents of the state; and there is only one state. A degree of tension may arise between plant-level representatives and those higher in the hierarchy. Competition among workers' organizations, however, is seen only as an evil, weakening the regime.

The revolutionary intellectual elite tends to create a limited number of labor organizations, industrial in form, with a high degree of centralization over district and local groups and at the confederation level. The structure reflects the deliberate design of labor organizations by the elite rather than more gradual evolution or conformance to the market. This structure also reflects the function of the organizations: to serve as the organ of education and communication between the party and the industrial workers and to stimulate industrial output. This narrow range of functions reflects a design in which the party and the state fulfill the functions of regulating or constraining managers which is elsewhere performed by labor organizations and the market. This type of organizational structure may be vulnerable to the rise of plant-level worker organizations from below as illustrated by works councils in Hungary.

In the country led by the revolutionary intellectual elite, labor organizations are relatively well financed by assessments levied upon all workers. The organizations are particularly well supplied with buildings appropriate to their status as an arm of the regime. Finances and resources are no problem.

The leadership of the labor organizations in the revolutionary-intellectual-led country tends to be drawn from reliable party leaders, many of whom have devoted a career to the work of the party in labor organizations. They are financially secure and are in a sense (with a different type of assignment) professionals or bureaucrats of the labor organization and the party. They are concerned with the administration and implementation of policy and ideology developed by the party.

Labor organizations under the revolutionary intellectuals have no ideology apart from the ruling elite. They seek to preserve the true revolution envisaged by the elite.

The Colonial Elite. The indigenous worker is envisaged as personally dependent upon the foreign manager as the agent of the colonial power. The role of labor organizations of indigenous workers tends to be largely a part of the nationalist and independence movement. After a country has passed through the portals of political independence, the dilemma of the function of labor organizations arises with perplexing urgency. There is, of course, the purpose to "consolidate independence," to "liquidate the evil remains of colonialism," and to push for the more practical objectives, in foreign firms particularly, of training local citizens to replace foreigners in managerial, technical, and highly skilled positions. The dilemmas which confront labor organizations in the newly industrializing countries are explored in a later section of this chapter.

Labor organizations under the colonial elite tend to be united on the theme of independence, but they are likely to be divided on a wide range of ideological, regional, and tactical grounds, as well as on the basis of personal leadership. The rivalry is one of slogans, programmes, and personal leadership rather than of representation or constraints on management. Under the colonial elite the workers' organizations among the indigenous workers tend to reflect a wide variety of structures. Organizations are not well developed, and they are often the reflection of personal leadership.

Labor organizations have no systematic dues collection, and they are poorly supplied with funds. Their funds may come largely from other nationalist groups. The leaders of labor organizations in the colonial community are drawn from the nationalist and independence movement; they tend to be intellectuals with a personal following. The ideology of these labor organizations is built around independence and anticolonialism.

Nationalist Leaders. Workers in the new nationalist state regard foreign managers as a lingering vestige of colonialism and indigenous managers ideally as partners in the new nation.

The nationalist leader seeks the support of the rising group of industrial workers and is concerned to insure their reliability. Industrial workers are a strategic group to the nationalist elite. The elite tends to bestow favors upon reliable organizations and to assist in the opposition to rivals for worker support in exchange for subordination to the nationalist objectives.

This elite tends to develop more explicit and more advanced organizational structures than under the colonial elite, largely industrial in form. The tendency is to adopt the organizational forms of labor organizations from some more economically advanced country held in high prestige by the nationalist elite. The nationalist elites tend to promote reliable and loyal labor organizations and encourage the collection of membership dues for them. These dues may even be required of all workers. The elite may also provide funds directly for local organizations, and it may support reliable groups by government grants to worker education and by employment on public payrolls of a number of leaders of labor organizations.

The reliable leadership of labor organizations is drawn from nationalist leaders in the first generation after independence. The leadership includes many intellectuals responsive to the nationalist elite, except in cases in which leadership is specifically confined to manual workers. The ideology of labor organizations under the nationalist elites is that of partners in development.

The Dilemmas of Labor Organizations in Early Industrialization

Labor organizations in newly industrializing countries, particularly with a new nationalist elite, confront four questions of fundamental significance to the elites and to the labor organizations:

(1) *Wages vs. Capital Formation.* There are conflicting claims of economic development and immediately improved wages and other benefits for workers. The nationalist labor leaders' dedication to industrialization, which requires increased savings, conflicts with the labor organizations' declared purpose and their often promised gains from independence, to provide immediately

improved wages and working conditions. Within some limits, higher wages may increase worker productivity, but this is likely to be a narrow and a difficult range of wage policy to find.[38]

(2) *Strikes vs. Production.* The nationalist labor leader must choose again on strike policy. Strike action tends to decrease production where successful and may make development investments less attractive to foreign investors, but strike action may be necessary to achieve economic objectives of the labor organization, to build disciplined labor organizations, and to retain the interest of the membership.

(3) *Grievance-handling vs. Discipline.* Individual workers and small groups in an emerging industrial work force have numerous complaints, grievances, and frustrations. The national labor leader must choose in some degree between supporting the immediate reactions and grievances of workers or supporting the insistence upon higher standards of discipline, a faster pace, training, and production which are vital to economic development.

(4) *Organizational Prestige vs. Political Subservience.* The labor organization is often long on political influence and short on economic power. It must weigh the costs of faithful support and dependence on a political party or government against the benefits of governmental recognition and support in a variety of ways, including exclusive labor rights and favoritism in treating rival labor organizations and outright financial support. The immediate attractiveness of a strong legal position in dealing with managements, members, and rivals and financial solvency is to be balanced against the loss in independence of action in being subservient to the government.

These basic policy decisions, which are most difficult for labor organizations in a country led by a democratic and middle-class elite, present few difficulties for the labor organizations under the revolutionary intellectual elite. Economic development takes first priority over wage increases; production cannot be interfered with by strikes; labor organizations are designed to increase labor productivity, and they are always subservient to the party and government. There is more of a problem in a country under the dynastic elite, but in the main wages cannot be raised very much in the face of the slow rate of development, and strikes are little more than demonstrations. The labor movement cannot secure many concessions from the government or ruling elite, although individual leaders or factions of labor organizations may secure benefits in exchange for political support.

It is easy to understand why many leaders of industrializing countries and their labor organizations in countries outside the Eastern orbit find the choices posed above to be very hard, and they talk of ways to develop labor organizations that will make a more affirmative contribution to the national objective of industrialization. Neither the elite nor the leaders of labor organizations find congenial the traditional model of the "free trade union" drawn from advanced Western countries. As Dr. Nkrumah has said, ". . . . The trade union movement has a great part to play and a far wider task to perform than merely the safeguarding of the conditions and wages of its members."[39] The debate and the experimentation over the role of labor organizations in recently industrializing countries is one of the focal points of the competition among groups for leadership in the process of industrialization.

The distinctive characteristics of the labor organizations created in the industrialization process by each ideal type of elite (see Chart 7) indicate the interdependence of each separate feature. The functions exercised by labor organizations, for instance, are closely related to their structure, leadership, financial arrangements, and ideology. Further, the labor organizations that arise in a society in transition led by an ideal type of elite fit into the full range of policies of that industrializing elite. The universals of worker protest and organization are molded to conform and contribute to the grand strategy of the industrializing elite.

Worker Protest and Pressure as an Historical Force

Worker protest to Marx was not just *the* labor problem but, indeed, *the* important social force at a certain stage in history. It was the peaking of labor protest in a revolution that ushered in the new society. But it was not only Marx who thus raised the historical import of worker protest to a dominant position. In the century from 1850 to 1950, worker protest was often as feared by the conservatives as it was worshipped by the radicals.

As noted earlier in this chapter, however, theories to the contrary, worker protest has been a declining not an increasing force as the evolution of industrialization has unfolded; and it has seldom, in fact, occupied the center of the stage. This does not mean, however, that it has been of little or no significance. Nearly everywhere it has been a social force to be reckoned with and in a few situations it has been the critical social force.

The main impact of worker protest has been its glacial impact — this is the central observation. In certain specific cases, worker protest has additionally played a large role in revolutionary transformation.

Glacial impact. Everywhere workers have a sense of protest in the course of the changes that industrialization brings in its wake. Everywhere, or nearly everywhere, they organize or are organized. Through organization, whether autonomous or controlled, they bring pressures to bear on enterprise managers and the ruling elite — pressures through grievances, negotiations, strikes, elections. These pressures work in the direction of more formal rules, more equality of treatment, more checks and balances on managers, more accumulated rights for workers and, generally, toward a sharing of power — toward the "constitutional" approach to authority over workers. These pressures also lead toward the greater intervention of neutrals, usually through actions of the state, the greater development of formal procedures to settle controversies, the creation of experts to handle industrial relations problems. Whether faster or slower, deeper or shallower, this is the direction of penetration of the impact of worker protest.

This glacial pressure can bring substantial changes over a period of years. It can help change the nature of the strategy of a dynastic elite from unadulterated paternalism toward pluralism, as in Germany; soften the policies of a middle class society toward labor, as in England and the United States; lead a nationalist drive toward industrialization in the direction of more consideration for the workers, as in Egypt; and even bring greater consideration for the wishes of the masses as against the requirements of the ideology, as in Poland and Yugoslavia. It can be an evolutionary force of some consequence helping to change in essential ways the strategies of elite groups.

Revolutionary transformation. There are exceptional cases where worker protest has played a major role in a social transformation — in the rise of a new elite or the shift of power from one elite to another. Not all such social transformations, however, inherently involve a role for labor proest. The rise of a dynastic elite to control the industrialization process or the introduction of a foreign elite into control of a colony, are not processes in which worker protest can normally play an affirmative role. Also, the rise to supremacy of a middle class elite is usually achieved without the assistance of worker protest, although the case of England shows how worker protest may aid the new middle class in reducing the authority of the old society.

The only two elites which can count on worker protest as a key to their assumption of supremacy are the revolutionary intellectuals and the nationalist leaders. Both are likely to rely on force in taking over from an ineffective dynastic elite or from a colonial regime; and part of the force they may muster is the force of worker protest through the general strike, the urban mob, the revolution. This worker violence helped weaken and then displace the old regimes in Russia, Argentina, Iraq, Indonesia. If the old regime is not actually destroyed, as in Argentina, the organizations of workers may be held in readiness to descend again into the streets to preserve the new regime.

These revolutionary transformations, with the aid of labor protest, not only can occur only in some places (the taking over of power from a dynastic elite or a colonial regime) but also only at some times — those turning points in history when social change is made possible by the decay of an old system and often only when such decay is made more evident by the effects of depression or of war.

These are the specific cases, not the general rule; the specific cases where worker protest can be a climactic force in changing the rule from one elite to another. The general rule is that worker protest is available as a revolutionary force only in certain situations and at certain times, and also only to certain people — the revolutionary intellectuals and the nationalist leaders.

Alliances. Worker protest, by itself, has never brought a change in the ruling elite. Workers and the middle class, with the role of the new middle class quite dominant, helped end the old regime in England. Workers and intellectuals and sometimes army officers and peasants have joined under Communist or Nationalist auspices to supplant a dynastic elite or a colonial power in a number of countries. Worker organizations may even be the source of the leadership of such movements, as in Kenya and Guinea.

But ruling elites may form alliances with worker organizations and direct the sense of worker protest to the purposes of the regime; and this has been one of the significant historical discoveries of the revolutionary intellectuals and the nationalist leaders in a number of countries — Russia, China, Brazil, Pakistan, Mexico. Worker protest need not be against the ruling regime; it can be turned against the defunct regime, the foreigners, backwardness, national degradation; it can be turned in favor of mutual goals of industrial progress, military power, national self-sufficiency. Thus it need not be destructive of the existing regime.

The ruling elites may also form their own alliances against protesting worker organizations when these exist; alliances with the army, the middle class, the Church. And they may seek to split the workers, as in Germany, into white collar versus manual, Catholic versus Socialist, officials against subordinates; and to isolate them from the middle class and the peasants. Only the colonial administrators are really bereft of possible alliances with a long-term mass base; much as they may try to rely on tribal chiefs and "tame" native leaders.

Thus protest can be owned by many people; even by the ruling elite as well as by its opponents. Least of all is it likely to be solely owned by the workers themselves, since to be effective they must make alliances with others. Worker protest seldom loses its chains.

The lessons of the past century. The next century of industrialization as compared with the first century of world-wide industrialization (1850–1950) may see an even less central role reserved for social protest.

(1) Workers now protest more in favor of industrialization than against it. "Machine breakers" are no longer heroes. Thus the new protest can be constructive toward industrialization and its ruling elites instead of destructive. The relations of leaders and led in the march to industrialization can be positive as well as negative.

(2) Workers have proved themselves much more adjustable to the impacts of industrialization on their technical and social skills,

and much more agreeable to the imposition of the web of rules than was once suspected. The led are more easily led.

(3) The elites have gained experience alike in the means of reducing protest — better housing, better personnel practices, greater social security — and in the means of controlling it — grievance procedures, incentives, development of joint goals — than they were a century ago. They appreciate more the need for consensus in society and understand better the ways to achieve it.

(4) The organizations of workers and their leaders have proved quite susceptible to the guidance involved in the development of consensus in an industrializing society; and even to more direct guidance by the elite through selection of goals and of men. Most labor organizations are, in fact, to one degree or another, a part of the established system. This explains, in part, the increasingly constant threat to them from "shop steward movements."

Earlier views on the role of worker protest reflected the facts of earlier times; periods when protest was more frequently against an authoritarian dynastic elite, a hard pushing middle class, harsh colonial masters; periods when protest was against the new technology itself. It then seemed reasonable to suggest the universal nature of class warfare, with the possibility of a few exceptions (Netherlands and the United States).

The conditions for class warfare still exist; but they are increasingly the exception. These exceptions are most likely to rest on the failure of an elite group — a dynastic elite that does not adapt fast enough or a colonial regime that does not transfer power fast enough. A related but separable phenomenon is where the incompetence of particular leaders among the revolutionary intellectuals or the nationalists created the basis for violent worker protest against those leaders.

The general phenomenon now to be explained is class collaboration on the road to industrialization; the collaboration of the new dynastic elite, the new middle class, the new revolutionary intellectuals, the new nationalists, with the workers and their organizations. What were thought to be the exceptions have become the rule; what was thought to be the rule, has become the exception. The road to industrialization is paved less with class warfare and more with class alliances.

The role of worker protest is both different and more complex than has been postulated in the past. It can affect the selection, the performance and the survival of each of the elites, but more frequently through its steady impact than through sudden exertion of massive force. It may also be a supportive feature to the elites more often than a destructive one. Thus the direction of its impact may be different as well as the force of its influence on history less decisive. Worker protest is more the fruit of the past, than the seed of the future. As a seed of the future, it leads both to more industrial progress and to more worker participation in society.

Industrialization does have an impact on workers. They do protest some aspects of this impact. Their protest does in turn have an impact on the course of history, but seldom as the single decisive force. This protest gets organized, channeled, controlled; and this is part of the larger process of the structuring of the labor force. The end result is the creation in each society of an industrial relations system which is the theme of Chapter 9.

CHAPTER 9

THE RULE MAKERS AND THE RULES

Industrialization necessarily creates industrial workers, managers, and a state active in industrial relations. Workers and managers evolve persistent attitudes and expectations toward each other and toward the state. Practices, rules, and regulations for the work place and the larger community develop to govern the relations between workers and managers, workers and the state, managers and the state and their multilateral and complex interactions. Each group takes on distinctive organizational forms and structure. Ideas and beliefs concerning the purposes of each group and their relations to other segments of society become formalized into an ideology. Career leadership emerges in the organizations of workers, in management, and in government agencies to assist in the formulation and administration of the rules of the work place and work community and to deal with opposite numbers in other organizations. In brief, industrialization creates industrial relations systems.[1]

Industrializing societies all face the task of organizing their institutions to confront certain common choices (Chapter 5). Industrializing societies similarly choose among alternatives in organizing the relations among workers, managers, and government agencies. The industrializing countries are everywhere debating the character of their projected economic systems; it is not so well recognized that the industrializing countries are engaged in a debate equally intense over the features of their industrial relations systems. There is a world-wide contest going on over industrial relations systems no less than over economic systems.

Every industrial relations system, regardless of its form, fulfills at least three major functions in industrializing societies: (1) It defines the relative duties and responsibilities of workers, managers, and the state; it defines and sets up power and authority relationships. (2) It controls and keeps within tolerable limits the responses of industrial workers and managers to the dislocations, frustrations, and insecurities inherent in the industrializing process. (3) It establishes the complex of rules, practices, and regulations, both substantive and procedural, which is requisite to the work place and work community. These three are interdependent functions. They are not necessarily performed the same way nor with the same arrangements in different industrial relations systems. But these are indispensable functions to the society in transition toward industrialism.

Industrial relations systems reflect the persistent theme of uniformity and diversity in industrialization. All industrial relations systems involve workers, managers, and the state. They all serve the functions of defining power and authority relationships, controlling worker protest, and establishing a complex of rules. They all resort to career leaders or professionals at national levels. They all establish many similar rules depending upon common technology and market conditions.

But industrial relations systems also reflect significant diversity. They were started at different historical periods, each of which has left its indelible mark. They started from different degrees of backwardness. They also differ at the present moment of time since they reflect different stages and speeds of economic development. They contend with quite dissimilar pre-industrial cultures. The industrializing societies are under the command of different elites with different visions and programs for the emerging industrial relations systems.

The Formative Period

The major characteristics of a national industrial relations system appear to be crystallized by the leading elite at a relatively early stage. In the absence of a violent revolution or postwar upheaval, the national industrial relations system appears to retain these early characteristics and institutions. The central and distinctive features of voluntarism in Great Britain, the arbitration courts in Australia and Denmark, and exclusive representation in the United States emerged early in the formation of these industrial relations systems. There have been changes in administrative forms, of course, but most of the distinctive elements were evident and widely commented upon a half-century ago. It would appear that the outstanding traits of industrial relations systems in India, Israel, the Soviet Union, Yugoslavia, and Brazil — to select a few illustrations — are even now well established.

The early and formative years shape an industrial relations system in important ways to be noted in this section. Two countries with similar resources and even similar cultural backgrounds, but industrializing at different historical periods, may be expected to develop industrial relations systems varying in significant respects.

The Soviet Divide.   Industrial relations systems established before the Soviet revolution may often show differences from those which evolved after the rise of the Soviet Union. In newly industrializing non-communist countries, the relations of labor organizations to the state may be arranged to insure against capture by the Communists and against subversion. The status of organizations of workers in Brazil, India, Egypt, and Greece, for instance, has been substantially shaped to prevent the Communists from capturing government-favored labor organizations. Only "reliable" organizations may be registered or recognized by government. Among more industrialized countries (outside the Eastern bloc), the status of competing labor organizations may be arranged to dilute and thwart a Communist challenge. Thus, the multiple representation in France in the postwar period was designed to encourage the noncommunist FO and CFTC. The rise of the Communist party, with an ideological mission to capture and to direct labor organizations, has created a new feature in the formation of an industrial relations system. In non-communist countries it has led to, or provided an excuse for, increased state surveillance of labor organizations and in communist countries it has led to the explicit design of labor organizations as an instrument of party policy and party education among workers.

The Prestige of the International Labor Organization.   The conventions and resolutions of the ILO have had a considerable effect upon shaping the formal relations among workers, managers, and the state in many countries currently at the early stages of industrialization. We refer to international instruments on rights of organization, freedom of association, collective bargaining, and collaboration at the plant level rather than to reso-

lutions on minimum economic and social standards. The drive
for economic development and against economic backwardness
often includes the imitation of the forms of modern labor and
social security legislation. The appeal to international instruments
in shaping an industrial relations system is a relatively new historical factor.

The Greater Role of Government as Employer. The government as an employer, directly in public utilities, military establishments, and executive departments, or more indirectly in public
corporations, development projects, and nationalized industries
exerts a much greater influence on the formation of an industrial
relations system than if government activity were confined to
functions approved by classical liberals. An industrial relations
system at the formative stages in the 1960's is more likely to
be influenced by the state than previously since the government enters the system, not merely as sovereign, but often as the
largest single employer of industrial labor. Thus, in Nigeria more
than 60 per cent and in Ghana more than 50 per cent of wage
and salary earners are employed by the government. The status
accorded to workers, the procedures for dispute settlement, and
the personnel practices by the government as employer come to
have a significant influence on the full range of emerging relations
among workers, managers, and government. The greater role of
government as employer in shaping industrial relations systems
is a factor of new magnitude.[2]

The Rise of Professional Management. This group is a relatively new force in emerging industrial relations systems. There
are, of course, great differences among managers in all industrializing countries, as there have always been since the days of
Robert Owen. Although the picture is spotty, there is a growing
interest among managers in the status of workers, in collective
relations, in eliminating unrest, in human relations techniques,
and in meeting some of the aspirations of the emerging industrial
workers (Chapter 6). To the extent that professional management emerges, industrial relations systems are likely to be characterized by fewer tensions and less primitive protest. Each new
labor movement does not have to fight through in the same way
the same issues that confronted the early British unions. Professional enterprise management is a new factor in handling the

tensions which arise with the development of an industrial labor force.

Labor Organizations and National Independence. The timing of independence movements with the early stages of industrial development may have a decisive effect on an industrial relations system. In many countries that have gained independence in the past several decades, the labor organizations have played a significant role in the successful nationalist drive. In the unique instance of Israel, Histadrut was in effect a joint founder of the state. In India, and to some extent in Ghana, the labor organizations were in large measure an arm of the nationalist movement among workers. In such a setting, the experience of successful struggle for independence (with or without military campaigns) is likely to establish a strong tie between a government or a ruling party and a labor movement. In this situation, a rival labor organization is not likely to be accorded equivalent status. The "struggle for independence" may be expected to give distinctive coloration to the emerging industrial relations system in contrast to a situation where independence was achieved without or prior to the rise of a labor movement. Compare the experience of Israel and India with the position of labor organizations in the Philippines, Turkey, or most Latin American countries. Where a country drastically recasts its industrial relations system in the aftermath of war or revolution, as in the Netherlands or Yugoslavia, the role of the labor organization in making such changes is significant to the new system.

Gradual Development or Drastic Transformation. An industrial relations system will be influenced significantly as the organization of workers and managers proceeds gradually, more or less in step with the growth in industrialization, or as it is retarded or suppressed and then suddenly emerges, transforming large sectors of industry. Wholesale transformations may also take place following a war or revolution. The postwar reorganizations of the relations among workers, managers and the state in the Netherlands, Germany, Yugoslavia, Argentina, Japan, and Italy are illustrative. When transformation proceeds by major break-throughs rather than by more gradual processes, there is likely to be more centralization in the system and less regional and industrial autonomy. The role of the government is accentuated. In one case the industrial relations system may evolve, or just grow up, while in the other it is more deliberately fashioned or refashioned.

Thus the formative period in which the relationships among workers organizations, managers, and stage agencies are first organized or drastically reorganized is likely to have decisive consequences for the emerging industrial relations system. The present generation takes on added significance when so many newly emerging nations and regions have embarked on industrialization. The relations among industrial workers, managers, and government agencies currently being established by ideological design of the industrializing elite or fashioned by pragmatic experiment are likely to persist in the absence of violent transformation.

The Various Elites and Their Industrial Relations Systems

There is an almost infinite variety of ways of arranging the actual network of relationships among workers, managers, and the state in an industrializing country to perform the common functions of establishing the web of rules and to control protest. Logically these functions could be performed primarily by managers, the state, or by worker organizations alone with the other two groups playing only a passive role. Managers and the state, or managers and labor organizations, or even the state and labor organizations paired together, could set the rules of the work place and constrict worker protest with the third group in each case taking only an inert part. Or, finally, in a pluralistic society, managers, workers, and the state could all share actively in a variety of ways in the operation of an industrial relations system.[3]

While actual experience may seldom conform to these extremes, the diverse industrial relations arrangements in Great Britain, Peronista Argentina, Franco Spain, Saudi Arabia, Israel, the Soviet Union, and French West Africa illustrate the wide range of actual industrial relations systems. These countries reflect vast differences in the locus of power and the distribution of rule-making authority among managers, the state, and workers' organizations.

Industrial relations systems also differ in fundamental structure according as worker and management organizations and the state confront rivals and as they enter into alliances with other sectors of the national community which command power or influence, such as organized religion, political parties, or the military. Labor and management organizations in some countries may comprise a unified federation or center while in others they may be sharply divided on religious, ideological, and racial or nationalist lines. Labor organizations at the industry or community level may confront significant competition at the work place from works councils or other plant-level organizations of workers with which they are compelled to share or to which they may yield their role in rule-making.[4] The shop stewards movement in Great Britain, the works councils of Germany, the workers' councils in Yugoslavia or in Hungary and the Spanish plant-level syndicates illustrate the range of work level organizations and the problems of their relations to national labor organizations.

The industrializing elites provide the organizing principles for industrial relations systems. The following discussion combines and builds upon the separate discussions in Chapters 6, 7, and 8 of management and labor organizations under each of the ideal type of elites. It treats each industrial relations system as an entity. The wide variety of actual relations among workers, managers, and the government can better be understood in terms of the industrial relations system which each ideal type of industrializing elite tends to create.

The following questions are confronted by every industrial relations system: What is the division of authority over rule-making? How broad or narrow and detailed are the rules? What role in rule-making or in the administration of rules is played by labor organizations at the work place? How is protest controlled, recognizing that each elite seeks to use both rewards and punishments to accommodate workers to industrial life?

The Dynastic Elite. Enterprise managers develop a paternalistic concern for the dependent industrial workers on a personal basis. The elite regards the class of industrial workers as paternal wards. Industrial workers in turn develop a personal dependence upon enterprise management and the state. The web of rules is established by general regulations issued by the state applicable to an industry or sector often under the predominate influence of management. The detailed administration of the work place is the prerogative of paternal management, and detailed rules of the work place are not generally prescribed but left to managerial discretion. The elite sets or reshapes the regulations of the work community. Competitive and rival labor organizations divided by religion and ideology play little role at the work place or in the community, but workers' councils may bring workers together at the work place and influence the application of the rules to a degree. The dynastic elite uses suppression when necessary to contain protest, and it appeals to the ideal of "partners in society" or to ordered relations to reconcile workers to their new industrial role in their society with its traditional values.

The Middle-Class Elite. Enterprise managers treat the employment relation as a market transaction with independent workers. The elite regards the class of industrial workers as fellow citizens. The web of rules is largely established jointly by management and workers in direct negotiations within a framework of procedural rules established by government with participation by workers' organizations and management. The rules at the work place are detailed, and managerial authority to administer the rules is subjected to constitutional limitations and review. Labor organizations play an active role in the administration of the rules of the work place within established limits and according to established procedures. The middle-class elite constricts protest through the labor market by appeal to industrial life and its rewards, and protest is fractionalized by the separation of the work place grievance from the protest related to the larger community. It also relies upon the exercise of political redress to dissipate the inevitable tensions aroused in the industrialization of the work force.

The Revolutionary Intellectuals. The enterprise managers have a paternalistic concern for the class of industrial workers, but not a personal paternalism. The elite regards industrial workers as a special class whose destiny is to be led and guided by the elite. The working class in turn regards itself as dependent upon the elite. The web of rules both at the industry and plant level is established by detailed regulations issued by the state with varying degrees of internal consultation by managers and labor organizations, both in turn subject to direction of the state and the party. Labor organizations have only a minor direct role in the administration of most rules affecting management at the work place, although they have a major role in social services, and they may exercise influence internally through the party. This elite also resorts to suppression when necessary to contain protest and to the appeal of monetary incentives and the ideology of the "workers' state" to motivate workers toward full reconciliation and acceptance of their place in the new industrial order.

The Colonial Elite. The colonial industrial relations system varies with the type of colonialism (Chapter 3). The managers adopt the pose of the "white man's burden" toward the colonial industrial worker. The elite treats workers as a labor force to be used for the best interests of the home country. The colonial workers in turn develop a personal dependence upon foreign managers. The web of rules is established by management under the authority of the home country. The rules tend to be general, allowing wide discretion for the colonial management at the immediate work place. Labor organizations are typically an arm of a nationalist movement, and hence they have little concern with the immediate work place, except to advance the nationalist cause; moreover, colonial managers do not willingly allow labor organizations of indigenous workers any significant influence at the work place. This elite also uses suppression when necessary to contain protest and appeals to the ideals and rewards for the home country to attract workers to a new role in an industrial work force.

Nationalist Leaders. The enterprise managers in this elite ideally regard the class of industrial workers as partners in the new nation. The elite sees the emerging industrial workers as a favored group, with heavy responsibility to press toward industrialization and the fulfillment of nationalist dreams. The working class in turn has a prestige and influence far beyond its numbers, and it comes to be sought after by political leaders. The web of general rules is largely established by authority of the nationalist government, which has a major role in their formulation. In some cases labor organizations and in other instances enterprise management may be more influential in affecting the rules announced by the government. The rules of the immediate work place are

more likely to be the preserve of management but labor organization influence is not unknown where labor is scarce or where the
labor organizations played a decisive role in bringing the nationalist leaders to power. Labor organizations have little systematic
and direct impact on the administration of the rules at the work
place. This elite may also use suppression when necessary to
contain protest and the ideal of devotion to the new nation to
accommodate industrial workers to the new ways of industrialization.

Chart 8 summarizes the idealized types of industrial relations
systems — the complex interrelations among managers, workers'
organizations, and the state — which tend to be established by
each of the elites. It is possible to see at a glance the logical implications for the structure of an industrial relations system of
industrialization led by each type of elite. The actual industrial
relations systems created in history are, of course, different from
these idealized types; they reveal many variations in detail, as the
growing number of comprehensive studies and reports of different
industrial relations experiences reflect. Moreover, the industrialization process itself significantly changes the status of managers,
workers' organizations, and the state in any system. These idealized industrial relations systems, however, provide a frame of
reference for the comparison of actual systems and for pressing
toward an understanding of the inherent tendencies in any
historical structure of relations among managers, workers' organizations, and the state.

Industrialization and the Substantive Rules

Economic growth has a systematic impact upon the substantive
rules of the work place, irrespective of which elite leads the
industrialization process. There are common developments in the
complex of rules.

The rule-making process itself becomes more explicit and
formally constituted in the course of industrialization (Chapter
8). The very idea of a rule and a complex of related rules including procedures and machinery to administer rules at the work
place is itself a part of the process of economic development. Industrialization brings more and more detailed rules and a larger

CHART 8.

Industrial relations systems of industrializing elites.

A. Structure of Industrial Relations Systems

Industrial-izing Elite	Dynastic	Middle-Class	Revolutionary-Intellectuals	Colonial Administrators	Nationalist Leaders
View of elite toward industrial workers	Paternal wards.	Another citizen.	Special class whose destiny is to be led by elite.	Labor force for the mother country.	Favored and critical group to help bring industrialization.
View of managers toward industrial workers	Paternal concern for dependent workers.	Constitutional rule.	Authoritarian and paternal to workers as a class.	Dictatorial or paternalistic.	Depends on nature of managerial class.
View of industrial workers toward managers	Personally dependent upon managers in time of need.	Independent workers.	Class of dependent workers.	Dependent upon the foreigners.	Partners in the new nation.
Division of authority on rule making	State and management dominant.	Pluralistic with workers, management and state having an active role.	Party and state, with management and labor organizations as instruments.	Manager dominant with support of mother country.	Nationalist state and enterprise managers.
Broad or detailed systems of rules	General rules at the industry level with management free at the work place.	Detailed regulation at the work place primarily through collective agreements.	Detailed regulation at industry and work levels prescribed by the state.	General rules prescribed by state with management free at the work place.	General rules prescribed by state with management often free at the work place.

CHART 8. (continued)

	Dynastic	Middle-Class	Revolutionary-Intellectual	Colonial Administrator	Nationalist Leader
Role of labor organization at work place	Little role, competitive with works councils. Cooperate with management.	Active role under established procedures. Regulate management.	Little direct role; influence through party. Increase productivity.	Little role, force for nationalism and independence.	Little direct role influence through government tribunals; increase productivity.
Control over protest	Suppression and the ideal of ordered relations.	Public opinion and political redress to dissipate protest.	Suppression and ideology of the workers' state.	Suppression and ideals of the mother country.	Suppression and ideal of devotion to new nation.

B. Rules of the work place.

Industrializing Elite	Dynastic	Middle-Class	Revolutionary-Intellectual	Colonial Administrator	Nationalist Leader
Recruitment and Commitment	Preserves for as long as possible labor contractors and family or tribal recruitment. Housing and community services regarded as desirable. Family rather than individual recruitment.	Very restricted use of labor contractors; primary reliance on labor market to recruit industrial workers. Housing and community services only rarely established by enterprises. Individual or family recruitment.	Agricultural policy designed to release labor; party and state apparatus directs flow of workers by plan and at times by forced orders. Housing and community services used where pragmatically essential.	Resort to labor contractors, money taxes, labor drafts and force to secure indigenous labor. While policies vary, community service only used when necessary to recruit labor. Preferred positions for colonialists.	Abolishes the colonial forms of recruitment and differences in job rights. Housing and community services allocated on nationalist grounds.
Training	Least concerned with training in enterprise or community. Traditional apprentice training.	Training in enterprise varies with shortage of workers. Broad training.	Elaborate training programs in enterprises and community required by rapid industrialization from backward levels. Narrow, specialized and rapid training.	Few training programs and indigenous workers to be maintained in their occupational status.	Little attention to enterprise training but an expansion of community education.

CHART 8. (continued)

Industrializing Elite	Dynastic	Middle-Class	Revolutionary-Intellectuals	Colonial Administrators	Nationalist Leaders
Redundancy	Severe restrictions on layoffs established by government.	Layoffs a normal condition of employment. Rules cushion layoffs and assign priorities.	Short-term fluctuations in employment reduced by concern of enterprise management to meet production plans.	Layoffs in the discretion of enterprise and colonial managers alone.	Layoffs often restricted, particularly in foreign enterprises.
Compensation and Wages					
Payments in Kind	Most likely to adopt payments in kind and to retain them longest.	Payments in kind regarded as inherently undesirable and only temporary departure from the market.	Use of payments in kind when necessary to direct the labor supply to particular uses or locations.	Use of payments in kind to recruit labor supply, to offset the tendency to work less with higher wages, and to supply food to workers.	Dismantle payments in kind as backward and as symbol of colonial arrangements.
Components of compensation	Components other than basic wages a high proportion of total compensation. High family allowances and social security.	Basic wages a high proportion of total compensation; against family allowances. Components of compensation designed to regulate management.	Components other than basic wages relatively large. Moderate family allowance and high social security. Components of compensation are directed to control work force rather than regulate management.	Components generally conform to home country except citizens of colonial power receive additional benefits and some components reflect colonial problems.	Components adopted to conform to full range of advanced industrial countries.

Wage-rate structure. (structure varies in the course of industrialization)	Wage rates not high ly interdependent. Relatively low skill differentials.	Highly interdependent wage-rate structure through the labor market. Skill differentials sensitive to labor market; typically moderate.	Wage-rate structure not highly interdependent. Skill differentials relatively large on account of rapid pace.	Wage-rate structure reflects differences for citizens of home country; wage differentials related to pre-existing nationality and total labor supplies; gross skill differential large.	Tendency to develop more equalitarian wage-rate structure than established by colonial power.
Methods of Wage Payments	Few piece rates. Ideological opposition to piece rates.	Moderate piece or differential rates; no ideological influence.	Extensive use of piece rates as influenced by ideology and pace of industrialization.	Extensive use of piece work for reasons of labor turnover and variations in labor force.	No distinctive policy.
Procedures for settlement of disputes	Ideology permits no room for open conflict. Neutrals are government representatives. Parties have little voice in their selection. Formal proceedings. Decisions seldom a form of agreement.	Some disputes left to agreement making for possible conflict. Neutrals need not be government representatives nor lawyers. Parties have large voice in their selection. Informal proceedings. Decisions often in the form of agreement.	Ideology permits no room for conflict. Government and party decisions. Formal proceedings. Decisions seldom a form of agreement although worker and management representatives may play a role through the party.	Institutions modelled after the home country. Conflict tends to be associated with independence and nationalism; considerable role for colonial administrator in making decisions.	The concern for the future of the new nation tends to deprecate conflict. Workers need to be re-educated on the use of the strike. Previously used against colonialists. Now Government plays a decisive role in dispute settlement; often compulsory settlement. Adoption of ILO conventions.

body of explicit rules as the history of labor legislation and the mere bulk of agreements, regulations, decrees, codes, or other forms of rules well illustrate.

Recruitment and Commitment. Every industrial relations system must recruit workers, including managerial staff, train them, and make temporary and permanent layoffs at the work place (Chapters 6 and 7). A body of rules emerges in every industrial relations system to govern the recruitment, training, and redundancy of the work force. The severity of these problems varies with the ratio of labor to other resources and the state of industrialization.

When workers are not fully substitutable for each other, either in the judgment of managers or in their own eyes, then a group of rules arises concerning the choices to be made among types and groups of workers. Thus, some jobs may be reserved for those of a certain age, sex, color, nationality, residence, organizational affiliation, qualifications, or these characteristics may be used as a basis for exclusions from jobs. The most significant and explosive differentiation among groups of workers in countries at the early stages of industrialization has to do with race and nationality.

When workers are not readily hired to fill a vacancy, or the need cannot readily be met from the existing work force, then a group of rules may be expected to arise concerning training as a part of the procurement of a labor force. Some training may be done at the community or local level, but a work force is seldom fully adapted to the needs of an enterprise. Hence, rules arise concerning probationary periods, physical examinations, apprenticeship, and a wage schedule with provisions for individual merit reviews, and mention should be made of the training within industry programs, supervisory training, job methods, work study, and the like. Rules on discipline are also related to the standards for quality and quantity of work performance and are an integral part of training of the work force.

One of the pivotal questions in the development of an industrial labor force, for the enterprise or community, concerns the breadth of training or the degree of specialization of workers and technicians. They may be trained to perform only a few operations or a wide range of skills and activities. The decision is closely related to the speed of development of the industrial work force and priorities for immediate performance. Rapidly industrializing countries tend to adopt a functional and specialized training program for the work force, and a work force with limited training places greater responsibilities of coordination upon managements.

Enterprise managers in the course of industrialization come to be concerned with the loss of workers from turnover and the costs of training new workers, and workers may be concerned with both insecurity and the issues of equity among different workers when there is to be a reduction in the working force. At the early stages of industrialization few, if any, rules on redundancy seem to arise. Sooner or later some workers become more committed to an enterprise or to industrial forms of employment; their ties with the larger family system and village are likely to become weaker, and a migratory pattern is broken. While enterprise managements may have imposed rules on the order of redundancy in order to be rid of the least efficient workers, or those which have proved most troublesome, or those least servile, the workers subsequently come to express, by formal organization or by social pressure, preferences on the vital issues of priority in redundancy.

The rules that are gradually developed take a variety of forms: there is often provision for a minimum period of notice of any layoffs; the distinction comes to be made between rules for temporary and permanent severance of the employment relation; hours of work or days of work may be varied, allowing the work force to share available work opportunities; certain probationary or temporary employees may be excluded from the rights created for longer-service workers; in the event of layoffs an explicit priority of rights is often established indicating the order in which different workers are to be laid off; workers in certain nationality, marital status, or sex groups may have to go first; there may be specific prohibitions or limitations against layoffs, or rules for the payment of a proportion of wages, or the payment of a number of weeks of normal pay in case of permanent layoffs (severance pay). A variety of rules arise applicable to the community as well; an unemployment compensation system is such a group of rules.

The following propositions relate a few of the rules concerning building a labor force to the course and pace of industrialization:

Early recruitment which may involve the enterprise in a wide range of services, such as housing, medical services, canteens, transportation and the like, gives way to arrangements under which these services are provided by the community.

The differentiations among groups of workers that characterize the pre-industrial society — racial and ethnic groups, sex, residence, and family — tend to be destroyed. A new set of priorities and differentiations is created based upon a wide range of occupations and job classifications, nationality, or membership in labor organizations.

The resort to recruitment from within the enterprise for higher-skilled jobs is increased.

The extent of formal training is increased within the enterprise and the larger community.

A body of rules develops to limit narrowly the range of discretion of enterprise management in making decisions on layoffs.

A body of rules tends increasingly to provide special compensation and advantages to long-service employees; special compensation is provided for long-service employees made redundant under the rules of the enterprise.

Compensation and Wages. The rules of the work place community regarding compensation are a central feature of the total body of rules; they often influence a variety of other rules since affecting wage costs and workers' income is often an effective method to induce action on the part of enterprise managers and workers. As an illustration, seventh-day pay for six days of work in a week (but five days' pay for five days' work) was probably designed in oil-producing countries of the Middle East to discourage absenteeism, a form of attendance bonus. The monthly contract in parts of Africa (Kenya) was no doubt designed to attract workers from the reserves for a stated period. Premiums for undesirable or even hazardous working conditions are in part designed to provide an incentive to managements to eliminate or to control these aspects of work operations. Compensation rules are thus often used as an effective instrument for other purposes. They are particularly varied to meet problems of the recruitment and commitment of a labor force.[5]

Payments in Kind. At the early stages of industrialization the proportion of total compensation paid in kind, sometimes called "hidden emoluments," may be substantial. This proportion tends to decline with the growth of an industrial community so that in more economically developed communities the fraction is quite small and may be confined to certain types of medical services. In very highly developed communities with progressive income taxes, significant payments in kind may return, at least for elite and high income individuals. In the early stages, lodging for single men or housing for some family units, furnished by the enterprise, may be necessary to recruit a labor supply to isolated localities or from reserves as in Northern Rhodesia and Peru. In the early stages the furnishing of meals or canteens as a part of compensation is quite common; the provision of food is likely to have a direct impact upon worker productivity where caloric intake is low and where diet is poor and unbalanced and where money income would go to others in the extended family. Payments in kind are often a carry-over from arrangements practiced for agricultural and migratory labor.

As development proceeds, the value of payments in kind tends to be incorporated into the money wage, and even when those services are continued by an enterprise, there is often some money charge for the services. The rise of communities around a work place and the greater role of local authorities, the heavy capital costs of tying up the funds of an enterprise in housing, the problems of housing with discharged, laid-off, or retired workers are all factors tending to curtail or to eliminate this form of payment in kind. A combination of manager and landlord has often proven an endless source of difficulty. Although some new types of payment in kind arise as industrialization proceeds, they do not constitute for most workers a significant fraction of total compensation.

Components of Compensation. The money terms of compensation are customarily divided into wage rates, which may be set in terms of time or related to a measure of output or performance, and other components of compensation, such as vacations or holidays with pay, pension plans, and a wide range of supplementary-pay practices or fringe benefits.[6] In the course of economic development the total number of components tends to grow, although some components, such as family allowances, are characteristic of particular countries.[7] The proportion of supplementary pay components to total compensation varies to some degree with the industrializing elites, and the late starters have from the outset adopted many of the supplementary pay practices of the economically advanced countries. It is nonetheless valid that economic growth seems to add additional components to compensation, not merely to increase the value of existing components.

There is a tendency to earmark leisure (nonworking time) and compensation for particular purposes or to provide compensation in the event of particular contingencies. Rising incomes may be distributed in a variety of ways; inflation or a wage stabilization or wage restraint program has often added components to compensation. A number of the additional components to compensation can be directly related to the increasing role of government in industrial relations systems; social security programs in their full range of components constitute the largest contribution of governments.

Wage-Rate Structure. In the early stages of industrial development in small enterprises only personalized wages are likely to exist; the notion of wage rates for job classifications is a relatively advanced practice. Indeed, one of the early effects of industrial development is to create within enterprises, particularly larger enterprises, an explicit wage scale for more or less defined occupations or jobs. A time rate for a job requires some degree of standardization in performance among different workers in the labor force that are grouped together in one job category. A piecework or performance method of payment is compatible with much wider variations in training, skill, and performance among members of the labor force. It is no accident that on account of wide differences among workers piecework is prevalent in hired agriculture and on plantations. Piecework is predominant in many of the earliest industries to arise in the classical pattern of industrialization, such as textiles, clothing and shoes. It is customarily used in early industrial-type agriculture.

During the early phases of industrialization, it is well established that skill differentials tend to be relatively wide. The supply of skilled labor tends to be short compared to unskilled workers.

The types of skilled jobs required in industrial activity are not found extensively in pre-industrial countries, and the requisite workers must be trained or imported. Either method results in relatively wide skill differentials. In many parts of Africa and the Middle East the skilled manual jobs pay three or four times the unskilled rates, compared to 1.2 or 1.3 times in many economically advanced countries. The actual skill differentials may be further widened in the early stages by differentials according to race.[8] The skilled manual workers may be white and the unskilled black. In such cases some of these gross skill differentials may be often as high as ten or twelve times, or even higher.

In the course of economic development skill differentials tend to narrow. As a rough generalization, the skill wage differential among manual workers in enterprises in economically advanced countries tends to be 20 to 30 per cent more than unskilled rates, compared to the two to four times that skilled manual rates exceed unskilled rates in the early stages of industrialization. The narrowing process is related to the rise of general levels of education and the spread of technical education, the creation of a stable work force in enterprises that can increase the supply of skilled wokers by gradual upgrading and training on the job, the emergence of a local supply which reduces the need to import skilled labor incurring the costs of transport and movement, the rise of labor organizations which may press for more equalization in wage rates, and inflationary periods in which relatively uniform general wage increases are made on grounds of equity.[9] The elimination or narrowing of wage rate differentials based on race, nationality, or sex will also tend to narrow the gross skill differentials.

The process of creating a labor market tends to eliminate many of the differentiations among workers which are a carry-over from the pre-industrial society and which are frequently reflected in wage-rate differentials at the early stages. The assignment of manual jobs by tribe, nationality, sex, or race creates wage differentials which later tend to be narrowed or eliminated. Assignment of the work force between manual and clerical operations or between mechanical and menial tasks by nationality or tribe are common illustrations. At times the reduction of such wage-rate differentials directly reflects labor-market developments in the economically underdeveloped country, but just as often it reflects the importation of industrial values and specific legislation or international conventions from abroad.

Not only does an explicit wage-rate structure emerge in the rules of an enterprise, but a hierarchy of wage rates also emerges among enterprises in the same industry, among industries, and among localities and regions. It does not matter for present purposes what part of the total interenterprise wage-rate structure of a country is subject to explicit rules and decisions and which wage-rate relationships are left solely to the workings of the market. In some countries there comes to be a high degree of centralization of wage-rate changes and wage-setting institutions. The arrangements in Australia, New Zealand, the Netherlands, Scandinavia, and Italy are illustrative, although the rule-making processes formally provide for quite different decision making institutions. In other countries the interdependence of wage rates among enterprises is reflected more exclusively through the market. In the course of industrialization wage rates in an enterprise tend to become relatively more interdependent (whether or not formally recognized in wage-setting machinery) with the wage rates established in other enterprises.

The course of economic development tends to narrow inter-enterprise differentials in the wage-rate structure of a country. The development of the transportation system historically has affected both the movement of products and workers and hence the interdependence of wage rates in different enterprises. The interdependence of wage rates among enterprises in similar product markets, particularly in one locality or region, tends to emerge before the general interdependence among regions. As economic development proceeds further, as levels of employment rise, as capital flows more readily among regions, the wage rates among localities tend to become more interdependent and pure geographical wage-rate differentials also tend to narrow percentage-wise from what they were in the early stages of economic growth.

The industrial wage-rate structure shows a high degree of similarity (rank correlations of industrial average hourly earnings are high) among countries at comparable levels of development. This similarity among countries in the process of industrialization is to be explained by the fact that the same industries in different countries use roughly similar technologies which implies roughly similar proportions of workers in occupations or jobs of varying skills and wage-rate levels. Although the percentage differentials for skill among countries varies, as has been observed, the relative ordering of the wage rates for job classifications in an industry shows a high degree of similarity among countries. Combining a similarity in the proportion of workers at different occupations in an industry with a similarity in ranking of rates for these occupations yields industrial averages of wage rates or earnings that tend to be relatively quite similar among countries at the same stage in the process of industrialization.[10]

As economic growth proceeds, new industries arise to be slotted into the industrial wage structure, in part determined by the proportions of workers of varying skiils, by the requirements for new skills, and by the level of rates that are required to attract workers into an expanding industry. Many of these newer industries tend to be higher-wage industries for these reasons. Industrialization thus imparts an upward drift to the average wage in the country by virtue of an increasing proportion of higher wage industries.

Method of Wage Payment. The relative distribution between time and piece or incentive methods of wage payment shows little consistent pattern in the course of economic development, although there are marked differences in methods of payment among countries and in the policies of industrializing elites. The circumstances which give rise to piece or incentive rates at the early stages of industrialization are replaced by others in the course of economic growth. At the outset there are likely to be very wide differences in the quality and performance of members of the work force; payment by time places a heavy burden on supervision which is likely to be in very short supply and relatively expensive. If turnover rates are high and labor plentiful, the enterprise can avoid substantial costs of training involved in time rates and need be less concerned about higher earnings resulting in a smaller amount of labor inputs, as is often held to characterize workers in the early stages of economic growth.

As industrialization proceeds and a more stable and committed industrial work force is established, the factors leading to the use of piece or incentive rates tend to change. Piece rates are often designed to stimulate a greater rate of effort among trained workers to get the largest utilization of expensive capital equipment; some workers are on nominal incentives to preserve wage-rate relationships and to prevent complaints arising out of comparisons with other workers on piece or incentive earnings; the selling field often leads to a compensation system which includes commission rates on account of the difficulties of supervision with changing work places and the complex salesman-customer relationship. The process of industrialization changes the problems and the opportunities for using time or piece and incentive methods of wage payment.

The following propositions relate the rules concerning compensation and wages to the course of industrialization:

The proportion of total compensation paid in kind generally declines.

The number of components of compensation tends to expand.

An explicit wage-rate structure of job classifications or occupations arises in the enterprise.

Wage-rate differentials in percentage terms among types of skill tend to narrow.

Many wage-rate differentials that arise at the outset of economic development and which reflect differentiations (for example, by sex, tribe, nationality, or race) among workers significant to pre-industrial society tend to narrow or to be eliminated.

New differentiations arise, such as by occupation and industry.

A national wage-rate structure or hierarchy of rates arises exterior to an enterprise, and this structure may in varying degrees be the subject of explicit rules or left largely to the market in different countries.

A greater degree of interdependence in the interenterprise wage structure is likely to emerge first among enterprises in the same or closely allied product markets in a locality. Wage-rate differentials among such enterprises tend to narrow, or the wage rates become uniform. Uniformity spreads to enterprises in more distant localities in the same product grouping.

The geographical differentials in the wage-rate structure tend to narrow only at a later phase in economic development.

The interindustry wage-rate structure among countries tends to be somewhat similar, and new industries emerge often at the higher end of the wage-rate structure.

Procedures for the Settlement of Disputes. Another significant group of rules developed by an industrial relations system concern the procedures for the settlement of disputes, particularly over the application of existing rules. The distinction between procedures to resolve disputes over the application of existing rules and those concerned with disputes over a change in the rules or a new rule is a fundamental characteristic of an industrial relations system. Not all systems make this distinction. In some countries there is relatively integrated machinery for the resolution of disputes (Denmark), while in others there may be no single vertex in the procedures with a variety of autonomous bodies (England), and in still others there may be a number of procedures relatively specialized by type of issue with possible conflicts in jurisdiction among these procedures (France). The present concern is with the way economic development affects the procedures to settle disputes.

In the course of development of an industrial relations system rules tend to limit stringently the resort to force, including the strike and lockout.[11] The established procedures are designed as a substitute for open conflict. In some systems a limited place for open conflict (strike and lockout) is deliberately retained while in other systems group conflict is entirely prohibited or suppressed and forms of protest are largely by the "strike in detail."

In the earliest stages of industrialization, the development of dispute-settling machinery frequently utilizes the preexisting tribal and family system among the work force. In the course of development, procedures for handling disputes create neutrals (often government representatives) who have final authority to decide certain disputes. The emergence of neutrals is a necessary corollary to the limitation on conflict.

Industrial relations systems tend to develop specialists or professionals to administer the rules of the workplace and work community and to process disputes. The rules tend to provide that all disputes must be channeled on each side through these specialists. In the course of development there is a tendency for the neutrals to become continuing or permanent, subject often to some term of office, rather than limited to a single dispute.

Industrial relations systems tend to develop a constantly expanding body of precedents in the settlement of disputes. These are normally in written form. But the way in which precedents are used and the weight attached to them shows a wide spectrum among systems. Systems differ depending upon whether or not decisions are accompanied by elaborate opinions and explanations. They differ in the extent to which procedures are formal and the extent to which precedents are regarded as binding on the settlement of future disputes.

The following propositions show the relation between the rules concerning procedures for the settlement of disputes in an industrial relations system and the course of industrialization:

The resort to force and open conflict tends to decline.

Formal disputes settling machinery and procedures arise at the plant, industry, and national level.

At the plant level, the machinery in the initial stages may be related for a period to the system of authority in the traditional society.

There arise professionals to handle disputes in the organizations of workers, management, and state agencies.

There arise private neutrals or government representatives to settle disputes.

The rules of the work place and work community require an industrial jurisprudence.

Industrializing Elites and Rules of the Work Place

The industrialization process has been shown to have systematic impact upon the rules of the work community; the important rules on recruitment and commitment, compensation and on dispute settlement have been used as illustrations. But there is significant variation in these rules established in the industrial relations systems of different ideal types of elites directing industrialization. Each elite adopts policies and strategies for compensation and wages and dispute settlement which are distinctive in some major respects.

Recruitment and Commitment. As was observed in Chapter 7, each of the ideal types of industrializing elites tends to approach the development of an industrial labor force and labor markets with somewhat different interests, objectives, and methods. The dynastic elite is anxious to preserve as much as possible of the preexisting social and family arrangements and the traditional differentiations among groups of potential workers. It is least concerned with the training of the labor force in the enterprise or the community, and there develop stringent restrictions against layoffs established by law.

The middle-class elite has no particular attachment or animus toward the preexisting arrangements, but it advocates changes brought about by the working of a labor market in which movements of workers are ordered by the choices of individual workers registered in the market against the demands of enterprises. Training is substantially a community responsibility in which enterprises engage when impelled by labor shortages. Priorities are established in layoffs and in the remaining jobs by detailed rules regulating enterprise management.

The revolutionary intellectuals seek rapidly to sweep away the preexisting differentiations; agricultural policy is designed to separate potential workers from the land requiring them to go to the cities, and strong indirect pressures and even enforced direction is used to secure the rapid creation and allocation of the industrial labor force. Elaborate training programs are established in both enterprises and the community to furnish labor skills required by the rapid pace of industrialization. The training is narrow and technical. Redundancy is less a problem.

The colonial elite often resorts to money taxes, labor drafts, labor contractors, force, and coercion in the development of a labor force from indigenous groups. Technical and managerial positions, and even in some cases the skilled jobs, are reserved for the citizens of the home country. Some recruitment policies vary with the type of colonialism. The colonial elite is unconcerned with the development of skill levels and training of indigenous workers beyond the immediate needs of the enterprise. Layoffs are entirely at the discretion of enterprise and colonial managers.

The nationalist elite seeks to eliminate the preferred position of the former colonialists, particularly in managerial and skilled positions. This elite seeks to place into effect advanced community training programs, although training in enterprises may be neglected. Layoffs are often restricted and inefficient use of labor develops, particularly in large foreign enterprises.

Payments in Kind. The dynastic elite is most likely to adopt payments in kind and retain them longer. These payments are consistent with the paternal attitudes of the state and management toward the work force. Payments in kind are well regarded in themselves. The middle-class elite regards such payments as temporary and exceptional departures from a market economy, while the revolutionary intellectual elite is more inclined to use those methods of compensation when essential to the direct allocation of the labor force. The colonial elite makes considerable use of payments in kind to recruit a labor supply, to offset the tendency of individuals to work less with higher money payments, to increase the calories directly available to manual workers, and to recruit and to commit a labor force without relying to the same extent upon money wage-rate increases. The nationalist leaders often seek to dismantle payment-in-kind arrangements as symbols of colonialism and as largely alien to an economically advanced country.

Components of Compensation. The dynastic elite multiplies the components of compensation by placing emphasis upon family allowances, social-security benefits, and the like, so that basic wage-rates constitute a relatively smaller proportion of total compensation.

In the society of the middle-class elite there is a tendency to pay a much larger fraction of total compensation in basic wage rates and to look to individual workers to allocate income among competing uses rather than to predetermine the allocation. There is relatively little interest in family allowances. The separate components of compensation that arise are frequently designed to regulate enterprise management or to meet specialized industry problems rather than solely to increase income.

The revolutionary intellectual elite tends to develop a larger number of components than the middle-class elite, and these are designed to affect the direction and supply of workers rather than to circumscribe management.

The colonial elite tends to conform to the compensation components of the mother country, except that citizens of the mother country receive additional benefits such as home leave and allowances, and the indigenous workers may not receive some of the components of compensation of the mother country. The nationalist leaders adopt the full range of compensation of more advanced countries. Programs of unemployment compensation, social security, vacations and the like are imposed by regulations at an early date as a symbol of advancement.

Wage-Rate Structure. The dynastic elite tends to establish much lower wage-rate differentials for skill. This elite does not need wide differentials to recruit skilled labor with a relatively slower pace of industrialization. The wage structure of the country as a whole is less highly interdependent, and product market competition is a much less active factor influencing relative wage rates and the allocation of the labor force.

In the economy of the middle-class elite, all wage-rate differentials are relatively more interdependent and more responsive to labor and product-market competitive conditions. Skill differentials tend to be determined in the same way by relative labor scarcities.

The revolutionary intellectual elite establishes relatively wide skill differentials to help to attract the large amount of skilled labor needed in a short period of time. The wage structure, as the price structure, on the whole plays a less immediate and short-run role in the allocation of resources. The wage-rate structure is less responsive to changes in product prices, and accordingly it is less interdependent than in the middle-class led economy.

The wage-rate structure of the colonial elite is likely to be dominated by the differences between workers from the mother country, who receive the high skilled and managerial and technical jobs, and local residents who are employed in semiskilled and unskilled jobs, at least at the outset. The gross skill differentials are accordingly very wide. Other wage rates are likely to reflect the recruitment policy of the colonial elite; thus, the wage structure may be designed for bachelors or for a family worker.

The nationalist leader elite is likely to follow a policy of eliminating the extent of wage-rate differentials of the colonial period. A more egalitarian wage rate structure is adopted.

Method of Wage Payment. The dynastic elite tends to use piece rate and incentive methods of pay least frequently. It is ideologically objectionable since it magnifies differences in earnings among workers. The revolutionary intellectuals, in their drive for production, seek to use these methods of wage payment as universally as possible. The middle-class elite utilizes piece rates only moderately, depending upon the characteristics of the particular industry; there are few ideological considerations involved in the choice. The colonial administrators tend to make extensive use of piecework on account of the variations in the quality of the labor force and the turnover of workers. The nationalist elite has no distinctive policy, and in most cases tends to continue the existing methods of wage payment.

Procedures for Disputes Settlement. The procedures established by the industrializing elites for the settlement of disputes also tend to reflect some characteristic differences. The dynastic elite seeks to establish an industrial relations system which formally leaves no role for conflict. Conflict is abhorred since it would destroy the paternalistic view of the work community. The neutrals are government representatives, and labor and management organizations have little direct role in their selection or in direct shaping of the decisions. The proceedings tend to be formal, and decisions are seldom a form of agreement. The neutrals tend to be lawyers, and great weight is attached to formal precedents.

The middle class establishes industrial-relations systems which deliberately leave some room for conflict on some types of disputes in the event of failure to achieve an earlier agreement. Labor and management organizations play a large role in the selection of neutrals whether or not they are appointed by governments. The proceedings tend to be more informal, and decisions are frequently mediated and constitute real agreement between the parties. Neutrals need not always be lawyers. Precedents are more flexibly used.

The revolutionary intellectuals establish industrial relations systems which provide no room for conflict which would violate the accepted ideology. The neutrals are government-appointed, and procedures tend to be formal. Neutrals are likely to be trained as lawyers. Any mediation of a dispute is likely to involve the party and governmental agencies rather than the managers and workers' organizations, although some of the same individuals may be involved.

The colonial elite establishes industrial relations systems modeled after that of the mother country. Industrial conflict tends to be associated with independence and nationalism and is likely to be less tolerated than in the mother country. Labor organizations are seldom encouraged by the elite, but where disputes do arise the pattern in the mother country is adopted with an even greater role for the colonial administrators.

The nationalist leaders tend to abhor conflict on the grounds that it interferes with national efforts to industrialize. Strikes which were used to harass and dislodge the colonialists are not to be used against the interests of the new nation. The forms of the conventions and resolutions of the ILO have great appeal, although actual practice is likely to reflect considerable government control over labor organizations and management. The government plays a large role in the settlement of disputes, and compulsory arbitration or settlement of disputes on terms determined by the government is most common.

Industrialization universally creates industrial relations systems which establish a web of rules relating the managers and the managed. In all systems managers share rule making functions, in varying ways and degrees, with workers and the state. In the course of industrialization rule-making tends to become more formal. There have been pointed out many common features to the substantive rules which are derived from the logic of industrialization and the common features of technology and market constraints. But there is also diversity in these rules derived from the policies of the industrializing elites.

Chart 8 summarizes the diversity in the rules relating to recruitment and commitment, compensation and wages, and procedures for dispute settlement which tend to be established by each of the idealized types of elites leading industrialization. It is essential to see how the inner logic and implications of industrialization for the work place are given diverse form by the policies and ideologies of particular elites. The stage of industrialization also affects the content of the rules. The history of rule-making at the work place in any particular industrializing country is illuminated by appraising the influences inherent in economic growth and the impact of coherent policies of industrializing elites.

PART III

THE ROAD AHEAD

The first five chapters developed the theme of the uniformities and the diversities in the industrialization process. The inherent logic of industrialism interacts with the diversity of cultural factors, economic constraints, and the strategies of the industrializing elites.

The next four chapters were concerned with the theme of the managers and the managed. The universals are enterprise managers, industrial workers, the commitment of the labor force, the web of rules, labor organizations, and industrial relations systems. The diversities and the particularities in the relationships of the managers and the managed reflect the time in history at which industrialization begins, the stage of development, the distinctive cultural and economic settings, and the strategies of the industrializing elites including those concerning the pace of transformation.

The final chapter turns from industrial relations to the industrialization process as a whole. It turns from the past to the long-term future. The chapter starts by examining the question of how the various elites have achieved their supremacy, and the tendencies for change within each ideal type. The chapter then projects the road ahead, focusing upon both the threads of diversity and the sources of uniformity. The industrialization process converges toward pluralistic industrialism.

CHAPTER 10

PLURALISTIC INDUSTRIALISM

Industrialization has been abroad in the world only about two centuries. One century ago perhaps only England had crossed the great divide on the road toward the industrial society. By the mid-twentieth century, at least a third of the population of the world, or close to one billion people, lived in countries well established in the process of industrialization, and most of the other two-thirds of the world's population was in countries in the throes of starting to industrialize. Relatively few remnants of mankind were as yet untouched by this new and vital force. By the middle of the twenty-first century, industrialization will have swept away most pre-industrial forms of society, except possibly for a few odd backwaters.

This is the great transformation in the long history of mankind on this planet — more basic, more rapid, and more universal than any earlier transformation.

Modern industrial civilization, with its technical evolution and intellectual drive, is, as we know, the most aggressive form of civilization that mankind has ever known. Its twin impact of science and industry is one that involves a total transformation of all aspects of life — not only of organization and technique but of fundamental habits of thought and social behavior. You have only to consider the impact of this type of society upon people who have not yet moved beyond the simplest patterns of living and working to see that, without immense patience, understanding, and restraint, the incoming settlers will annihilate the whole social apparatus of the backward local peoples. Yet these qualities are not usually the qualities of conquerors or pioneers.[1]

Industrialization creates vast urban areas; makes possible a great explosion of population; yields a new standard of living and of leisure: draws on new skills both social and technical; requires a vast network of rules to guide and coerce men in the complex and interrelated tasks essential to its successful growth; spawns new centers of organized power and furthers the concentration of authority in old centers, particularly the state; forges new methods of attaining and retaining this power; links men together in new chains of subordination and invites frictions at each of the links in these chains; and provides a new culture based on mass tastes and mass consumption which gradually overwhelms the many and varied preexisting cultures. It is the great transformation — successful, all-embracing, irreversible.

Central to this transformation are the relations of managers and the managed. Much of the working lives of men is spent in constant contact with the reciprocal relations of manager to managed; and these relations set the occupational roles and working behavior of most members of the labor force. But manager and managed do not form any separate and clear-cut classes. Many of the managers are in turn managed from above, and many of the managed in turn manage someone below. Few are those who only manage, and many are those who are only managed; but there is a hierarchy of managerial relations far too complex to compress into simple class relations. Instead a society develops of the semimanagers and the semimanaged.

Industrial man develops new patterns of relations different from those of tribal members and chieftain, serf and lord of the manor, craftsman and merchant prince, or even worker and capitalist. These relations are more varied and more complex than in preexisting societies. Industrial man leads a new kind of life and, in the course of it, becomes a new kind of person. He views himself and others, society and the universe in new ways. The old ideologies and the old theories lose their meaning.

How may we interpret what is happening; what the new forms of relations really are and will be? Earlier we sought to explain the developments in part as due to the logic of industrialism itself and in part to specific cultural and environmental influences within nations. But we also related them to the strategies of the several industrializing elites, and sought to describe how the nature of these elites affected the selection and behavior of managers, the structuring of the labor force, the response of the workers, the interweaving of management, labor, and the state. We did not, however, seek to explain how each elite came

into its dominant position; or how these elites have changed
their strategies or were replaced; or what the future trends may be
affecting the character and behavior of these elites; and how
these trends may in turn affect the nature of industrial relations.
This chapter seeks to give some impressions of the dynamics of
the total situation as compared with the more sectional approach
in earlier chapters.

The Sources of the Elites

Some elites have achieved supremacy in some places and
others in others; some for one reason and some for another. The
dynastic elites with their paternal community, the middle
classes with the market system, the revolutionary intellectuals
with their centralized state, the colonial administrators with
their service to the home market or the compatriot settlers
or the home ideology, and the nationalist leaders with their state-
guided development all have their areas where they exercise
the dominant authority in society.

How did they happen to get this authority? In each single
case the explanation involves a great deal of historical detail.
Viewed broadly, however, there appear to have been four major
considerations variously involved: the nature of the preexisting
society, the role of geography, the stage of history, and the accidents of history.

The Preexisting Society. Industrialization began in Western
Europe. It is one of the mysteries of history why it began there and
at the time it did. Ancient Greece and Rome and before them
Mesopotamia and Egypt had developed a capacity for new ideas
and new ways of doing things. In each of these societies,
they could build buildings, organize men, engage in elaborate
commerce, develop transportation, keep accounts. But they never
developed science nor got the machine capable of repetitive
operations and the secret of constant sources of power other than
man or beast. The Chinese and even the Mayan civilizations
also had many of the conditions necessary for the start of industrialization; but it never started.

In the cities of Western Europe, commerce and craftsmanship
rose to high levels. When the new machines and the new sources

of power came along there was already a substantial urban middle class oriented toward profit and sufficiently independent of the older feudal order to undertake the industrializing process. The early industrialization in England and the Lowlands fell largely to the lot of the new middle-class entrepreneurs accustomed to and in congruence with a market economy and a democratic polity. Here was a new and better way of getting things done and making profit. The new held no terror for them because they were already in opposition to the old feudal order. No other elite group at this time could have so easily and quickly embraced and encouraged the new productive techniques.[2]

The new industrialization found acceptance elsewhere, and sometimes in the most unlikely places. Dynastic elites still in control of their societies, as in Germany, Japan, and Iran, saw the success of the new technique and came to use it. In Germany with the competition of England, in Japan with its fear of foreign conquest, and in Iran with its fear of social revolution, the obvious hand of the future impelled the established elites to accept the unaccustomed methods while still seeking to preserve as much as they could of the old order. Some dynastic elites elsewhere, however, either refused to come to terms with the new modes of production or were so ineffective they could not make proper use of them. Only when the dynastic elites were at the same time realistic, patriotic, and strong did they seize control of the industrializing process. Once they had hold of it they had enough authority to introduce the new system of production rapidly and efficiently; but the introduction was still an act of necessity and not of desire. By a strange turn of fate, in recent times, the old has come to embrace the new. The old dynastic elites which once scorned commercial and industrial pursuits, as in England, have come to seize upon industrial endeavor, as in parts of Latin America and the Arab world, as the source of their salvation. The old dynastic elite has taken the place of the new middle class as carrier of change.

The middle-class and dynastic elites alike, and for much the same reasons, took industrialization into many more primitive societies in the interests of the home country. These societies were sufficiently primitive economically so that they could not develop or at least had not developed industrially. In some cases the idea of industrializing was totally new to them. In any event, they did not have the means of effective resistance in the face of the weapons placed in the hands of the colonial powers by their machines. Industrialization under these conditions usually affected only a segment of the economy, most often plantation agriculture or extractive pursuits, but the society was impregnated by the new industrial order. Thus industrialization initially came to Indonesia, India, the Congo, and many other parts of the world under colonial auspices.

In reaction to colonialism or to a resistant or ineffective dynastic elite or a combination of both, nationalist leaders have seized control in many parts of the world customarily in the name of national progress, as in Egypt, Mexico, Indonesia, and now lead the industrializing process. Also in reaction to colonialism or to a resistant or ineffectual dynastic elite or to a combination of both, revolutionary intellectuals have also captured nations for the sake of forced draft industrialization; as they took over in Russia from a crumbling aristocracy and in China from a society too often run by war lords in the country and foreign firms in the treaty ports. Never have the nationalist leaders or the revolutionary intellectuals attained control, by means of internal action, from a vigorous middle class or dynastic elite. In areas and times mutually conducive to their ascendancy, the nationalist leaders and the revolutionary intellectuals often stand as alternatives to each other, and are thus inherently competing for power. The one responds to national and the other to international considerations; and out of this arises the necessity for their enmity.

Thus a successful commercial society is predisposed toward middle-class leadership of industrialization; a feudal or semifeudal system toward continued leadership by the dynastic elite if it is realistic enough and forceful enough; a truly primitive society toward guidance, although often involuntarily, by the representatives of a colonial power; the evolving colonial or the decaying feudal society toward either nationalist leaders or revolutionary intellectuals. The middle-class leadership attains supremacy by its mere existence and its inherent temperament; the dynastic, by the right of its hereditary authority; the colonial, by virtue of its technical and military superiority; the nationalist

and revolutionary intellectuals through the weakness of others
and their own will to power.

The Fact of Geography. This factor affects the advent to
power of each of the several elites through the influence of pro-
pinquity, of discovery, and of conquest. The British system
had its impact in Western and Northern Europe, the North
American in Latin America, the Soviet in China; in each case
both through example and through influence. The British colo-
nized North America and Australia. The British conquered India;
the Dutch, Indonesia; the Soviets, Eastern Europe; the Chinese, Tibet. Africa was divided up by Western European powers.
Each dominant nation favored its own system of industrialization.

The Stage of History. This third factor has had its impact on
the selection of the elites. Before World War I, industrialization
was undertaken by middle-class, dynastic, or colonial elites;
since World War I, and particularly since World War II, by nationalist leaders and revolutionary intellectuals. The great rise
of new nationalist leaders intent on industrialization has
taken place since 1918. They have risen against alien control
and against backwardness. By 1918, colonialism had passed its
zenith as an international influence and in many colonial countries, with the spread of skills and education, a new class of
indigenous leaders was arising. By 1918, industrialization was
so obviously the road to power, to better health, to higher standards of living, and to education that it became the goal of mankind and the essence of national aspiration. Turkey was among
the first to seek modernization under nationalist leaders.

By 1918, the Bolsheviks had attained power in Russia and
set about the successful and rapid industrialization of that country, with visions of ultimate world-wide conquest. Also by 1918,
middle-class elements and most dynastic elites which had the
vision and the vigor to industrialize their countries had, by and
large, already begun to do so. Thus the large new areas for
industrialization since 1918 have largely fallen under the leadership of the nationalists or the revolutionary intellectuals, both
of whom were promising progress; except that, as noted earlier,
some still reigning dynastic elites have in recent times undertaken industrialization in the interests of self-preservation.

The middle class began the process of industrialization, the dynastic elite borrowed it, the revolutionary intellectuals seized it by force, the colonial administrators spread it, and the nationalists in turn wrested it from them.

The Accidents of History. Finally, among our four considerations, the accidents of history help explain who seizes the reins. War and depression have determined a great deal of history. The revolutionary intellectuals would not so certainly have taken over Russia except for World War I and China except for World War II. Colonialism came to a quicker end in India and Indonesia because of World War II. The chief beneficiaries of violent eruption have been the nationalists and the revolutionary intellectuals.

The preexisting society, geographical considerations, the time period in history, and climaxes of events each serve to explain, in part, the supremacy of a particular elite and its preferred system of organization in particular countries.

The Natural History of the Elites

The actual industrializing elites are seldom, if ever, as we have noted earlier, pure or ideal types. They are often both mixed and changing by type, although there is usually enough of the central theme of the ideal type to permit differentiation and classification of systems. At this stage in history, in the middle of the twentieth century, we can still identify many countries which adhere to one or another of these types; but relatively few of them illustrate the particular type in all its purity. Each type, however, seems to have its own natural tendencies for evolution and thus there exist more or less parallel evolutions for countries equally patterned after a certain type.

The Erosion of the Dynastic Elite. Where the dynastic elite governs ineffectually, as it frequently has done, the country will, in modern times, shift either to nationalist or revolutionary intellectual leadership. If it governs effectively, however, it is also subject to changes. As industrialization proceeds, the hereditary elite expands, recruiting new members from lower strata in its society and particularly by the process of selection through the mechanisms of higher education. It becomes less of a class apart. Also, industrialization requires a great deal of mobility in the labor force, from one occupational level to another, from one area to another, from one enterprise to another. This tends to break down the paternal plant community as does the growth of social services provided by other institutions than the enterprise. Class lines are softened. The political parties of the working class and the labor organizations become gradually less ideological, although this can take a long time and involve many conflicts between the traditionalists and the revisionists. Both the managerial and working classes converge toward the upper and lower ranges of the middle class in their habits and beliefs. Tradition and status mean less; competition and contracts mean more. The worker becomes more independent and the manager more professional. Attitudes toward industrial conflict also have softened. The labor organizations come to share more of the rule-making authority.

The society is moving more toward the middle-class ideal type. But it may retain for a long time remnants of the earlier ideological struggle which is so typical of such societies: permanently enhanced power for the state, a heightened attention to the role of occupation in determining the standing of an individual. The society, however, is no longer so traditional and the managers no longer so paternal.

The Middle Class and the Organization Society. The middle-class system is the most stable of our several types, partly because the middle class is also the mediating class in society and makes its adjustments a little at a time rather than in dramatic bursts. In fact, the middle class once in full control of the industrialization process has never in history lost its authority for internal reasons. This does not mean, nevertheless, that the middle-class system does not itself change significantly.

The size of enterprise becomes larger. A separation takes place between ownership and management. Workers add to their power through their own large-scale organizations. The state takes on ever new duties. It provides social security, regulates competition and industrial conflict, redistributes wealth, assures a minimum level of economic activity and employment, and enters the internal life of private organizations to guarantee equality of treatment and opportunities for participation. It becomes the biggest single employer.

The market loses some of its influence. Decisions are supplied by rules and by group actions as well as by atomistic interchanges in the market place. The worker becomes more closely tied to his particular employment through seniority rules and security benefits. Individual self-advancement gives way increasingly to efforts at group advancement. The middle class becomes less and less a definable leadership elite, as many elements in society share urban middle-class status. The middle class still rules, but less obviously so; and the markets are still major instruments for making decisions, but they are no longer so open.

The Non-Revolutionary Intellectuals. The revolutionary intellectuals are committed to the view that the great climactic change through which they seize power is the last great change in social relations. The classless society will emerge, and, according to Marx, the only other really substantial change in prospect is the "withering away of the state." Thus far it has not withered, and it is highly unlikely it ever will. But other changes can and do take place.

There is in communist society, as noted earlier, the great contradiction between the demands of the ideology and the desires of the populace. These desires are particularly hard to deal with if they arise from a subjugated people (Poland, Hungary) who are also resistant to essentially alien rule of an alien system. They have their nationalism around which to rally opposition and pressure. Aside from the pressure of nationalism against the "total colonialism" of the Communists, there may also be the antagonistic interests of some national minorities, as in the Soviet Union itself.

The desires of the populace, however, are basic under any circumstances, whether encouraged by nationalism or not. The ideology calls for an attack on the old culture, and there are those who cherish it. The ideology requires an immense national effort of hard work and austerity, and there are those who resent it. The ideology calls for a great centralization of power, and there are those who seek to share it. The most persistent drive is probably in the direction of sharing power. The military makes its demands. The scientists and the new managers make theirs. Even the workers, as they get more skill and responsibility, and thus power, can make demands of their own. These groups may come to have their own areas within which they can govern; and, while they may not share authority over society, they may be able to bring greater influence to bear upon those who do. Universal education, which is an imperative of successful industrialization, may even open up an eventual possibility of sharing political power widely throughout the society.

The requirement of efficiency itself may force some fractionalization of power. As there are more enterprises and particularly as more enterprises are involved in the production and distribution of a myriad of consumer goods and the provision of an increasing range of personal services, central control becomes less possible. The more successful the process of industrialization, the more reliance has to be placed on localized decisions and on markets, instead of on centralized decisions and plans; and markets bring the middle-class approach in their wake.

The new generations of leaders become more secure, more professional, more bureaucratically interested in standard performance than in all-out effort, further removed from the old ideological considerations and the traditions of the revolution. The wolves give way to the watchdogs. With greater educational opportunities and a less desperate need for trained people, the class stratification of the society declines, and a new equality seeps into the society. Here, too, more people become middle class; the status of the ruling class is no longer so comparatively high. Forced-draft industrialization becomes less forced; the peak of each new cycle of effort declines toward the norm.

The masses also will come to crave more of the product of their own labor; and the drive for more consumers' goods and better housing will change the society too.[3]

The revolutionary intellectuals appeal particularly to the "transitionals"[4] in societies in the very early stages of industrialization. They promise an end to the old ruling elite or the colonial power, to the old tribal or feudal culture, to economic and educational backwardness. They have much less to offer to others than to the "transitionals" and particularly have they little to offer to the members of a developed middle-class society. They may have some continuing appeal to the workers in a class society under a dynastic elite, but if this elite is successful in managing industrialization and moves over time toward the middle-class approach, the appeal lessens. In the nationalists, they meet competitors who offer the same things and can hold the allegiance of the "transitionals" if they are reasonably successful in delivering what they promise.

The revolutionary intellectuals also have programs for the handling of the problems of the transition — rapid commitment of a labor force, the fast buildup of an educational system, the quick encouragement of labor discipline and productivity, the enlargement of the gap between current consumption and current production for the sake of investment, development of an export surplus from the agricultural segment to feed the cities, suppression of industrial conflict.

Again, however, they have much less in the way of programs for an advanced industrial society. They are inept, because of the rigidity of their ideology, in handling diversified production, in responding to the insistent calls for fractionalized power, in giving the freedom for inquiry which goes along with highly developed educational and research institutions.

Their historical message may be only to the "transitionals" anxious to have behind them a decaying feudal or alien colonial society; and their greatest historical impact may be, not the creation of the "classless" society, but the firm, even forceful handling of the economic and political problems in the immediate transition from the traditional to the technological society. They respond to the problems at one stage in history and to the defaults of others in the handling of those problems; their rule is neither inevitable nor necessarily everlasting. It is communism that withers away. However that may be, any society they run, despite any reluctant tendency toward gratification of the desires of the masses, will be comparatively disposed toward the managerial state, to the use of force, to the service of technology, to the supremacy of the party, to the suppression of conflict so long as their ideology has any hold either in theory or in continued practice and acceptance.

The Fate of All Colonies. The colonial system likewise has its natural history. It is the most transient of the several ideal types of elites. "Colonialism spawned its destroyer — nationalism."[5] The segmented colonialism and settler colonialism, although the latter much more reluctantly, give way to nationalism or, in extreme cases, to the rule of the revolutionary intellectuals.

Total colonialism may be successful, but in that event ceases to be colonialism by becoming the system of the country itself. No advanced industrializing society has ever yet been run by aliens.

The Nationalists as Experimenters. Nationalism too has its inherent tendencies. It relies heavily on the state, but not so rigidly as the revolutionary intellectuals. Consequently, private enterprise and markets not only have a chance to survive, but the opportunity to take over larger areas of the economy as they are capable of doing so. Nationalism often conduces to one-party rule or domination, but again this is not based on ideology and, as consensus develops in the society and education spreads, a greater distribution of political power can occur. The nationalist leaders, having many of the same goals as the revolutionary intellectuals, are, however, not bound by an all-pervading ideology. They are opportunists and experimenters. This has its disadvantages and its advantages. The lack of an effective ideology leads to much stumbling and uncertainty in the early stages; but it also helps avoid confining rigidities in the later stages of industrialization. Generally, nationalism, if successful, will tend toward a modified version of the middle-class approach, modified by heavier emphasis on the state; if unsuccessful, however, only the revolutionary intellectuals can readily attain leadership.

The natural history of each of our five types is to change; some completely (colonial), some drastically (dynastic elite and nationalist), and some substantially (middle-class, revolutionary intellectual); but they all do change. Chart 9 summarizes the natural history of these ideal types of elites. Will these changes keep on occurring in the future as in the past and, if so, in what direction?

The Road Ahead: The Threads of Diversity

Industrialization came into a most varied world; a world with many cultures, at many stages of development from the primitiveness of quasi-animal life to high levels of civilization, under the rules of many different elites and beliefs. It was a world marked by great diversity; in terms of the contrast between the least and the most civilized societies, a world more diverse than at any time during the earlier history of mankind on this planet.

CHART 9.

The sources of the elites and the natural history of their systems.

Industrializing Elite	Dynastic	Middle-Class	Revolutionary-Intellectuals	Colonial Administrators	Nationalist Leaders
Pre-existing society	Strongly led feudal or quasi-feudal.	Commercial.	Weakly led quasi-feudal; or colonial.	Primitive.	Weakly led quasi-feudal; or colonial.
Stage in history	Relatively early.	Relatively early.	Relatively late.	Relatively early.	Relatively late.
"Normality" of development	"Normal."	"Normal."	Development at a crisis point (war or depression).	Most transient.	Development often at a crisis point (war or depression).
Inherent direction of change	Less elitist and paternal.	More group and state action.	Less ideological; more bureaucratic; more sensitive to the wishes of the masses and of other emerging elites.	Nationalism; and occasionally rule by revolutionary intellectuals.	More middle-class influence, if successful; revolutionary intellectuals, if unsuccessful.
Changing relation to markets	Larger role.	Markets lose some of their influence.	Larger role.	Larger role internally and externally.	Markets qualified by nationalist state.

Into the midst of this disparity of systems there intruded a new and vastly superior technique of production; a technique which by its very nature always pushed for identity since the more modern was always the more superior. This technique knew no geographical limits; recognized no elites or ideologies. Once unleashed on the world, the new technique kept spreading and kept advancing.

Men ignored or rejected or accepted this new method of production in many different reactions. Different elites undertook its sponsorship, some effectively and some ineffectively; and sought to organize society in such a way as both to use the new technique and to serve their own goals, whatever they might be. Ideologies were formulated in an effort to understand, to control, to attack, and to defend the new arrangements.

In the intervening two centuries since the new techniques began to be a real force in parts of the world, many changes have taken place and are still taking place. This is part of the long and as yet unconcluded process of man's adaptation. The arrangements made by men are still quite various, although one might argue that with a single productive technique there should be one best way to organize its use. If there is one best way, men certainly have not yet agreed upon it. Diversity continues to mark the process of adjustment. The sources of this continued diversity are several.

The Persistence of the Strategies. To begin with, the differing elites each tend to organize the process in a different fashion. Once structured, the institutions and the ways of doing things tend to develop a life and a persistency of their own, provided the ruling elites are reasonably successful in handling the problems of industrialization and the other problems of a society. There are, after all, several possible ways of organizing an industrial society. Aside from wars and depression, the normal tests of adequacy are not too hard to meet when using a technique which, with competent direction, is capable of improving many of the aspects of the lives of men. Only the colonial system is sure to fail at some point because of its alien character. The basic test for the dynastic elite, the middle class, and the nationalist leaders is whether they can make reasonably rapid progress. Only the middle class has fully proved that it can. The

dynastic elite may be held back by tradition and the nationalists by uncertainty.

The basic test for the revolutionary intellectuals is whether
they can avoid going too fast, for their ideology tends to draw
them into pushing the population to its very limits of endurance,
particularly in the earlier stages; and, in the later stages, whether
they can adjust adequately to the changing nature of the masses.
The colonial aside, each of the other elites can maintain itself
from sudden change, provided it pushes the new process neither
too little nor too much, and the leeway between too little and
too much is quite substantial. But none of the elites can insulate
itself from gradual change.

As each elite maintains itself, it seeks to preserve, even though
changed over time, the essential elements of its system — its role
for the state, its place for the leaders, its preferred rate of development and source of capital, its place for labor organizations,
and its attitude toward industrial conflict, its policies toward
the preexisting culture. Not only the elites but also the workers
tend to preserve their particular institutions and their special
beliefs. Each system has a degree of endurance.

This durability is strengthened by the rigidity of the ideology.
Since the middle-class and the nationalist approaches have the
least static ideology, they are most subject to experiment and to
change, painful as experiment and change always are; since the
dynastic elite and the revolutionary intellectuals have a firmer
ideological base and class identification, they are likely to be the
most rigid and the most resistant to changes, and they can
easily become the most "old fashioned" and the least adaptable.
But the slogans, the heroes, the vested interests that collect around
an ideology and a strategy for organizing society give any system
considerable tenacity and are a great source of diversity in an
industrializing world.

The Imprint of Culture. The culture of a nation and the
degree of its continued adherence to that culture also affect
world-wide diversity in the process of industrialization. The family
and the class carry on, particularly under the dynastic elite. Education often adapts quite slowly from its traditional forms, again
particularly under the dynastic elite. But other national traits
carry on as well — the discipline and energy of the Germans,

the individualism of the French, the easy-going approach of the Indonesians. France is a particularly good example of how attitudes from an earlier stage of political and economic development can carry on and give a very special cast to the face of industrialization. The French are particularly conscious of their national identity and character, and intent on preserving their national traits; but they are not alone in this. Rather there seems to be a new consciousness in a number of countries of their special national heritages.

The Hour on the Clock of Evolution. The stage of development, regardless of the nature of the leadership, is another source of variation. Early industrialization, regardless of the overall strategy, has its own special problems, its own special attitudes, its own special approaches. Mature industrialization, with its well-developed institutions and web of rules, its full complement of industries and services and trades, its settled labor force, its greater consensus, is a different phenomenon, regardless of the organizing forces. Degree of development, of course, relates both to the date of the start and the rate of change.

The Culture of the Industry. The special character of the basic resources and the central industries is another factor causing variations from one country to another. Plantation agriculture, crude oil production, heavy industry, light industry, each give a tone to their society. Some industries are more prone to industrial unrest than others; some are more likely to engage in paternalistic practices; some are occupationally more highly stratified; some are more subject to a system of norms; some have more large-scale enterprises. Each industry has its own character — the waterfront, coal mining, banking — and these cast their reflections on the surrounding society. A small or a newly industrialized economy is more likely to reflect the special character of one or a few industries than is a large and mature economy. Oil gives a special flavor to Iraq, as textiles and coal mining once did to England.

People and Performance. Finally, the demographic aspects of a nation impart to its industrialization continuing characteristics. A relatively empty country, like Australia, has quite a different course of development than a heavily populated one, like India; wages tend to be higher, recruitment more difficult, a significant increase in the standard of living more possible, a high evaluation of the worth of the individual worker and the attention he deserves more likely; and so forth.

Among all these forces for diversity, or rigidity, as it may also be viewed, the two most forceful are a clear ideology held by a distinct ruling class and a persistent, recognized series of cultural traits developed in earlier times.

The Road Ahead: The Sources of Uniformity

Time moves along and, as it does, many a battle is joined between the forces perpetuating diversity and those promoting uniformity; many of these battles are the impersonal clashes of old ways and new facts, but the drama has its human performers who carry the causes, large and small, of diversity and uniformity. These causes are found under many banners and are fought in a myriad of places. Ranged on the side of uniformity in industrialization are some powerful developments.

History and Homogeneity. The passage of history itself is a force. Each industrializing nation moves farther along from its introduction into the industrial world, from its preexisting forms, from its original leadership. The early elites bring in new recruits from other strata. The elite group grows in size and becomes less identifiable, merging into each successively lower level in the new hierarchy. The second and third and fourth generations of the leaders and the led alike are different from the first.

The age of ideology fades. When man first entered the irreversible journey into industrialization there were innumerable views about the best way to organize the society. Some of them have almost completely disappeared from the scene: anarchism, syndicalism, communalism, cooperativism. Others of them have been blunted and revised from their original form, particularly capitalism and socialism. The age of utopias is past. An age of realism has taken its place; an age in which there is little expectation of either utter perfection or complete doom. One of the results of the past century is the accumulation of experience about the realistic alternatives.

Industrial society conduces toward "realism" through the

elimination of certain alternatives which are unworkable, through the development of expectations by the mass of men which lie above despair but below utopian hope; and through the rise of men and institutions devoted to the compromise of differences. It requires "realism" because an industrialized society is such a complicated mechanism with such interdependence of its parts, that keeping it going without major disruption becomes an over-riding concern. A fierce ideological battle, for example, among social democrats, communists, and Catholics, as in certain Latin American countries, can get in the way not only of progress but even of current production. Aspiration and attainment come closer into accord; and a leading aspiration becomes the attainment of reasonable continuity.

Thus we see the phenomenon of the one-party society which relies on a coalition of several elements, as in Egypt and Mexico; or the nonparty government, as in Pakistan; or a government operated by a coalition of parties, as in Austria, Venezuela, and Columbia. Even where the parties still contend, they draw closer together, as in the United States, and may even drop their ideological inheritance in favor of a new pragmatism, as in England and Germany. Industrial man is seldom faced with real ideological alternatives within his society.

Solutions are negotiated among representatives of the leading interest groups rather than being fought out on the level of principle. "Veto groups" can veto any action which threatens their survival. The negotiator takes the place of the prophet, the idealist, the demagogue.

Industrial society must be administered; and the administrators become increasingly benevolent and increasingly skilled. They learn to respond where response is required; to anticipate the inevitable. The benevolent political bureaucracy and the benevolent economic oligarchy are matched with the tolerant mass.

The "new realism" is essentially conservative. The *status quo* is changed only gradually. "Balance" must be maintained. However, considerable individual liberty and social mobility are compatible with and even essential to the "new realism."

Parliamentary life may appear increasingly decadent and political parties merely additional bureaucracies; the great political causes of old may become little more than technical issues; and oratory may give way to committee work; but the "new realism" conforms to the realities of industrial society. The century of the "great debate" from the mid-nineteenth to the mid-twentieth century, gives way to the era of the great and little compromises; ideology is dead but industrialism is alive — industrialism and the "new realism" that is its companion. Not only all dictatorships but also all democracies are "guided."

As the conflict of ideologies is blunted and fades between societies, so also consensus develops within such societies as industrialize successfully. The labor force becomes committed to and settled into industrial life. It accepts the pace of work, the web of rules, the surrounding structure. The sense of protest subsides. The enterprise managers, left to their own devices, push less hard. Society provides more of the amenities of life. Men learn from experience how better to do things and the rough edges are evened off. Industrialization has been accepted.

The elites become less differentiated, the ideologies become more pragmatic; the old culture becomes dimmer in the memory. The elites all wear grey flannel suits; the ideological controversies become more barren; the cultural patterns of the world intermingle and merge. These changes are in evidence, even though the majority of nations in the world have been in the active throes of industrialization only two generations or less.

Technology and Social Arrangements. Technology is also a unifying force. At one moment of time there may be several best economic combinations or social arrangements, but only one best technology. The technology can be up to date or antiquated, but there is no question which is which, and the modern is constantly replacing the ancient. The same technology calls for much the same occupational structure around the world — in steel, in textile, in air transport. The occupational role of a man gives him a place in society and affects his behavior in many ways. Also there comes to be a growing diversity of occupations and of levels of management, and no really clear-cut dividing lines visible to all. The occupation takes the place of the class.

The technology is dynamic and it calls for change. Men change their locations and their occupations. A labor market must be created with substantial mobility within it. A fully paternalistic system at the plant level becomes less possible. Mobility calls at least for the semi-independent rather than the dependent worker.

The skill level rises. Men are given responsibility for more expensive equipment and more essential processes. Their consent becomes more important. The need for their consent gives them influence. It may even give them organized power, for there is a tendency to organize around the occupation; only scientists may be given this right at first, but the pressure will always exist to spread professional and occupational organization.

Social arrangements will be most uniform from one society to another when they are most closely tied to technology; they can be more diverse the farther removed they are from technology.

The Push of Progress. The thrust of progress also serves the cause of uniformity. The industry mix, country by country, becomes more balanced and thus more like that elsewhere. A labor supply is recruited one way or another, or a labor surplus is handled one way or another. There is insistent pressure to obtain a rough balance of supply and demand in the labor market. The duality of economies, as in Japan with the industrial and the handicraft economies, tends to disappear in favor of the unified economy. Even agriculture becomes an industry, although this may take a very long time, as the history of France still attests.

The development of consumer goods industries and service trades requires the creation of markets despite the addiction to plans; and the market mentality and the planning mentality are quite different. The rising standard of living and increasing leisure create the capacity to read and travel and compare. They also encourage an aggressive materialism on the part of people, and the "age of faith" takes its place in history. Also progress brings the great metropolitan center and the city as the natural habitat of man; and the city has been the home of variety and of freedom throughout the centuries.

Progress reduces the diversity of economies, however different their levels of output may be, and creates urban, materialistic man around the globe making his choices in labor and product markets.

Education and Equality. An industrial society must educate its people. There are at least two imperatives. First, the vast bulk of the population must be literate in order to receive instruction, follow directions, keep records. Second, managers, engineers, and civil servants must be trained to operate the new productive system. Beyond that are the needs for doctors, lawyers, scientists, and university professors. Education becomes a leading industry.

Out of education come several results. Education is intended to reduce the scarcity of skilled persons and this after a time reduces the wage and salary differentials they receive; it also pulls people out of the least skilled and most disagreeable occupations and raises wage levels there. It conduces to a new equality which has nothing to do with ideology; in fact, it may come faster and more fully in a middle-class society than in a society under the revolutionary intellectuals who proclaim equality as a primary goal. This equality is at first economic, but it also affects class status and political outlook. The miners and longshoremen view themselves and others differently when they become the aristocrats of labor. Middle incomes make for a middle class.

Out of education may also come a new call for freedom. This call will be most insistent at the highest levels in the educational pyramid, for knowledge knows no geographical boundaries; but it may spread down through many of the ranks of society. Education and personal independence have usually walked the road together.

With an educated labor force, jobs tend to change or be changed. On the average, more responsibility adheres to them; they are made more interesting; their incumbents are treated more individually and humanely.

For the first time in history all men become literate, and this common literacy leads to a more common equality and humanity.

The Omnipresent State. The state, everywhere, becomes an important instrument in society. It becomes responsible for the general rate of growth, and the level of activity in the economy; for the distribution of power within society; the settlement of conflicts; the prevention of economic or other sabotage of the economy by special interest groups. It may, of course, do much more. But at least it must set the many basic rules for the economy and it inevitably becomes a partner, if not the sole partner, in labor-management relations. Industrialization has been accompanied by the growth of the directing, guiding, managing state as never before so universally in history.

The Managerial Evolution. The productive enterprise, whether public or private, becomes a large-scale organization in many industries. It comes to be run by professional managers, recruited and trained through the educational system, and separated from both ownership and political power. These enterprise managers must be placed under the constraints of the market or planning budgets to assure their suitable performance, and the structuring of these pressures and controls is an essential task in society. The professional manager has great power but power subject to checks and balances in all developed industrial societies.[6]

The managers are basically responsible for the web of rules within the plant and industry which relate them to the managed, although they do share this responsibility with the state and the organized workers. This web of rules is a universal phenomenon and many of the same rules turn up in the same industries, regardless of the contrasting nature of the societies within which they are found. Basically, this web of rules must spell out the authority of the managers. Economic enterprise is always basically authoritarian under the necessity of getting things done, and the limits to this authority must be specified. The distribution of power comes to be as important as the distribution of income, and much more unequal.

The large-scale enterprise, the professional enterprise manager, the web of rules are important features of any advanced industrialized society.

The Compulsion of Comparisons. Man everywhere wants progress and participation. The two are substitutes for each other and often, for a time, progress will be accepted in lieu of participation; but in the end industrial man wants both and will keep pressing for both. Progress means a higher standard of education, better health, more consumer goods and services; participation means choice of jobs, choice of consumer goods, a chance to influence the web of rules, even an opportunity to influence those who guide society itself. These same pressures develop, regardless of culture and ideology.

These pressures for progress and participation are enhanced by the world-wide character of industrialization, by international trade, by travel, by the exchange of ideas. We may never reach Sir William Beveridge's utopia where each man could pick and choose around the world the society he would like to live in, but already people are making comparisons and these comparisons are having their impact. Generally the impact will be to bring greater uniformity in the direction of the societal product which people widely judge to be the best. People may not be willing to settle for much less in their own systems than the standards and performance in competing systems.

Over the past few decades the threads of diversity and the sources of uniformity have been in conflict, and they will continue to be certainly for many decades ahead. Essentially, it is a contest between ideologies and national traits on the one hand, and technology and the changes that progress brings on the other. This opposition of forces is at work throughout the world. Our age, in particular, is witness to this titanic struggle.

The Road Ahead: Pluralistic Industrialism

The future can be really penetrated only when it becomes the present, but visions of the future also help determine the future by the time it has become the present. So men attempt to peer ahead, to understand the structure of history, to alter the process of history, if possible, in accord with their preferences. As we have seen, the history of industrialization to date has not been a smoothly unilinear one; it has been uneven and multilinear. It is likely that in the future it will continue to be both somewhat uneven and multilinear; and there will continue to be some latitude for choice and for chance. Chance may elude man, but choice need not; and the choice of men, within fairly broad limits, can shape history. To predict the future with any accuracy, men must choose their future. The future they appear to be choosing and pressing for is pluralistic industrialism.

Industrialism is a system of social organization where industries, including many large-scale industries, are the dominant method of production. Such a system cannot be an atomistic one with infinite fractionalization of power and distribution of decision making. Authority must be concentrated, although individuals may still have areas in which they can make free choices. Authority may be concentrated in a monistic or pluralistic arrangement. It is our view that the dominant arrangement will be pluralistic. Where there is one locus of power, there will come to be several; where there are many, there will come to be fewer.

Among the factors discussed above pressing for uniformity in industrialization, several push for uniformity in the direction of pluralistic industrialism. The complexity of the fully developed industrial society requires, in the name of efficiency and initiative, a degree of decentralization of control, particularly in the consumer goods and service trades industries; but it also requires a large measure of central control by the state and the conduct of many operations by large-scale organizations. Industrialism cannot function well according to either the monistic or atomistic models.

As the skill level rises and jobs become more responsible, as noted before, any regime must be more interested in consent, in drawing forth relatively full cooperation. For the sake of real efficiency, this must be freely given. The discipline of the labor gang no longer suffices. Higher education and research become two of the larger and more important industries. In them, in particular, the consent and cooperation of the individual producer is particularly important; but more and more other industries take on some of the aspects of the university with its faculty. The university becomes more the model for the enterprise than the enterprise for the university. With skill and responsibility go the need for consent, and with consent goes influence and even authority. Occupational and professional groups, of necessity, achieve some prestige and authority as against both the central organs of society and the individual members of the occupation or profession.

Education brings in its wake a new economic equality and a consequent new equality of political outlook; the universal industrial mass. This in turn, along with many other developments, helps bring consensus to society. The harsh use of power by the state is not so necessary to hold society together by the seams. Education also opens the mind to curiosity and to inquiry, and the individual seeks more freedom to think and to act. Education brings a demand for liberty and can help create conditions in

which it is safe to grant it. Education leads to comparisons among
nations; to comparisons of progress which often rests on central
control and of participation which always rests on a distribution
of authority.

This is industrialism at work; centralizing and decentralizing
at the same time; creating areas of control and areas of freedom;
weaving a web of rules and liberating the individual. No one of
these contrary tendencies reigns supreme, many visions of the
future to the contrary. An uneasy balance arises among these
tendencies; in one situation, one is stronger; in another, another.
The fully developed industrial society is too dynamic and complex to yield to the dictates of a single imperative; and a theory
about it which yields sole place to any single imperative is too
simple to do more than mislead.

Industrialism is so complex and subject to such contrary internal pressures that it never can assume a single uniform un-
changing structure; but it can vary around a general central
theme and that theme is pluralism. It will, however, take generations before this theme will become universal in societies around
the world; but the direction of the movement seems already sufficiently clear. The complexity of industrial society, the ever higher
skill levels, the impacts of universal education all work in this direction.

The State That Does Not Wither Away.   The state will be powerful. It will, at the minimum, have the responsibility in an industrial society for the rate of growth of the economy; the over-all
distribution of income among uses and among individuals; the
basic security of individuals thus replacing the family as the basic
security unit; the stability of the system; the provision of the
essential public services of education, transportation, recreational
areas, cultural facilities, and the like, which will become more
important as the standard of living rises, leisure increases, education improves, and men multiply in numbers; particularly the
state will take on the responsibility of providing a favorable physical environment for urban man.

Any pluralistic society is subject to three great potential internal problems and the state is responsible for handling each. One
is the conflict among the several power elements in a pluralistic society. The state must set the rules of the game within

which such conflict will occur, enforce these rules, and act as mediator; conflicts between managers and the managed are the most noticeable, but by no means the only ones. Another is the control of collusion by producers against consumers, by a profession against its clients, by labor and management against the public. The undue aggrandizement of sectional interests is always endemic if not epidemic in a pluralistic society; in fact, one of the arguments for monism and atomism alike is the avoidance of sectionalism. Additionally, the state will come generally, under pluralistic industrialism, to set the rules relating members to their organizations — who may get in, who may stay in, what rights and obligations the members have, what are the boundaries for the activities of the organization. It will, almost of necessity, be against too much conflict among or collusion between or domination of the members by the subsidiary organizations in society.

All these responsibilities mean the state will never "wither away"; that Marx was more utopian than the despised utopians. It will be the dominant organization in any industrial society. It may, however, itself be less than fully unitary; itself be subject to checks and balances including the check of public acceptance of its current leadership and policies.

The Crucial Role of the Enterprise — The Middle Class and the Middle Bureaucracy. The productive enterprise under pluralistic industrialism, whether it is private or public, will be in a dominant position. It will often be large and it must always have substantial authority in order to produce efficiently. This authority will not be complete for it will be checked by the state, by the occupational association, by the individual employee; but it will be substantial.

The managers, whether private or public, will be professionals, technically trained and carefully selected for their tasks. They will be bureaucratic managers, if private, and managerial bureaucrats, if public; each responding to the rules and the technical requirements of the job. The distinction between the private and the public manager will decrease just as the distinction between the private and the public enterprise; distinction among managers will be more according to the size, the product, and the nature of their enterprise. The controlled market and the controlled budget will bring more nearly the same pressures on the managers. The private enterprise, however, will usually have more freedom of action than the public enterprise; but the middle class and the middle bureaucracy will look much alike.

Associated Man. The occupational or professional association will range alongside the state and the enterprise as a locus of power in pluralistic industrialism; and there will be more occupations and particularly more professions seeking association. Group organizations around skill and position in the productive mechanism will be well-nigh universal. These organizations will affect output norms, comparative incomes, access to employment, codes of ethics in nearly every occupational walk of life. Their containment within reasonable limits will be an all-enduring and all-pervading problem; and some of the groups will always seek to invade and infiltrate the government mechanisms which are intended to supervise them. Class warfare will be forgotten and in its place will be the bureaucratic contest of interest group against interest group. The battles will be in the corridors instead of the streets, and memos will flow instead of blood.

The Web of Rules. Uniting these organizations — the state, the enterprise, the association — will be a great web of rules set by the efforts of all the elements but particularly the state. This web of rules will also relate the individual to each of these elements. In the contest over who should make the web of rules, the end solution will be that they will be made or influenced by more than one element; they will not be set by the state alone or the enterprise alone, or by the association alone. The web of rules will not equally cover all aspects of life.

From Class War to Bureaucratic Gamesmanship. Conflict will take place in a system of pluralistic industrialism, but it will take less the form of the open strife or the revolt and more the form of the bureaucratic contest. Groups will jockey for position over the placement of individuals, the setting of jurisdictions, the location of authority to make decisions, the forming of alliances, the establishment of formulas, the half-evident withdrawal of support and of effort, the use of precedents and arguments and statistics. Persuasion, pressure, and manipulation will take the place of the face-to-face combat of an earlier age. The conflict also will be, by and large, over narrower issues than in earlier times when there was real disagreement over the nature of and the arrangements within industrial society. It will be less between the broad programs of capital and labor, and of agriculture and industry; and more over budgets, rates of compensation, work norms, job assignments. The great battles over conflicting manifestos will be replaced by a myriad of minor contests over comparative details.

From Class Movement to Special Interest Group.   Labor-management relations will conform to this new context. Labor organizations will not be component parts of class movements urging programs of total reform, for the consensus of a pluralistic society will have settled over the scene. Nor may they be very heavily identified by industry, particularly with the increasing multiplication and fractionalization of industries. Rather they may tend to take more the craft, or perhaps better, the occupational form. With skills more diverse, at a generally higher level and obtained more through formal education, and with geographical mobility greatly increased, the professional association may become the most common kind of organization, like those of doctors, lawyers, teachers, nurses, airline pilots in many countries already. These occupational and professional associations will not be united by a single program of social reform, but rather divided by the separate and often conflicting interests of their occupational or professional groups. The day of ideological labor movements as we have known them will have passed.

The purpose of these occupational and professional associations will be relatively narrow, mostly the improvement of the status of the occupation in terms of income, prestige, and specification of the rights and duties that accompany it. Generally these organizations will be a conservative force in society, opposed to new ways of doing things, resistant to increased efforts by members of the occupation. The enterprise managers will be the more progressive elements in the society, although they too may become heavily weighted down by checks and balances and rules.

The techniques of the professional associations for achieving their ends will be those of the bureaucratic organization everywhere; a far cry from the individual withdrawal, or the guerilla warfare, or the strike or the political reform movement of earlier times. They will constitute the quarrels between the semimanaged and the semimanagers.

Individuals will identify themselves more closely with their oc-

cupation, particularly if it involves a formal training period for
entry, and mobility will follow more the lines of the occupation
than the lines of the industry or the job possibilities of the immediate geographical area. In terms of identification, the orientation will be more nearly that of the member of a guild than
of a class or of a plant community. Mayo will turn out to be as
wrong as Marx. Just as the class will lose its meaning, so also
will the plant community fail to become the modern counterpart
of the primitive tribe. The occupational interest group will represent the employee in his occupational concerns and the occupation will draw his allegiance. Status in the tribe will not give
way to status in the plant; nor will status have given way to the
individual contract through the march of civilization; rather interest identification will take the place of both status and individual contract in ordering the productive arrangements of men.

Education, occupation, occupational organization will all be
drawn together to structure the life-line and the economic interests of many if not most employees.

Organization Man and the New Bohemianism.   The individual
will be in a mixed situation far removed either from that of the
independent farmer organizing most aspects of his own life or
from that of the Chinese in the commune under total surveillance. In his working life he will be subject to great conformity
imposed not only by the enterprise manager but also by the state
and by his own occupational association. For most people, any
true scope for the independent spirit on the job will be missing.
However, the skilled worker, while under rules, does get some
control over his job, some chance to organize it as he sees fit,
some possession of it. Within the narrow limits of this kind of
"job control," the worker will have some freedom. But the productive process tends to regiment. People must perform as expected or it breaks down. This is now and will be increasingly
accepted as an immutable fact. The state, the manager, the occupational association are all disciplinary agents. But discipline is
often achieved by a measure of persuasion and incentive. The
worker will be semi-independent with some choice among jobs,
some control of the job, and some scope for the effects of morale;
but he will also be confined by labor organizations, pensions, and
seniority rules, and all sorts of rules governing the conduct of
the job.

Outside his working life the individual may have more free-dom under pluralistic industrialism than in most earlier forms of society. Politically he can be given some influence. Society has achieved consensus and it is perhaps less necessary for Big Brother to exercise political control. Nor in this Brave New World need genetic and chemical means be employed to avoid revolt. There will not be any revolt, anyway, except little bureaucratic revolts that can be handled piecemeal. An educated population will want political choice and can be given it. There will also be reason-able choice in the controlled labor market, subject to the confining limits of the occupation, and in the controlled product market.

The great new freedom may come in the leisure of individuals. Higher standards of living, more leisure, more education make this not only possible but almost inevitable. This will be the happy hunting ground for the independent spirit. Along with the bureau-cratic conservatism of economic and political life may well go a New Bohemianism in the other aspects of life and partly as a reaction to the confining nature of the productive side of society. There may well come a new search for individuality and a new meaning to liberty. The economic system may be highly ordered and the political system barren ideologically; but the social and recreational and cultural aspects of life diverse and changing.

The world will be for the first time a totally literate world. It will be an organization society, but it need not be peopled by "organization men" whose total lives are ruled by their occupa-tional roles.

The areas closest to technology will be the most conformist; those farthest from the requirements of its service, the most free. The rule of technology need not, as Marx thought it would, reach into every corner of society. In fact, there may come a new em-phasis on diversity, on the preservation of national and group traits that runs quite counter to the predictions of uniform mass consumption. The new slavery to technology may bring a new dedication to diversity and individuality. This is the two-sided face of pluralistic industrialism that makes it forever a split per-sonality looking in two directions at the same time. The new slavery and the new freedom go hand in hand.

Utopia never arrives, but men may well settle for the benefits of a greater scope for freedom in their personal lives at the cost of considerable conformity in their working lives. If pluralistic industrialism can be said to have a split personality, then the individual in this society will lead a split life too; he will be a pluralistic individual with more than one pattern of behavior and one dominant allegiance.

Social systems will be reasonably uniform around the world as compared with today's situation; but there may be substantial diversity within geographical and cultural areas as men and groups seek to establish and maintain their identity. The differences will be between and among individuals and groups and subcultures rather than between and among the major geographical areas of the world. Society at large may become more like the great metropolitan complexes of Paris or London or New York or Tokyo, urbanized and committed to the industrial way of life, but marked by infinite variety in its details.

Pluralistic industrialism will never reach a final equilibrium. The contest between the forces for uniformity and for diversity will give it life and movement and change. This is a contest which will never reach an ultimate solution. Another eternal battle will be between the manager and the managed all up and down the line of all the hierarchies that will mark the world; quiet but often desperate little battles will be fought all over the social landscape. The themes of uniformity and diversity, and manager and managed which mark the world today will characterize it in the future as well. There will be constant adjustments between these eternally conflicting themes, but no permanent settlement. They will constitute the everlasting threads of history: the uniformity that draws on technology and the diversity that draws on individuality; the authority that stems from the managers and the rebellion, however muted, that stems from the managed. These threads of conflict will continue when class war, and the contest over private versus public initiative, and the battle between monistic and atomistic ideologies have been left far behind in the sedimentary layers of history.

CHART 10.

Pluralistic industrialism.

Industrial leadership	Professional managers -- private and public.
Central purpose of industrial leadership	Effectiveness of the enterprise.
Central characteristics of the society	Checks and balances and the web of rules in a society of ever-changing technology.
Sources of variation in approach	Shifting balance between forces of uniformity and diversity.
Basic rule-making authority in labor-management relations	State, manager, associations.
View of worker	Semi-independent.
Attitude toward conflict	Bureaucratic quarrels within highly structured situations.

APPENDIX

THE INTER–UNIVERSITY STUDY OF LABOR PROBLEMS IN ECONOMIC DEVELOPMENT

Organization and Orientation

Industrialism and Industrial Man is only one of many publications growing out of the "Inter-University Study of Labor Problems in Economic Development." This informal organization was formed by the four authors of this volume in 1954 to bring together people, projects, and funds for the purpose of making studies of human agents in the industrialization process. The study, and the preliminary investigations which led to it, have received generous financial support of the Ford Foundation.

In its first five years of existence, the Inter-University Study has sponsored over forty projects involving work in thirty-five countries. A total of seventy-eight persons of eleven different nationalities have been involved in some phase of the research. Those associated with the Inter-University Study have published twelve books, and a Reprint Series contains twenty-one articles. A number of other articles have also appeared; an additional fourteen books are in the press or in manuscript; and several other projects are at the research and writing stages. The publications are listed and the books and articles in the Reprint Series are annotated in this appendix.

From 1954–1959 the Inter-University Study was concerned primarily with industrialization, managerial organization and ideology, the development of industrial working forces, and the role of labor organizations. Studies of "labor problems" as thus broadly defined were undertaken in industrially advanced countries such as Germany, Japan, the Soviet Union, and Italy. The range of underdeveloped economies and newly industrializing societies included India, Egypt, and Indonesia. The "cross-cut," or topical studies have dealt with managerial ideologies, management organization and development, wage structures, the problems of worker protest, labor organizations, the recruitment and commitment of working forces, and the comparative analysis of industrial relations systems.

In collaboration with other research and educational institutions, the Inter-University Study has held conferences on labor and management problems in economic development in Turkey, Lebanon, Iran, Pakistan, India, Indonesia, Japan, and the United States. Thus, through publications, jointly sponsored research projects, and international conferences, the Inter-University Study has sought to establish a means of communication — and a common language — among those who have a professional interest in the labor and management problems of modern societies.

The arrangements for financial support of various projects have been as diverse as the number of countries in which inquiries were made. In some cases, such as, for example, the country studies of India and Egypt, as well as the cross-cut analysis of industrial relations systems, the entire cost was underwritten by the Inter-University Study. In other cases, grants from the Inter-University Study were matched with resources already available to individuals or institutions. In a few instances, the Inter-University Study took care only of the marginal cost of projects which were financed mostly with other resources. The conferences were financed jointly by the Inter-University Study, the Ford Foundation, and institutions in the various countries.

During the course of the next several years, the Inter-University Study hopes to continue and extend both its cross-cut and country studies. In the future, more emphasis probably will be given to policy issues and to the communication of research findings in conferences. One of the new analytical concerns is the comparative analysis of patterns of utilization of high-level manpower in societies at various stages of development and the critical examination of the role of education in the modernization process. The two objectives of this new interest are to find a means of making long-range projections of manpower requirements in newly developing countries and to establish guideposts for determining patterns of investments in education which are most appropriate for such countries. This part of the project will proceed with the support of a recent grant from the Carnegie Corporation of New York.

In the future, as in the past, therefore, the objective of the Inter-University Study will be to promote and sponsor comparative studies of the role of human agents in the processes of economic development. The purpose is both to conduct research and to help to develop people in different countries as experts in the analysis of industrial relations and manpower development problems. The Inter-University Study has been interested in the past and will be concerned in the future with both research and operations, with fundamental knowledge and policy applications. *Industrialism and Industrial Man,* therefore, is not the final volume of our joint enterprise. It is rather an interim analytical report.

We are deeply indebted to all the persons associated with the Inter-University Study for their contribution to the project in general and to our thinking in particular. Their names and the institutions of their affiliations at the time of their association with the project appear below. We wish to express at this time our particular debt to a few additional persons who contributed directly in conversations and writing to the central ideas expressed in this volume. At our request they read earlier drafts of the manuscript and made many detailed and stimulating comments. They are: E. Wight Bakke, Everett E. Hagen, Edward S. Mason, Abraham J. Siegel, and David Williams. During the five years of this project, we have also benefitted greatly from an exchange of views and close association in overseas seminars with Dr. Thomas H. Carroll, Vice-President of the Ford Foundation, who has officer responsibility for its program in Economic Development and Administration. To Marie Klein, the administrative secretary of the Inter-University Study for the first four years, we owe a special debt of gratitude for holding together the procedural strings of the entire project. Mrs. Ruth Houghton edited the manuscript.

Clark Kerr
John T. Dunlop
Frederick H. Harbison
Charles A. Myers

April 1960

Individuals Associated with the Inter-University Study
(Academic Affiliation during Work with the Study)
(1954–1959)

Ahmedebad Textile Industry & Research Institute, Ahmedebad, India.

Chowdhry, Kamla, Psychology Division
Pal, A. K., Human Relations Division

American University of Beirut

Badre, Albert Y., Economic Research Institute
Nabulsi, Hikmat, Economic Research Institute
Bawarshi, Tewfick, Economic Research Institute
Klat, Paul J., Economic Research Institute
Sayigh, Yusif A., Economic Research Institute
Siksek, Simon G., Economic Research Institute

California, University of (Berkeley)

Anspach, Ralph, Institute of Industrial Relations
Bendix, Reinhard, Department of Sociology and Institute of Industrial Relations
Burgess, Eugene W., School of Business Administration
Conroy, John, Institute of Industrial Relations
Coontz, Sidney, Institute of Industrial Relations
*Fisher, Lloyd, Institute of Industrial Relations
Galenson, Walter, School of Business Administration and Department of Economics
Kerr, Clark, President, University of California
Kisch, Herbert, Institute of Industrial Relations
Lange, M. G. (Institut für Politische Wissenschaft, Berlin-Dahlem, Germany)
Leibenstein, Harvey, Department of Economics
Linz, Juan, Institute of Industrial Relations
Morgenstern, Otto, Institute of Industrial Relations
Roth, Gunther, Institute of Industrial Relations
Scalapino, Robert, Department of Political Science
Schran, Peter, Institute of Industrial Relations
Wachenheim, Hedwig, Graduate Research Economist

Chicago, University of

Harbison, F. H., Industrial Relations Center
Hoselitz, Bert F., Division of Social Sciences
Klein, Marie E., Industrial Relations Center
Lorwin, Val R., Division of Social Sciences
Massey, Ralph J., Industrial Relations Center
Nash, Manning, Department of Anthropology
Rottenberg, Simon, Department of Economics
*Slotkin, J. Sydney, Division of Social Sciences
Willner, Ann Ruth, Graduate Student in International Relations
*Wohl, Richard, Division of Social Sciences

Colorado, University of

Ehrmann, Henry W., Department of Political Science

Council of Personnel Administration, Stockholm, Sweden

Lahnhagen, Rolf, Director
*Lohse, Lennart

* Deceased.

Florence, University of, Florence, Italy

Ferrarotti, Franco, Social Sciences

Harvard University

Berg, Elliot, Department of Economics
Dunlop, John T., Department of Economics
Horowitz, Daniel, Research Associate
Palekar, S. A., Research Associate, Littauer School of Public Administration
Rothbaum, Melvin, Department of Economics
Ulman, Lloyd, Department of Economics

Indian Institute of Technology, Kharagpur, India

Ganguli, H. C.

Institut für Politische Wissenschaft, Berlin-Dahlem, Germany

Lange, M. G.
Stammer, Otto

Liverpool, University of, Liverpool, England

Matthews, David, Department of Social Science
McGivering, Ian, Department of Social Science
Scott, William H., Department of Social Science

Massachusetts Institute of Technology

Abbott, Jarold G., Industrial Relations Section
Baldwin, George B., Department of Economics and Social Science
Bauer, Raymond A., Department of Economics and Social Science
James, Ralph C., Department of Economics and Social Science
Kalacheck, Edward, Industrial Relations Section
Kannappan, Subbiah, Industrial Relations Section
Kotler, Philip, Industrial Relations Section
Munson, Fred C., Industrial Relations Section
Myers, Charles A., Department of Economics and Social Science
Siegel, Abraham J., Department of Economics and Social Science
Williams, David, Industrial Relations Section

Mount Holyoke College

Hawkins, Everett D., Department of Economics

Northeastern University

Rosen, Sumner, Department of Economics

Princeton University

Blumenthal, W. Michael, Industrial Relations Section
Eason, Warren W., Industrial Relations Section
Harbison, F. H., Industrial Relations Section
Hartmann, Heinz, Industrial Relations Section
Ibrahim, Ibrahim A., Industrial Relations Section
Klein, Marie E., Industrial Relations Section
Rimlinger, Gaston V., Industrial Relations Section
Shearer, John C., Industrial Relations Section

Roosevelt University

Sturmthal, Adolf, Philip Murray Professor

Rutgers University

Alexander, Robert J., Department of Economics

Vassar College

Brown, Emily Clark, Department of Economics

Washington University (St. Louis)

Sobel, Irvin, Department of Economics

Yale University

Leiserson, Mark, Department of Economics

Miscellaneous

de Möy, Gérard, Industrial Consultant, Paris, France
Montjoie, René, Inspecteur de Mines, Metz, France
Thorner, Daniel, Bombay, India

Publications of Inter-University Study of Labor Problems
in Economic Development
(1954–1960)

Books

Bendix, Reinhard. *Work and Authority in Industry; Ideologies of Management in the Course of Industrialization.* New York. John Wiley & Sons, Inc. 1956. 466 pp. $7.50.

The author distinguishes between "entrepreneurial ideology," associated with the early stages of industrialization, and "managerial ideology," found in fully industrialized societies. His case histories are drawn from eighteenth- and nineteenth-century England and Russia, from twentieth-century United States, and from East Germany. The link between these two parts of his analysis is formed by a chapter on the bureaucratization of economic enterprises. He concludes with a discussion of East-West alternatives in dealings with developing states.

Dunlop, John T. *Industrial Relations Systems.* New York. Henry Holt and Company, Inc. 1958. 399 pp. $5.75.

An attempt to develop a general theory of industrial relations which can be used for analysis of "the widest possible range of industrial relations facts and practices." After developing the concept of an industrial relations system, the author tests it against the rules developed by bituminous coal mining in eight countries, the building industry in nine, and the national industrial relations system in Yugoslavia. The impact of change over time and of economic development upon industrial relations systems are also considered.

Ehrmann, Henry W. *Organized Business in France.* Princeton, N.J. Princeton University Press. 1957. 514 pp. $7.50.

The writer is concerned with French business as a private pressure group — an organized lobby — seeking to acquire and wield political power. Using published data and the interview responses of 130 high government and business officials, he analyzes the post-1936 acts and ideology of French employers' and trade associations. Attention is also paid to the prospects for French economic growth.

Galenson, Walter, editor. *Labor and Economic Development.* New York. John Wiley & Sons, Inc. 1959. 304 pp. $6.75.

A volume of essays concerned with the creation and commitment of nonagricultural labor forces, as well as with the development and role of labor organizations in India, Japan, Egypt, French West Africa, and the British West Indies.

Harbison, Frederick and Ibrahim Abdelkader Ibrahim. *Human Resources of Egyptian Enterprise.* New York. McGraw-Hill Book Company, Inc. 1958. 230 pp. $5.50.

An analysis of the human aspects of Egyptian industrialization. The authors chart the dimensions of the labor problems of industrialization in Egypt and suggest some general approaches toward solutions. The book has three major sections: "The Setting," "Development of Manpower Resources," and "Management of Labor Protest."

Harbison, Frederick and Charles A. Myers. *Management in the Industrial World, an International Analysis.* New York. McGraw-Hill Book Company, Inc. 1959. 413 pp. $7.00

The first part of this book is concerned with the formulation of "an international concept of management" applicable to various stages of economic development. The second part provides a comparative analysis of management in twelve countries. In both sections attention is paid to the nature of management as an economic resource, as a system of authority, and as a class. The authors find that there is a definite relationship between "the competence and performance of management and the facilities for developing managerial resources."

Hartmann, Heinz. *Authority and Organization in German Management.* Princeton, N.J. Princeton University Press. 1959. 318 pp. $6.00.

Devoted to an analysis of the system of authority as it relates to the internal organization of modern industrial enterprises in West Germany. The author suggests that German industry has evolved its own unique system of authority which is firmly rooted in the traditions and values of German society. He compares general administration, industrial relations, and management development in four case studies of patrimonial and professional management as well as of management under codetermination.

Leibenstein, Harvey. *Economic Backwardness and Economic Growth; Studies in the Theory of Economic Development.* New York. John Wiley & Sons, Inc. 1957. 295 pp. $6.75.

The author first suggests that various characteristics of densely populated underdeveloped economies are interrelated in a mutually sustaining pattern ("quasi-equilibrium"). He then deals with the factors that underlie a country's transition to sustained economic growth. Particular attention is paid to the "critical minimum effort thesis" which warns that certain efforts to raise per capita income (e.g. the creation of entrepreneurship, the expansion of productive knowledge) can fail if they prove less significant than the depressing effects of retardation factors. The last two chapters suggest the relative magnitudes of the main variables and of investment policies.

Lorwin, Val R. *The French Labor Movement.* Cambridge. Harvard University Press. 1954. 346 pp. $6.00.

A history of the French labor movement and an analysis of the structure and functions of French unions from 1789 to mid-1953.

McGivering, I. C., D. G. J. Matthews and W. H. Scott. *Management in Britain: A General Characterisation.* Liverpool. Liverpool University Press. 1960. 157 pp. 25s.

> This study describes the characteristics and organization of British management, its relations with unions and with individual employees, with particular reference to the changes in the industrial environment which have occurred during the postwar years. It also evaluates the adequacy of management's adjustment to these changes.

Myers, Charles A. *Labor Problems in the Industrialization of India.* Cambridge, Massachusetts. Harvard University Press. 1958. 297 pp. $6.50. (Also published as *Industrial Relations in India,* Bombay, Asia Publishing House. 1958.)

> An analysis of the dimensions of the industrial labor force in India, its recruitment and commitment, the growth and development of an organized labor movement, the managerial response, and the role of government in labor-management relations in India.

Slotkin, James Sydney. *From Field to Factory: New Industrial Employees.* The Free Press, Glencoe, Illinois, and Research Center in Economic Development and Cultural Change, The University of Chicago. 1960. 156 pp. $4.00.

> A conceptual development of labor force recruitment and commitment, based on other studies and a special study of southern migrants to northern industrial centers in the United States.

Articles in Reprint Series

Baldwin, George B. "Public Enterprise in Indian Industry." *Pacific Affairs,* March 1957. pp. 3-21. $1.00.

> The writer suggests that over the next generation the most interesting experiments in the field of public enterprise may well be found in Asia. He reviews the history and performance of industrial enterprises established by the Indian government. Particular attention is paid to ideological issues, reliance on the "private limited company" form of organization, and the key operating problem — the provision of competent management.

Brown, Emily Clark. "The Local Union in Soviet Industry: its Relations with Members, Party, and Management." *Industrial and Labor Relations Review.* January 1960. pp. 192–215.

The article presents a report on first hand interviews with plant-level representatives of labor organizations in the Soviet Union during 1955 and 1959. Attention is directed to changes in recent years.

Dunlop, John T. and Melvin Rothbaum. "International Comparisons of Wage Structures." *International Labour Review.* April, 1955. pp. 3–19.

Presents a generalized framework for the comparative study of wage structures in different countries and indicates the uses which could be made of such comparisons. Sample comparisons are included, as well as hypotheses for future research.

Galenson, Walter and Harvey Leibenstein. "Investment Criteria, Productivity and Economic Development." *Quarterly Journal of Economics,* August 1955. pp. 343–370.

The writers contend that the criterion of allocating investment on the basis of the marginal productivity of each unit of capital invested is not suitable for contemporary underdeveloped areas. In such areas, the facts of rapid obstacles to technological change suggest that "successful economic development hinges largely upon the introduction of modern technology upon as large a scale as possible." Underdeveloped countries are advised, therefore, to consider the twin desiderata of up-to-date equipment and relatively high capital/labor ratios when allocating available capital resources.

Harbison, Frederick. "Entrepreneurial Organization as a Factor in Economic Development." *Quarterly Journal of Economics,* August 1956. pp. 364–379.

Argues that the concept of organization is "more precise and meaningful" for the study of economic growth and development than traditional notions of entrepreneurship. The author discusses the following tentative propositions: "(1) industries requiring large capital investment probably require a correspondingly large investment in organization; (2) organization is the principal factor in determining the productivity of labor, assuming capital and natural resources to be constant; and (3) because of noneconomic factors . . . all organizations are probably 'inefficient' in effecting the optimum combination of economic resources which is theoretically possible."

Harbison, Frederick. "Two Centers of Arab Power." *Foreign Affairs,*
July 1959. pp. 1–12.

Contrasts the problems of economic development in Iraq and Egypt,
paying particular attention to what the differences might mean, both for
strategic relationships within the area and for the larger power struggle
in which the Middle East "is not a pawn but a queen." The writer
suggests that in the long run the economic development of the Middle
East will require some kind of union which will effectively combine the
different, but complementary assets of Egypt, Iraq, and other Arab
states as well.

Harbison, Frederick H. and Eugene W. Burgess. "Modern Management in Western Europe." *The American Journal of Sociology,* July
1954. pp. 15–23.

Compares American management with that in France, Belgium, and
Italy. Particular attention is paid to the organizational development of
the enterprise, the means of access to managerial positions, and the
goals of management. Concludes that dynamic changes may be taking
place in the static enterprise systems of Europe.

Hartmann, Heinz. "Managers and Entrepreneurs: A Useful Distinction?" *Administrative Science Quarterly,* March 1959. pp. 429–451.

Attempts to demonstrate the usefulness of a distinction between
manager and entrepreneur in terms of their relationship to formal
authority in the industrial organization. Schumpeter's classical concept
of the entrepreneur is evaluated along with Selznick's recent definition
of decision-making, and both are found lacking in precision and em-
pirical comprehension. Weber's definitions are thought adequate and
are tested in a case study of German management. The writer concludes
with a call for further tests of Weber's definitions in different cultural
environments.

Hoselitz, Bert F. "The City, the Factory, and Economic Growth."
American Economic Review, May 1955. pp. 166–184.

A discussion of the relation of urbanization to industrialization in underdeveloped countries with particular reference to the impact of each
upon social relations. Although acknowledging the anxieties and stress
which are "the price paid by peasants who come to the city where they
are forced to become industrial workers," the author feels that the
tendency of city life to break down old social patterns makes integration
into the social system of the factory easier to accomplish and thereby
facilitates industrialization.

Kerr, Clark. "Collective Bargaining in Postwar Germany." *Contempo-rary Collective Bargaining.* Edited by Adolf Sturmthal. Ithaca, N.Y. State School of Industrial and Labor Relations, Cornell University. 1957. pp. 168–209.

A discussion of German employer associations and trade unions and of their mutual relationships. Pre-Hitler patterns of collective bargaining were quickly restored at the end of the war with only two principal differences: the unification of the trade union movement and the pro-hibition of compulsory arbitration.

Kerr, Clark. "Productivity and Labour Relations." *Productivity and Progress;* Proceedings of the 1957 Summer School of the Australian Institute of Political Science. Sydney. Angus & Robertson. 1957. pp. 1–35.

Discusses the major determinants of productivity rates in different economies, the impact of trade unionism and collective bargaining on productivity, and various "solutions" for productivity problems.

Kerr, Clark. "The Trade Union Movement and the Redistribution of Power in Postwar Germany." *Quarterly Journal of Economics,* No-vember 1954. pp. 535–564.

Considers the environment that influenced the postwar development of the German trade union movement, its strategy, the means by which its program has been effectuated, and the potential consequences involved. Particular attention is paid to explanations of three basic German labor decisions: (1) to have a politically and religiously neutral trade union movement, (2) to emphasize political instead of economic means, and (3) to strive for codetermination at all levels of the economy.

Kerr, Clark, Frederick H. Harbison, John T. Dunlop, and Charles A. Myers. "The Labour Problem in Economic Development, a Frame-work for a Reappraisal." *International Labour Review,* March 1955. pp. 1–15.

The authors consider traditional analyses of the labor problem too limited for application to newly industrializing countries because such factors as recruitment and commitment of the labor force, the nature of business organizations and of the elites that direct them, and the emer-gence and management of protest are neglected. They suggest that social scientists can best make useful contributions toward the solution of the policy issues which these countries face through comparative studies of diverse patterns of industrialization based upon an expanded framework of analysis.

Kerr, Clark and Abraham Siegel. "The Interindustry Propensity to Strike — an International Comparision." *Industrial Conflict.* Edited by Arthur Kornhauser, Robert Dubin, and Arthur M. Ross. New York. McGraw-Hill Book Company, Inc. 1954. pp. 189–212.

Using data for eleven democratic industrialized nations, the authors group industries according to their propensity to strike. They next examine various theoretical explanations for similarity of strike propensity. The theory of most general applicability seems to be that strikes occur most severely in industries which segregate large numbers of persons who have relatively unpleasant jobs. In conclusion, they consider the problem of reducing "the intensity of conflict" in certain industries and advise "integrating the worker and his associations, and the employer, as fully as possible into the general society without coercion."

Kerr, Clark and Abraham Siegel. "The Structuring of the Labor Force in Industrial Society: New Dimensions and New Questions." *Industrial and Labor Relations Review,* January 1955. pp. 151–168.

Examines critically traditional theorizing about the labor movement. As such theorizing is primarily concerned with a "labor movement" response to a liberal-capitalist challenge, and as neither such response nor challenge is characteristic of most developing countries, new theory is called for. Industrialization and the structuring of the labor force via "a web of rules" are thought to be keys to an improved theoretical framework.

Lorwin, Val R. "Collective Bargaining in Postwar France." *The Annals of the American Academy of Political and Social Science,* March 1957. pp. 66–74.

Characterizing the collective bargaining situation as "more interesting than happy," the author discusses the disorganization and strife that followed the 1946 Communist-inspired split in the General Confederation of Labor, the attempts of the state to regulate collective bargaining, the 1950 collective bargaining law, the role of plant-bargaining, and the forces facilitating, and those impeding, change in industrial relations.

Lorwin, Val R. "Working-Class Politics and Economic Development in Western Europe." *American Historical Review,* January 1958. pp. 338–351.

Considers these questions: How far has economic development conditioned working-class politics in the last 150 years? Are there stages of economic development in which labor protest is always sharp or dull? To what extent are national differences in protest due to national differences in economic growth or to different patterns of historical development caused by other factors? Finally, what type of studies may facilitate answers to these questions?

Myers, Charles A. "Labour Problems of Rationalisation: The Experience of India." *International Labour Review*, May 1956. pp. 1–20.

Uses the experience of the Indian cotton textile industry as a basis for analyzing the problems which arise in introducing technological improvements into industrially underdeveloped countries and for pointing out how a balance can be kept between "the need for increased productivity through rationalisation and the overriding threat of unemployment in a labour-surplus economy." Among the conclusions are that labor protest can best be avoided if job opportunities are expanded before rationalisation and if employers attempt to understand and meet the legitimate fears of the affected workers.

Myers, Charles A. "Lessons from Abroad for American Management." *Journal of Business*, Vol. XXXII, No. 1, January 1960. pp. 1–9.

An examination of recent trends in American management in the light of the studies of managerial structures and philosophies abroad. The author raises the question whether American management is as advanced as many believe.

Myers, Charles A. "Recent Developments in Management Training." *Indian Journal of Public Administration*, April-June 1958. pp. 154–164.

Stressing the importance to successful industrialization of investment in high-level human resources. Recent developments in management training in India are "encouraging evidence of India's determination to meet [the] need for high-level managerial resources." There are brief critical reviews of seven development programs and suggestions for the future.

Rimlinger, Gaston V. "Autocracy and the Factory Order in Early Russian Industrialization." *Journal of Economic History*, March 1960. pp. 67–92.

Rimlinger, Gaston V. "International Differences in the Strike Propensity of Coal Miners: Experience in four countries." *Industrial and Labor Relations Review*, April 1959. pp. 389–405.

Challenges the Kerr-Siegel hypothesis that a mining environment creates a strike-prone "isolated mass," regardless of the cultural milieu. Study of mining communities in the Saar, Germany, France, Great Britain, and the United States leads to the broad generalizations that: "(1) the conduct of miners everywhere reflects the impact of a peculiar environment; and (2) the inherent environmental tendency toward strike proneness may be counteracted or reinforced by socio-cultural factors."

Other Articles

Dunlop, John T., "The Role of the Free Trade Union in a Less Developed Nation." *American Labor's Role in Less Developed Countries,* Report on a Conference Held at Cornell University, October 12–17, 1958, New York State School of Industrial and Labor Relations, Cornell University, 1959, pp. 12–19.

Eason, Warren W. "Managers and the Managed in the Soviet Union." *Proceedings* of Princeton University Conference, November 23 and 24, 1959.

Harbison, Frederick, "The Development of Human Resources in the Newly Industrializing Countries." *High-Talent Manpower for Science and Industry,* Industrial Relations Section, Princeton University, Princeton, N.J. 1959.

Harbison, Frederick, and Ibrahim A. Ibrahim, "Some Labor Problems of Industrialization in Egypt." Annals of the American Academy of Political and Social Science, May 1956.

Harbison, Frederick, Ernst Köchling, Frank Cassell, and Heinrich Ruebmann. "Steel Management on Two Continents." *Management Science,* October 1955. Reprinted in *Comparative Studies in Administration,* University of Pittsburgh Press, Pittsburgh, 1958.

Hartmann, Heinz. "The Transfer of Managerial Know-How Between Advanced Economics." Proceedings of Princeton University Conference, November 23 and 24, 1959.

Hartmann, Heinz. *Education for Business Leadership — The Role of the German Hochschulen.* Organization for European Economic Cooperation, Paris, 1955.

Kannappan, Subiah. "The Impact of the ILO on Labor Legislation and Policy in India." *Labor-Management and Economic Growth.* The

Institute of International Industrial and Labor Relations. Ithaca, New York, Cornell University, 1954, pp. 175–190.

Manpower Problems in Economic Development — A Selected Bibliography, by Keith Simpson and Hazel C. Benjamin, Industrial Relations Section, Princeton University, Princeton, N.J. 1958.

Myers, Charles A. "Problems of Management in Less Developed Countries." *American Labor's Role in Less Developed Countries.* A Report on a Conference Held at Cornell University, October 12–17, 1958, New York State School of Industrial and Labor Relations, Cornell University, 1959, pp. 52–58.

Shearer, John C. "Overseas American Managers — Necessities or Luxuries." *Proceedings* of Princeton University Conference, November 23 and 24, 1959.

Forthcoming Books

In addition to the works already published, the following are either in the manuscript draft stage or actually in press. The university in parentheses after each title is the educational institution of the author.

Alexander, Robert. *Labor Problems in Brazil, Argentina, and Chile* (Rutgers University).

Bendix, Reinhard. *Class Relations and Industrialization* (University of California [Berkeley]).

Badre, Albert and Simon Siksek. *Manpower and Oil in Arab Countries* (American University of Beirut).

Eason, Warren. *The Labor Problem in the Soviet Union* (Princeton University).

Ferrarotti, Franco. *The Italian Managerial Elite* (University of Florence).

Galenson, Walter, editor. *Labor and Economic Development,* Volume II (University of California [Berkeley]).

Hartmann, Heinz. *Transfer of Managerial Know-How between Advanced Economies* (Princeton University).

Hawkins, Everett D. *Labor in Indonesia* (Mount Holyoke College).

Hoselitz, Bert F. *The Commitment of Workers to Industrial Employment* (University of Chicago).

Lorwin, Val R. *Labor and Economic Development in France* (University of Oregon).

Rothbaum, Melvin. *International Comparison of Wage Structures* (University of California, Los Angeles).

Scalapino, Robert. *The Japanese Labor Movement* (University of California [Berkeley]).

Shearer, John C. *High Level Manpower Resources in Overseas Subsidiaries: Experience in Brazil and Mexico* (Princeton University).

Sturmthal, Adolf. *Workers' Councils — A Comparative Study of Plant Representation in Four Countries.* (Roosevelt University).

NOTES

Chapter 1: The Task of Interpretation

1. T. S. Ashton, *The Industrial Revolution 1760–1830* (London: Oxford University Press, 1948), pp. 125–126.

2. W. Arthur Lewis, *The Theory of Economic Growth* (London: George Allen and Unwin Ltd., 1955), p. 144

3. "In this work I have to examine the capitalist mode of production, and the conditions of production and exchange corresponding to that mode. Up to the present time, their classic ground is England. That is the reason why England is used as the chief illustration in the development of my theoretical ideas." Karl Marx, *Capital*, Author's Preface to the First Edition.

4. *Ibid.*

5. No attempt is made to present the Marxian system as a whole. See, Paul M. Sweezy, *The Theory of Capitalist Development, Principles of Marxian Political Economy* (New York: Oxford University Press, 1942); Joseph A. Schumpeter, *Capitalism, Socialism and Democracy* (New York: Harper and Brothers, 1942), pp. 1–58.

6. Joseph A. Schumpeter, *History of Economic Aanalysis* (New York: Oxford University Press, 1954), p. 391; also see p. 573.

7. Paul M. Sweezy, *Theory of Capitalist Development*, p. 94.

8. Alexander Gerschenkron, "Reflections on the Concept of 'Prerequisites' of Modern Industrialization," *Scritti in onore di Giuseppe Ugo Papi*, Editrice L'industrie (Milano, 1957).

9. K. Marx and F. Engels, *Manifesto of the Communist Party* (Moscow: Foreign Languages Publishing House, 1955), pp. 57–58.

10. Thorstein Veblen, *The Theory of Business Enterprise* (New York: Charles Scribner's Sons, 1919), p. 374.

11. Frank Tannenbaum, *The Labor Movement, Its Conservative Functions and Social Consequences* (New York: G. P. Putnam's Sons, 1921), pp. 28–29.

12. The page citations in *Capital* are to vol. 1, English ed., published by Foreign Languages Publishing House, Moscow, 1954. Chapter XV is entitled, "Machinery and Modern Industry," pp. 371–507.

13. *Capital*, ch. XXV, sec. 4

14. K. Marx and F. Engels, *Manifesto*, p. 75.

15. "His [Marx's] preconceptions about the nature of the relations between labor and capital, in particular, he simply took from an ideology that was already dominant in the radical literature of his time." Joseph A. Schumpeter, *History of Economic Analysis*, p. 389.

16. K. Marx and F. Engels, *Manifesto*, p. 95.

17. F. Engels, *Origin of the Family, Private Property and the State*, translated by Ernest Untermann (Chicago: C. H. Kerr & Co., 1902), p. 130.

18. Paul M. Sweezy, *Theory of Capitalist Development*, pp. 243–244.

19. F. Engels, *Origin of the Family, Private Property and the State*, p. 211.

20. K. Marx and F. Engels, *Manifesto*, pp. 58–59.

21. Paul M. Sweezy, *Theory of Capitalist Development*, p. 305.

22. "The place of manufacture was taken by the giant, Modern Industry. . . ." K. Marx and F. Engels, *Manifesto*, p. 54.

23. "The fact that there is a new ownership class in Communist countries does not explain everything, but it is the most important key to understanding the changes which are periodically taking place in these countries. . . ." Milovan Djilas, *The New Class* (London: Thames and Hudson, 1957), p. 62.

24. For another recent interpretation, see W. W. Rostow, *The Stages of Economic Growth, A Non-Communist Manifesto*, (Cambridge, England: Cambridge University Press, 1960).

Chapter 2: The Logic of Industrialism

1. W. Arthur Lewis, *The Theory of Economic Growth* (London: George Allen and Unwin Ltd., 1955), p. 116.

2. V. I. Lenin, "Differences in the European Labour Movement" (December 1910). *Selected Works*, XI (London: Lawrence and Wishart Ltd., 1939), p. 741.

3. "The general conditions of an unstructured market, then, are five-fold: (1) there must be no unions with their usual accompaniment of seniority, preference of employment, and other limitations upon access to the labor market; (2) there must be an impersonal relationship between employer and employee, lest informal obligations and various types of moral tenure develop; (3) the productive employment must be largely unskilled so that it becomes accessible to a large and unspecialized labor force. . . ; (4) the method of compensation must be by unit of product rather than by unit of time; (5) the operation must employ little or no capital or machinery." Lloyd H. Fisher, *The Harvest Labor Market in California* (Cambridge, Massachusetts: Harvard University Press, 1953), p. 9.

4. The 32 labor grades in the basic steel industry and the many thousands of jobs described and rated in the manual in use in the United States are eloquent testimony to the way in which an industrial work force is structured. While the details of the ordering vary among countries, the steel industry of all countries reflects a highly differentiated and ordered work force. See Jack Stieber, *The Steel Industry Wage Structure* (Cambridge, Massachusetts: Harvard University Press, 1959). Compare American Iron and Steel Institute, *Steel in the Soviet Union* (New York: 1959), pp. 287–376.

5. Bert F. Hoselitz, "The City, The Factory, and Economic Growth," *American Economic Review*, (May 1955), pp. 166–184.

6. If industrializing countries are arrayed in groups according to product per capita, the proportion of the labor force in agriculture and related industries varies from 61.2 per cent in the least developed group to 14.4 per cent in the group with the highest product per capita. See Simon Kuznets, *Six Lectures on Economic Growth* (Glencoe, Illinois: The Free Press, 1959), pp. 44–45.

7. W. Arthur Lewis, *The Theory of Economic Growth*, p. 92.

8. Marion J. Levy, Jr., "Some Social Obstacles to 'Capital Formation' in 'Underdeveloped Areas,'" in *Capital Formation and Economic Growth,* A Conference of the Universities — National Bureau Committee for Economic Research (New Jersey: Princeton University Press, 1955), p. 461.

9. Daniel Bell, *Work and Its Discontents* (Boston: Beacon Press, 1956). "Although religion declined, the significance of work was that it could still mobilize emotional energies into creative challenges" (p. 56).

10. Eric Hoffer, "Readiness to Work" (unpublished manuscript).

11. J. Robert Oppenheimer, *The Open Mind* (New York: Simon and Schuster, 1955), p. 121.

12. G. Myrdal, *An International Economy* (New York: Harper and Brothers, 1956), pp. 9–16.

Chapter 3: The Industrializing Elites and Their Strategies

1. Everett E. Hagen, "The Process of Economic Development," *Economic Development and Cultural Change* (April 1957), pp. 206–214, and "How Economic Growth Begins: A General Theory Applied to Japan," *Public Opinion Quarterly* (Fall 1958), pp. 373–390.

2. E. Levasseur, *The American Workman* (Baltimore: the John Hopkins Press, 1900), pp. 443–440.

3. Reinhard Bendix, *Work and Authority in Industry* (New York: John Wiley & Sons, Inc., 1956), pp. 22–116.

4. The quotation from Lenin appears on the front of a collective agreement in the Soviet steel industry. See American Iron and Steel Institute, *Steel in the Soviet Union* (New York, 1959), p. 329.

5. A. J. Meyer, *Middle Eastern Capitalism* (Cambridge, Massachusetts: Harvard University Press, 1959), p. 64: ". . . Cyprus is still economically unviable and a ward of the West for its food and clothing."

6. Karl Mannheim, *Ideology and Utopia* (New York: Harcourt, Brace & Co., 1949), p. 219.

Chapter 4: The Conflict of Cultures in Industrialization

1. This is E. B. Tylor's definition, quoted in A. L. Krober and Clyde Kluckhohn, *Culture — A Critical Review of Concepts and Definitions,* paper of the Peabody Museum of American Archaeology and Ethnology, Harvard University, 47.1:43 (1952).

2. Ralph Linton, "Cultural and Personality Factors Affecting Economic Growth," *The Progress of Underdeveloped Areas,* Bert F. Hoselitz, ed. (Chicago: University of Chicago Press, 1952), p. 83.

3. See C. K. Yang, *A Chinese Village in Early Communist Transition and The Chinese Family in the Communist Revolution* (The Technology Press of the Massachusetts Institute of Technology, distributed by Harvard University Press, Cambridge, Massachusetts, 1960).

4. F. S. C. Northrup, *The Taming of the Nations: A Study of the Cultural Bases of International Policy* (New York: The Macmillan Co., 1952), p. 74.

5. Max Weber, *The Protestant Ethic and the Spirit of Capitalism,* translated by Talcott Parsons (New York: Charles Scribner's Sons, 1948). Talcott Parsons, *The Structure of Social Action* (New York: McGraw-Hill Book Company, Inc., 1937), pp. 500–558. R. H. Tawney, in his *Religion and Rise of Capitalism* (London: Harcourt, Brace & Company, 1926), was one of Weber's critics, raising the incisive question whether economic factors did not produce the change in religious ideas.

6. Daniel Lerner, *The Passing of Traditional Society: Modernizing the Middle East* (Glencoe, Illinois: The Free Press, 1958), p. 105.

7. For a corroborating view, see Milton Singer, "Cultural Values in India's Economic Development," *Annals of the American Academy of Political and Social Science,* 305:81–82 (May 1956).

8. William O. Douglas, *West of the Indus* (Garden City, New York: Doubleday & Company, Inc., 1958), pp. 445, 481.

9. Rudolf Schlesinger, *Soviet Legal Theory* (New York: Oxford University Press, 1945), p. 258. Vyshinsky quotes Marx as saying, "Society does not rest on law. That is a phantasy of jurists. On the contrary, law — in contrast to the arbitrariness of the separate individuum — must rest on society, must be an expression of society's general interests and needs. . . ." A. Vyshinsky, *The Law of the Soviet State* (New York: The Macmillan Company, 1948), p. 37.

Chapter 5: Shaping the Industrialization Process

1. W. Arthur Lewis, *The Theory of Economic Growth* (London: George Allen and Unwin, Ltd., 1955), pp. 225–226. Also see Simon Kuznets, "International Differences in Capital Formation and Financing," in *Capital Formation and Economic Growth,* A Conference of the Universities — National Bureau Committee for Economic Research (New Jersey: Princeton University Press, 1955), pp. 19–106.

2. Lord Salter, *The Development of Iraq, A Plan of Action,* Iraq Development Board, 1955, p. 2: "The main limiting factors to progress are not material but human." See Frederick Harbison, "Two Centers of Arab Power," *Foreign Affairs* (July 1959), pp. 1–12.

3. Alexander Gerschenkron, "Economic Backwardness in Historical Perspective," in *The Progress of Underdeveloped Areas,* Bert F. Hoselitz, ed. (Chicago: University of Chicago Press, 1952), pp. 3–29 and "The Rate of Industrial Growth in Russia Since 1885," *The Tasks of Economic History,* supplement, 7: 144–174 (1947).

4. "Rostow on Growth," *The Economist,* August 15, 1959, pp. 409–416, and August 22, 1959, pp. 524–531.

5. Alexander Gerschenkron, "Notes on the Rate of Industrial Growth in Italy, 1881–1913," *Journal of Economic History* (December 1955), p. 372.

6. Arthur D. Gayer, W. W. Rostow, Anna Jacobson Schwartz, *The Growth and Fluctuation of the British Economy 1790–1850,* vol. II (Oxford: Oxford University Press, 1953), p. 626; Alvin H. Hansen, "Factors Affecting the Trend of Real Wages," *American Economic Review* (March 1925) pp. 27–42; E. H. Phelps Brown and Sheila V. Hopkins, "The Course of Wage-Rates in Five Countries, 1860–1939," *Oxford Economic Papers* (June 1950), pp. 226–296.

7. Simon Kuznets, Wilbert E. Moore and Joseph J. Spengler, (eds.) *Economic Growth: Brazil, India, Japan* (Durham: Duke University Press, 1955), pp. 14–15. The quotation is from Chapter 1. "Problems in Comparisons of Economic Trends," p. 120, by Simon Kuznets.

8. Alexander Gerschenkron, "Notes on the Rate of Industrial Growth in Italy, 1881–1913," p. 365.

9. Edward S. Mason, *Economic Planning in Underdeveloped Areas: Government and Business* (New York: Fordham University Press, 1958), pp. ix–x.

10. Simon Kuznets, "International Differences in Capital Formation and Financing," pp. 26, 27.

11. United Nations, Economic and Social Council, E/2901, June 21, 1956, Financing of Economic Development, the International Flow of Private Capital, 1953–1955, *Report by the Secretary General*, p. 9.

12. Bert F. Hoselitz, "Patterns of Economic Growth," *The Canadian Journal of Economics and Political Science* (November 1955), pp. 416–431. Hoselitz uses the terms "dominant" and "satellitic" patterns of development to indicate the degree of dependence upon one or more countries.

Chapter 6: Managers of Enterprises: Their Power, Position, and Policies

1. For an elaboration of the definition of management, see Frederick Harbison and Charles A. Myers, *Management in the Industrial World; An International Analysis* (New York: McGraw-Hill Book Company, Inc., 1959), pp. 3–20.

2. Samuel E. Hill and Frederick Harbison, *Manpower and Innovation in American Industry* (New Jersey: Princeton University Press, 1959).

3. This discussion does not consider the relative priorities at the margin. Should more resources be put into expanding technological institutes, medical schools or centers for training of elementary school teachers? Manpower planning and manpower budgeting are complex problems, related to the stage and pace of industrialization. We intend to devote attention to these problems in a number of countries during the next few years. The observations above, therefore, should be considered as an interim report.

4. It is important to stress that these are points on a spectrum or a continuum rather than discrete instances of managerial philosophies and approaches. Some mixture of each of these ideal types may be present in the managerial philosophy of a particular enterprise and in the managerial philosophies found in an industrial society at any one time.

5. David S. Landes, "Observations on France: Economy, Society, and Policy," *World Politics* (April 1957), p. 336. There are exceptions to this generalization, and the rapid expansion of certain segments of French industry in recent years is associated with changes in the traditional pattern of French management.

6. See Joseph S. Berliner, *Factory and Manager in the USSR* (Cambridge, Massachusetts: Harvard University Press, 1957), pp. 9, 202.

7. James Burnham, *The Managerial Revolution* (New York: John Day Company, Inc., 1941). For a more balanced view, with particular reference to the United States, see Adolph A. Berle, Jr., *Power Without Property: A*

322 **CHAPTER 6**

New Development in American Political Economy (New York: Harcourt, Brace & Company, 1959).

8. Frederick Harbison and Ibrahim A. Ibrahim, *Human Resources for Egyptian Enterprise* (New York: McGraw-Hill Book Co., Inc., 1958), p. 65.

9. Reinhard Bendix, *Work and Authority in Industry* (New York: John Wiley & Sons, Inc., 1956), pp. 162–174.

10. Solomon B. Levine, *Industrial Relations in Postwar Japan* (Urbana, Illinois: University of Illinois Press, 1958), p. 36.

11. Quoted in Charles A. Myers, *Labor Problems in the Industrialization of India* (Cambridge, Massachusetts: Harvard University Press, 1958), p. 96.

12. For a fuller description of this type of democratic-consultative management, see Frederick G. Lesieur, ed., *The Scanlon Plan: A Frontier in Labor-Management Cooperation* (New York: The Technology Press and John Wiley & Sons, Inc., 1958); Allan Flanders and H. A. Clegg, *The System of Industrial Relations in Great Britain* (Oxford: Basil Blackwell, 1954), pp. 323–364.

Chapter 7: Developing the Industrial Labor Force

1. For example, the first natives to work in the South African diamond mines in the 1870's were the indentured servants of Europeans. These natives had originally been forced into indenture because of cattle killing and starvation among the tribes. See Shelia van de Horst, *Native Labour in South Africa* (London: Oxford University Press, 1942), pp. 28ff.

2. P. G. Powlsland, *Economic Policy and Labour*, edited by Walter Elkan, East African Institute of Social Research, study no. 10 (Kampala, Uganda, East Africa, 1957). See particularly pp. 28ff. for a discussion of imposition of forced labor by British administrations and danger to native institutions.

3. Elliott Berg, "French West Africa," *Labor and Economic Development*, edited by Walter Galenson (New York: John Wiley & Sons, Inc., 1959), p. 194.

4. For a brief account of forced labor in Russia, see Emily Clark Brown, "The Soviet Labor Market," *Industrial and Labor Relations Review* (January 1957), pp. 190–198.

5. See Solomon Schwarz, *Labor in the Soviet Union* (New York: Frederick Praeger, 1952), pp. 10ff.

6. This may occur even in advanced industrializing countries, such as the United States, when new recruits come to northern factory centers from southern or border state rural areas and return frequently for intermittent periods. See, James Sidney Slotkin, *From Field to Factory; New Industrial Employees,* Research Center in Economic Development and Cultural Change, University of Chicago (Glencoe, Illinois: The Free Press, 1960), p. 104.

7. Quoted from James C. Abegglen, *The Japanese Factory* (Glencoe, Illinois: The Free Press, 1958), pp. 133–134.

8. See, however, Arthur M. Ross, "Do We Have a New Industrial Feudalism?" *American Economic Review* (December 1958), pp. 903–920.

9. Bert F. Hoselitz, "The Recruitment of White-Collar Workers in Un-

derdeveloped Countries," *International Social Science Bulletin,* (1954), pp. 433–442.

10. Kingsley Davis, "The Unpredicted Pattern of Population Change," *Annals of the American Academy of Political and Social Science* (May 1956), pp. 53–59.

11. Bert F. Hoselitz, "Urbanization and Economic Growth in Asia," *Economic Development and Cultural Change* (October 1957), pp. 42–54; Kingsley Davis and Hilda H. Golden, "Urbanization and the Development of Pre-Industrial Areas," *Economic Development and Cultural Change* (October 1954), pp. 6–24.

Chapter 8: The Workers: Impact and Response

1. T. S. Ashton, *The Industrial Revolution 1760–1830* (London: Oxford University Press, 1948), p. 99.

2. George Macauley Trevelyan, *British History in the Nineteenth Century and After* (London: Longmans, Green and Co., 1941), p. 156.

3. J. L. Hammond and Barbara Hammond, *The Town Labourer 1760–1832; The New Civilization* (London: Longmans, Green and Co., 1925), p. 19.

4. David Ricardo, *The Principles of Political Economy and Taxation,* Sraffa edition, I, (Cambridge, England: Cambridge University Press, 1951), p. 390.

5. Frederick Engels, *The Condition of the Working-Class in England in 1844* (London: George Allen and Unwin, Ltd., 1950), p. 177. See, however, F. A. Hayek, *Capitalism and the Historians* (Chicago: The University of Chicago Press, 1954).

6. T. S. Ashton, *The Industrial Revolution,* p. 123.

7. Sidney and Beatrice Webb, *The History of Trade Unionism* (London: Chiswick Press, 1913), p. 22

8. J. L. Hammond and Barbara Hammond, *The Skilled Labourer 1760–1832* (London: Longmans, Green, and Co., 1920), p. 259.

9. Elliot Berg, "French West Africa," in *Labor and Economic Development,* ed. Walter Galenson (New York: John Wiley & Sons, Inc., 1959), p. 227.

10. Wilbert E. Moore, *Industrialization and Labor* (Ithaca: Cornell University Press, 1951), p. 122.

11. W. Arthur Lewis, *The Theory of Economic Growth* (London: George Allen and Unwin, Ltd., 1956), p. 161.

12. Norman Ware, *The Industrial Worker 1840–1860, The Reaction of American Industrial Society to the Advance of the Industrial Revolution,* reprinted (Gloucester, Massachusetts: Peter Smith, 1959), p. 107.

13. Frederick Engels, *The Condition of the Working Class in England in 1844,* pp. 178–179. For a detailed description of some rules in the United States in the 1890's, see E. Lavasseur, *The American Workman* (Baltimore: The Johns Hopkins Press, 1900), pp. 170–177.

14. *The American Workman,* p. 171.

15. Kazuo Okochi, *Labor in Modern Japan,* The Science Council of Japan, Division of Economics, Commerce and Business Administration, Economic Series no. 18 (Tokyo, March 1958), p. 15.

16. Charles A. Myers, *Labor Problems in the Industrialization of India* (Cambridge, Massachusetts: Harvard University Press, 1958), p. 48.

17. Daniel Bell, *Work and Its Discontents* (Boston: Beacon Press, 1956), p. 54.

18. Jawaharlal Nehru, *Independence and After, A Collection of Speeches, 1946–49* (New York: John Day Company, 1950), p. 389.

19. Frederick Nessel, "Peiping Stresses Doctrine of Work," *New York Times*, City Edition, November 9, 1959, p. 18, col. 1.

20. J. L. Hammond and Barbara Hammond, *The Town Labourer 1760–1832, The New Civilization*, pp. 39, 40.

21. Bert F. Hoselitz, "The City, the Factory, and Economic Growth," *American Economic Review* (May 1955), pp.180–181.

22. James Morris, "The Power of the Street in the Arab World," *The New York Times Magazine*, October 18, 1959, p. 11.

23. Carleton H. Parker, *The Casual Laborer and Other Essays* (New York: Harcourt, Brace and Howe, 1920), p. 76.

24. Charles A. Myers, *Labor Problems in the Industrialization of India*, p. 44.

25. Wilbert E. Moore, *Industrialization and Labor*, p. 116. For a discussion of turnover in East Africa, see Walter Elkan, "Migrant Labor in Africa: An Economist's Approach," *American Economic Review* (May 1959), pp. 188–197.

26. *Ibid.* p. 118.

27. Daniel Katz, "Satisfactions and Deprivations in Industrial Life," in *Industrial Conflict*, Arthur Kornhauser, Robert Dubin, Arthur M. Ross, eds. (New York: McGraw-Hill Book Company, Inc., 1954), pp. 86–106.

28. *Report of the Commission Appointed to Inquire Into the Unrest in the Mining Industry in Northern Rhodesia in Recent Months* (Lusaka: The Government Printer, 1956), pp. 13–14.

29. V. I. Lenin, *What Is to be Done?* (New York: International Publishers, 1929), p. 90.

30. Albert Y. Badre and Simon G. Siksek, *Manpower and Oil in Arab Countries* (Beirut: American University Press, 1960), ch. 6.

31. Subbiah Kannappan, "The Tata Steel Strike: Some Dilemmas of Industrial Relations in a Developing Economy," *Journal of Political Economy* (October 1959), pp. 489–90; also see Morris David Morris, "Order and Disorder in the Labour Force, the Jampshedpur Crisis of 1958," *The Economic Weekly*, November 1, 1958, pp. 1387–1394.

32. For a more detailed treatment, see Clark Kerr and Abraham J. Siegel, "Industrialization and the Changing Nature and Impact of Worker Protest (unpublished manuscript).

33. Arthur M. Ross, "The Natural History of the Strike," in *Industrial Conflict*, pp. 23–36.

34. "Bonn Socialists Meet on Revision," *New York Times*, November 14, 1959, p. 5.

35. The term "job consciousness" was used by Selig Perlman, *A Theory of the Labor Movement* (New York: The Macmillan Company, 1928), p. 6. The present authors reject the claim for universality made by Perlman: "It is the author's contention that manual groups, whether peasants in Russia, modern wage earners, or medieval master workmen, have had their economic attitudes basically determined by a consciousness of scarcity of

opportunity. . . . Starting with this consciousness of scarcity, the "manualist" groups have been led to practicing solidarity. . . ." Perlman also uses the concept of job control (see pp. 7, 263–279). For the present authors job control finds its origins not in universal scarcity, nor in universal characteristics of the mentality of manual workers, but rather in the characteristics of the middle-class elite and the middle-class-led society.

36. John Clarke Adams, "Italy" in *Comparative Labor Movements*, Walter Galenson, ed. (New York: Prentice-Hall, Inc., 1952), p. 419.

37. In a consistent and stable industrial relations system these attitudes are the converse of the views of managers toward industrial workers (see ch. 6).

38. Harvey Leibenstein, *Economic Backwardness and Economic Growth, Studies in the Theory of Economic Development* (New York: John Wiley & Sons, 1957), pp. 62–76.

39. Quoted in R. B. Davison, "Labour Relations in Ghana," *The Annals of the American Academy of Political and Social Sciences* (March 1957), p. 139.

Chapter 9: The Rule Makers and the Rules

1. For an extended discussion, see John T. Dunlop, *Industrial Relations Systems* (New York: Henry Holt and Company, 1958).

2. International Labor Office, *Report of the Committee on Freedom of Employers' and Workers' Organizations, 131st Session, Governing Body, Seventh Item on Agenda, 6–10 March, 1956* (The McNair report), pp. 27–73.

3. Clark Kerr and Abraham Siegel, "The Structuring of the Labor Force in Industrial Society: New Dimensions and New Questions," *Industrial and Labor Relations Review* (January 1955), pp. 151–168.

4. Marcel David, *La Participation des Travailleurs à la Gestion des Entreprises privées dans les Principaux Pays d'Europe Occidentale* (Paris: Librarie Dalloz, 1954); Adolf Sturmthal, "Workers Councils — A Comparative Study of Plant Representatives in Four Countries" (1960), unpublished manuscript.

5. Elliot Berg, "The Recruitment of a Labor Force in Sub-Saharan Africa" (1960), unpublished manuscript.

6. "Wages and Related Elements of Labour Cost in European Industry, 1955: A Preliminary Report," *International Labour Review* (December 1957), pp. 558–587.

7. John T. Dunlop and Melvin Rothbaum, "International Comparisons of Wage Structures," *International Labour Review* (April 1955), pp. 3–19.

8. "The Interracial Wage Structure in Certain Parts of Africa," *International Labour Review* (July 1958), pp. 20–55.

9. International Labor Office, *Problems of Wage Policy in Asian Countries*, Studies and Reports, new series, no. 43 (Geneva, 1956), pp. 24–27; Lloyd G. Reynolds and Cynthia H. Taft, *The Evolution of Wage Structure* (New Haven: Yale University Press, 1956), pp. 355–360.

10. Clark Kerr, "The Prospect for Wages and Hours in 1975" in *U.S. Industrial Relations: The Next Twenty Years*, Jack Stieber, ed. (East

Lansing, Michigan: Michigan State University Press, 1958), pp. 169–204; Pamela Haddy and N. Arnold Tolles, "British and American Changes in Inter-Industry Wage Structure under Full Employment," *Review of Economics and Statistics* (November 1957), pp. 408–414; Melvin Rothbaum, "National Wage-Structure Comparisons" in *New Concepts in Wage Determination*, George W. Taylor and Frank C. Pierson, eds. (New York: McGraw-Hill Book Company, Inc., 1957), pp. 299–327.

11. Arthur M. Ross and Paul T. Hartman, *Changing Patterns of Industrial Conflict* (New York: John Wiley & Sons, Inc., 1960).

Chapter 10: Pluralistic Industrialism

1. Barbara Ward, *Five Ideas that Change the World* (New York: W. W. Norton & Company, Inc., 1959), p. 87.

2. For a discussion of the sources of industrializing elites, see Everett E. Hagen, "The Process of Economic Development," *Economic Development and Cultural Change* (April 1957), pp. 193–215.

3. W. W. Rostow, *The Stages of Economic Growth, A Non-Communist Manifesto* (Cambridge, England: Cambridge University Press, 1960), pp. 103, 133.

4. Daniel Lerner, *The Passing of Traditional Society* (Glencoe, Illinois: The Free Press, 1958), uses this term to denote the people on the margin between traditional and modern society.

5. John Scott, *Democracy is Not Enough: A Personal Survey of the Hungry World* (New York: Harcourt, Brace & Company, 1960), p. 19.

6. For a discussion of this point with reference to management in the United States, see Adolf A. Berle, Jr., *Power Without Property: A New Development in American Political Economy* (New York: Harcourt, Brace & Company, 1959).

INDEX

Absenteeism, 30, 131, 173, 203
Accra, 182
Africa, 5, 18, 81, 91, 167, 171, 182, 239, 253, 271
Agriculture, 2, 28, 38–40, 52, 99, 101–102, 106, 110, 113–116, 122, 124, 143, 168, 171, 184, 198, 252, 259, 276, 281, 285
Algeria, 64
Anarchists, 7, 195
Argentina, 8, 180, 106, 230, 238, 239
Ataturk, Mustafa Kemal, 88, 90, 92, 93
Australia, 3–4, 17, 45, 63, 183, 235, 254, 271, 281
Austria, 288

Bagdad, 182
Basrah, 206
Beirut, 5
Belgium, 169
Belgrade, 5
Beveridge, Sir William, 288
Birmingham, 7
Bombay, 182, 200, 203
Brazil, 18, 90, 180, 231, 236
Brazzaville, 200
Broken Hill, 207
Burnham, James, 145

Cairo, 182
Calcutta, 182
Canada, 17, 57, 63, 83, 183
Capital, sources, 28, 106, 125; capital accumulation, 27–28, 99, 109–113, 134, 226–227
Capitalism, 12, 20–21, 23–24, 28, 208, 282
Carroll, Thomas H., 4
Ceylon, 169, 181
Chartists, 7
Chile, 90, 180, 181
China, 7, 18, 61, 79, 81, 83, 84, 85, 88, 90, 91, 92, 93, 176, 181, 182, 200, 231, 270
Church, 56, 86, 231
Cities, 39, 85, 103, 181–182, 184, 193, 200–202, 285

Civil Service, 68, 101, 126, 176, 179
Class, 19, 26, 31, 52, 78, 82–86, 94–95, 133, 140–146, 157, 160
Class consciousness, 212, 221
Colonial administrators, 50, 62–66, 74–76, 81, 84, 91, 108, 112, 115, 117, 119, 120–121, 122, 125, 146, 157, 161–162, 167, 188–189, 213–214, 225, 232, 242, 259, 260, 261, 262, 268, 276–277
Colonialism, 10, 27, 62, 272, 276–277; segmental colonialism, 63–66, 276; settler colonialism, 64–66, 276; total colonialism, 64–66, 277
Commons, John R., 4, 6, 8, 12, 23
Communists, 9, 10, 26, 43–44, 68, 72, 83, 105, 140, 200, 206, 208, 236, 274, 200
Congo, 80, 178, 270
Culture, 6, 8–9, 11, 16, 21, 50, 59, 63, 77–97, 174, 186, 211, 235, 265, 267, 280–281
Cyprus, 63

Denmark, 102, 209, 235, 257
Discipline, 40–41, 97, 98, 124, 199–200, 204, 209, 227, 248, 276, 294
Disputes settlement, 92, 235, 237, 256–258, 262–263
Dudinstev, Vlidmir, 85
Dynastic elite, 50, 52–55, 65, 74–76, 80, 83, 87, 90, 108, 111, 115, 116, 118, 120, 121, 123, 146, 151, 155, 157, 160, 187, 212, 213, 214, 217, 220–221, 227, 232, 240–241, 258–259, 260, 261, 262, 268, 269, 272–273

Economic development, 5, 8, 10, 17, 19, 21, 69, 88, 93, 98–130, 153–154, 204–205, 235, 237, 243, 251, 252, 253, 254, 257
Economic systems, 98–130, 234
Education, 11, 19, 27, 29, 36–37, 43, 55, 60, 100, 102, 106, 113, 118–119, 137, 139, 159–162, 175–176, 178, 202, 253, 272, 275, 286, 289